Pole Raising and Speech Making

Pole Raising and Speech Making

Modalities of Swedish American Summer Celebration

Jennifer Eastman Attebery

Volume 3
Ritual, Festival, and Celebration
A series edited by
Jack Santino

Utah State University Press
Logan

© 2015 by the University Press of Colorado

Published by Utah State University Press
An imprint of University Press of Colorado
5589 Arapahoe Avenue, Suite 206C
Boulder, Colorado 80303

 The University Press of Colorado is a proud member of
The Association of American University Presses.

The University Press of Colorado is a cooperative publishing enterprise supported, in part,
by Adams State University, Colorado State University, Fort Lewis College, Metropolitan State
University of Denver, Regis University, University of Colorado, University of Northern
Colorado, Utah State University, and Western State Colorado University.

Cover design by Daniel Pratt

ISBN: 978-0-87421-998-2 (cloth)
ISBN: 978-0-87421-999-9 (ebook)

Library of Congress Cataloging-in-Publication Data

Attebery, Jennifer Eastman, 1951–
 Pole raising and speech making : modalities of Swedish American summer celebration /
Jennifer Eastman Attebery.
    pages cm. — (Ritual, festival, and celebration ; volume 3)
 Includes bibliographical references and index.
  ISBN 978-0-87421-998-2 (pbk.) — ISBN 978-0-87421-999-9 (ebook)
1. Festivals—Rocky Mountains Region. 2. Holidays—Rocky Mountains region 3. Folklore—
Rocky Mountains. 4. Swedish Americans—Rocky Mountains region—Social life and customs.
5. Rocky Mountains Region—Social life and customs. 6. West (U.S.)—Social life and cus-
toms. I. Title.
 GT4808.A88 2015
 394.260978—dc23
                                    2014049392

24   23   22   21   20   19   18   17   16   15   10   9   8   7   6   5   4   3   2   1

Cover photograph by Susan Duncan, Idaho State University Photographic Services

For Stina and Tom

Contents

Foreword

Pole Raising and Speech Making, Jennifer Attebery's contribution to the Ritual, Festival, and Celebration series, focuses our attention on the diversity of celebration in the United States. Unlike many other countries, the United States does not celebrate St. John's Eve (June 23) or St. John's Day (June 24), as midsummer—at least, not nationally. While a case can be made that Independence Day, on the Fourth of July, functions in many ways as a midsummer celebration, it is not called such. However, the United States is famously a nation of immigrants. Not only does the country boast many ethnicities, but as a result, it can also point to a multitude of religious faiths. In turn, certain ethnic groups who practice various faiths often, for histori-cal reasons having to do with economic opportunity, tended to cluster in certain regions.

It may surprise many that European-style midsummer celebrations are found traditionally in the United States. Scandinavian—especially Swedish—immigrants erect traditional "Maypoles" (although these are in fact erected for the summer solstice in June rather than in May) in areas where these groups have settled, such as Utah. Often, the ethnic traditions have melded with the Mormon religious identities of many practitioners, resulting in a set of local and regional holiday celebrations.

The Ritual, Festival, and Celebration series is intended to be broad in certain ways and narrowly focused in others. The kinds of events it may include are manifold: rituals, festivals, and celebrations of many different kinds, times, and places. One such manifestation of the celebratory that I am particularly interested in are calendrical holidays. With this book, Jennifer Attebery brings much-needed attention to a tradition that is not widely rec-ognized. She contributes a careful historical and ethnographic account of an important example of this country's plurality. In doing so, she demon-strates the value of celebration as a means of ritualizing a group's sense of place, identity, time, and their place in the larger scheme of life.

Jack Santino

Acknowledgments

I am deeply grateful to those institutions and their staff who helped me bring this project to fruition. My search for evidence of Swedish holiday celebrations took me to Denver Public Library, History Colorado, Utah State Historical Society, Montana Historical Society, Idaho State Historical Society, Latah County Historical Society, Brigham Young University–Perry Special Collections, University of Utah–Special Collections, Utah State University–Special Collections, the Swenson Swedish Immigration Research Center at Augustana College, and the Emigrant Institute at Växjö, Sweden. In all cases, I was assisted by highly competent professional staff whose knowledge of and interest in providing access to their collections made my work efficient and rewarding. I am grateful, too, for these depositories' permission to use the quotations from collections that are the backbone of this book—the words of the immigrants.

I am also grateful to Idaho State University for a Faculty Research Committee grant, which funded my travel to archives in the Rocky Mountain West during 2010, and the US Fulbright Program, through which, as a Distinguished Fulbright Chair at Uppsala during 2011, I was able to pursue further research into Swedish contexts for holiday celebration, share my thinking with scholars of Swedish immigration, and begin drafting my results.

The staff at Utah State University Press/University Press of Colorado have been exceedingly patient and thorough in their work with the manuscript, photographs, permissions, and other editorial and marketing processes. Many thanks go to them for shepherding my work to press.

The Minnesota Historical Society Press has kindly allowed reuse in expanded and revised form of my chapter in *Norwegians and Swedes in the United States*, edited by Philip J. Anderson and Dag Blanck (Minneapolis: Minnesota Historical Society Press, 2011).

Pole Raising and Speech Making

1

Spring-to-Summer Celebration
Abundance and Redundancy

EVERY JUNE SINCE 1985, ON A SATURDAY CLOSE to the summer solstice, a Midsummer pole has been raised on the lawn at Sealander Park, on the centennial farm established by Carl Sealander and still run by his grandson Dave. The park is a grassy oasis surrounded by Russian olive, cottonwood, and juniper trees among the sagebrush, lava beds, and irrigated fields of New Sweden, Idaho, just southwest of Idaho Falls. When I participated in the pole raising on June 23, 2001,[1] we had a perfect day at Sealander Park: pleasantly warm, windless, and bright with sunshine. On the edges of the park, we early arrivals got to work, our first step unwinding twine to strip off last year's dried greenery. Dave Sealander likes to leave the pole up throughout the year and bring it down the evening before or even the morning of the Midsummer gathering. In 2001, that happened precipitously—when one of the ropes securing the pole snapped in a windstorm a few weeks before. The pole toppled, worrying Dave and spurring him to design a new method for securing it. While the rest of us decorated and reassembled the pole, he spent the afternoon in his shop in the barn, welding a new cap for the top of the pole that would hold guy wires rather than rope.

We worked on through the afternoon: stripping the old materials, cutting fresh vegetation from areas along the park margins that needed pruning, gathering shasta daisies from a neighbor, braiding daisy chains, and wrapping the pole with the fresh greenery and flowers. Workers drifted in and out of the process, taking breaks for horse drawn wagon rides or conversations in the shade. On the wagon ride I joined, the riders sang rounds in English and German. Gradually more people arrived, including Dave Combs, accordianist in the group "Squeeze Play," who strolled among the workers and spectators playing Nordic[2] music and chatting. Dave Combs

DOI: 10.7330/9780874219999.c001

3

planned to leave the next day for Norway, where he and his family would be visiting relatives.

With Dave Sealander still busy in his shop, we carried the long mast to the site in the middle of the park where the pole would be raised. Those participants who had raised the pole before tried to remember how the pieces fit together. Where should the large rings be placed? The smaller ones? Even annual participants were puzzled. A runner was sent to consult with Dave. Further discussion ensued. Collective memory eventually produced a crosslike configuration with one large ring at the crossing, two smaller ones above it, and two large rings suspended by ropes in a skirt-like fashion below the crossing. On top, we placed the rooster, decked with flowers and feathers that Dave had fashioned as a decoration in imitation of poles he had seen elsewhere in the United States. Finally, the pole was ready, although without the ringed top piece needed for securing the pole with guy wires. We took a break to eat.

On his postcard invitations to Midsummer at Sealander Park, Dave always specifies times: pole decorating beginning at 1:00 p.m., pole raising and long dance at 5:00 p.m., and potluck to follow. In my experience, these times are hypothetical. When one enters the park and joins the work parties decorating the pole, one's sense of time shifts. Rather than consulting watches, we consulted the sun and our appetites. It was probably well after 5:00 p.m, and the pole wasn't ready, but we were ready to eat the food we had brought to share.

The potluck supper began with a blessing said by a participant who was asked, good-naturedly, because he "is a good Mormon"[3] and because others denied knowing how to say grace. Everyone joined in the potluck line, where, alongside American-style cold cuts, rolls, salads, cakes, and lemonade were enough distinctively Nordic dishes to fill a plate: flavored herring, hard bread, lingonberry jam, red beet salad, rice pudding, dipped rosette cookies, boiled potatoes with skins partially peeled, scalloped potatoes with cheese. No alcohol—Dave Sealander's mother Edith was a Latter-day Saint (LDS); her non-Mormon guests respectfully did not bring alcohol to the park. As we ate, Dave Combs continued to play, joined by another accordionist, a Danish American from Soda Springs—about three and a half hours' drive from New Sweden. Interspersed with the Nordic folk music was a varied repertoire of popular tunes. After eating, a Finnish immigrant from nearby Firth joined in on guitar. Those so inclined joined in song, puzzling out lyrics from a songbook that the Finnish immigrant had brought.

Diners and musicians lingered as dusk approached, until Dave Sealander emerged from his shop with the essential top piece, attaching

Figure 1.1. The Midsummer pole goes up at Sealander Park, New Sweden, Idaho, in June 2007. Courtesy of Susan Duncan, Idaho State University Photographic Services.

it to the assembled pole. Everyone gathered in the clearing for the pole raising. The only gender- and age-specific role was at the center, where the most physically able of us used crossed poles to push the Midsummer pole higher—with a "one-two-three-ho"—and higher yet, until it was erect and ready to be lashed. Nearly everyone else helped with the three guy wires, holding them until Dave could securely fasten each one to poles at the edge of the clearing. Those few not working exclaimed at the sight: the pole suddenly taking on life as an upright focal point in the center of the park. "How lovely," the woman next to me exclaimed, and truly, it is hard not to be moved by a Midsummer pole's transformation as it rises to become a mast. It was 8:30 p.m., and light was beginning to fade as folk dancing around the Midsummer pole began.

MIDSUMMER IN THE SPRING-TO-SUMMER SEASON

What could be more Swedish American than Midsummer? On June 24, or close to that date, Swedish Americans throughout the United States followed a process very similar to that at Sealander Farm. Along with St. Lucia's Day festivals, Midsummer can be used as an index of Swedish Americanness. Writing about Midsummer in Brevort, Michigan, Lynne Swanson (1996, 24) estimates that "nearly 95 percent of the 163 Swedish American organizations affiliated with the Swedish Council of America mark the holiday in some way." He characterizes Midsummer as "an activity strongly rooted in their [Swedish Americans'] collective identity" (Swanson 1996, 24).

The Midsummer holiday, located on the calendar either in relationship to the summer solstice or to the Catholic/Lutheran St. John's Day (June 24), is especially important to Scandinavians and to Scandinavian emigrants to North America and elsewhere. Although often thought of as the height or middle of summer, the holiday technically marks the beginning of summer and also, ironically, the beginning of the waning of daylight. Perhaps because this phenomenon is especially apparent in northern countries such as Sweden, Norway, and Denmark, Midsummer is heightened in their calendar customs as well as in the ethnic customs of those emigrating from the Scandinavian cultural region.

In celebratory activities, people elevate ideas that they especially value, making any holiday celebration worth our attention for the sake of probing the shared values of a community. Midsummer, along with the holidays that surround and influence it in America, is well worth our attention, then, not just for its intrinsic interest as a fascinating celebratory practice but also as a window into the values of an important nineteenth/twentieth-century ethnic group, Swedish Americans. The Swedish Americans of the Rocky Mountain West are of particular interest for their continuation and reinterpretation of Swedish customs in a region where they were also very successful in adapting to Western American cultural patterns. The Rocky

Mountain West's demographic complexity, with a population including Mormon enclaves, mining towns, urban centers, and farming communities, also allows us to explore some interesting contrasts in adaptations of ethnic culture.

The Mormon enclaves are of special interest in the ways their Swedish immigrant populations both reflect some of the patterns found throughout Swedish America and counter those patterns with customs peculiar to LDS immigrants. Furthermore, because most of the ethnic Mormon population immigrated close on the heels of conversion by missionaries, we see in this part of the Rocky Mountain population a syncretic religious-ethnic identity that is neither easy nor necessarily appropriate to disaggregate. Thus, the close relationship between Swedishness and Mormonness surfaces at several points throughout the chapters to come.

In this study, I will focus on the beginnings of Midsummer and the surrounding spring-to-summer seasonal celebrations in the Rocky Mountain West during the height of Swedish immigration to the Rockies (1880 to 1917). The passage from spring to summer was celebrated by Swedish Americans and the larger Scandinavian community alike with abundance and redundancy. Abundance was produced through observation of multiple celebrations drawn from both the Swedish and American cultures to heighten this time of year. These celebrations were redundantly meaningful through their expressing and re-expressing the turn in the season and its many associations, which could include national and ethnic patriotism. Abundance and redundancy resulted from many processes. With the Swedish Americans, what comes to mind most immediately is the process of ethnic recontextualization—immigrants reshaping their existing customs within a new context, negotiating their transition from immigrant to ethnic identity. But processes other than ethnicity were also important.

Addressing those other processes takes one into interesting territory. The key contexts within which the spring and summer celebrations can be understood range from everyday to sacred spheres of activity. Spheres of everyday activity, such as the routines of factory work or agricultural labor, shaped peoples' participation in seasonal holidays. The prime national holiday (the American Fourth of July) and a prime religious holiday for the Mormons (the Latter-day Saint Pioneer Day on July 24) competed and resonated with the Swedish idea of celebration. The nineteenth-century perceptions of sacred and secular spheres of activity frequently collapsed into each other when people enacted their holiday traditions. Another significant nineteenth-century pattern is the way in which activities like Midsummer were elevated through rhetorical culture. A redundancy of verbal activities, such as orating and praying, surrounded customary activities to create a ritualized sense of space and time.[4] In addition, the season as a whole represented an embodiment of human-nature connections, interweaving eco-cultural meanings with Swedish patriotism.

Although these processes could well be addressed by focusing on Scandinavian groups in other American regions, I have taken up Swedish immigration to the five-state area of the northern Rocky Mountains—Idaho, Montana, Wyoming, Utah, and Colorado—as a means of expanding our understanding of ethnic culture in an understudied portion of the country. Swedish immigration was an important contributor to Anglo-European movement into the West. Swedish immigrants and westering Swedish Americans came into the northern Rocky Mountain region in significant numbers beginning in the 1880s in response to labor demands in the logging and lumber, mining and smelting, and railroad construction and maintenance industries. Subsequent growth of cities in the region encouraged single women to move to the region to work as domestic servants. These patterns replicated the trends of Swedish American settlement in the upper Midwest. The immigration of Latter-day Saint converts into Utah, however, stands in contrast to these familiar patterns. The Swedish LDS came mainly as families and established themselves on small family farms along the Watsatch Valley, stretching north and south from Salt Lake City.[5]

Today, the people of the American West tend to elide substantial ethnic imprints on Western culture. Along with the three other largest immigrant groups that could disappear into "whiteness," (Jacobson 1998, 7–8, 69, 247, 256)[6] namely the Germans, Norwegians, and Irish, the Andersons and Johnsons of the West could go unmarked in the telling of Western local history, being instead collectively depicted as actors in "first white settlement" or "Mormon settlement" rather than ethnic settlement. The Swedish immigrants themselves helped create this impression by rapidly adopting English, explicitly claiming to be Americans and Westerners—especially in histories written during the World War I to World War II era—and leaving implicit their ongoing practice of ethnic traditions (Attebery 2001). In Utah, conversion to the LDS faith further complicated the development of a Swedish American ethnic culture, sometimes reinforcing ethnicity as religious practices that included mission work abroad permeated everyday activities and social life.[7] In spite of these claims to Westernness or Mormonness, Swedish American cultural activity can be found throughout the turn of the century period beginning in 1880 and, indeed, continuing throughout the twentieth century.[8] Documentation of much of this activity is often tucked away, though, in Swedish language sources preserved in specialized archives.

Within Swedish American culture, one might ordinarily focus on the winter holidays, St. Lucia Day and Christmas (*jul*). The winter season holidays have, indeed, been selected and intensified by Swedish Americans themselves. St. Lucia Day traditions practiced within the private space of family households have been developed into public St. Lucia festivals, often sponsored by towns, churches, or colleges with Swedish American roots. The annual festivals at Lindsborg, Kansas; Bethlehem Evangelical Lutheran Church, Elgin, Illinois; and Gustavus Adolphus College in St. Peter, Minnesota, are representative of many such celebrations held on or near December 13 each year.[9]

Also selected and intensified is the idea of a "Swedish Christmas," which was supported in nineteenth-century popular publications such as the Chicago magazine *Julgranen*, aimed at the Swedish American middle class as a part of a larger pattern of the nineteenth-century reinvention of Christmas that included Christmas annuals in nineteenth-century Scandinavian American and other literatures (Skårdal 1977, 238; Svensson, 1992, 157; Risley 2003, 58; Stokker 2000; Gradén 2004; Berry 1978).[10] This picture of the ongoing significance of Swedish Christmas customs is supported by evidence from a questionnaire for the Swedish Information Bureau in 1946–47. When Swedish Americans were asked, "Which holidays throughout the year do you celebrate?" Christmas, especially cited as the Swedish *jul*, was the most frequently cited observance, and 86 percent of those responding specified that Christmas was celebrated with *julgranen* (the candle-lit evergreen tree) and *julkakor* (cookies and baked goods). A few additionally cited *jultomten* (the Christmas brownie or elf), giving gifts, and serving special foods such as lutefisk, ham, and porridge as part of their holiday customs.[11]

Yet, the part of the year opposite the Christmas season offers an intriguingly complex pattern of celebrations that follow closely on each other's heels, both Swedish American and American. From Swedish tradition, Walpurgis Night (*Valborgsmässoafton*, or *sista april*, the last day of April), the first of May (traditional beginning of summertime but also International Workers' Day), and especially Midsummer (Swedish *midsommar*) mark and welcome the beginning and the apex of long days and warm weather in Sweden. This last tradition is elevated and elaborated as a high point in the yearly calendar, set at the summer solstice almost directly opposite Christmas. The Midsummer holiday experienced a renewal in the turn of the century period coincident with Swedish American settlement in the Rocky Mountain region. Therefore, as a pivotal celebration in the passage from spring to summer, Midsummer will take center stage in the chapters to come.

MIDSUMMER IN SWEDEN

Prior to Rocky Mountain settlement, Swedish celebration of the Midsummer holiday has its roots in northern Europe and in the American Midwest. In Sweden today, Midsummer is celebrated with a cluster of outdoor activities—Midsummer pole raising, dancing and music, children's games, and drinking and feasting out of doors—on the weekend closest to June 24 (Klein 1996; Swahn 1997, 26–27). But traditional observances at or near the summer solstice have also included bonfires, mumming by *lövgubbarna* (leaf-covered men), mock weddings, processions with *Midsommarspiror* (handheld poles decorated similarly to Midsummer poles), decorating churches with *Midsommarstakar* (decorated stakes), wreath-making, and drinking spring water (perhaps a reference to St. John the Baptist) for health or luck (Bringéus 1976, 198–219; Tidholm and Lilja 2004, 22). Another important set of practices revolved around foretelling one's future spouse, through, for example, sleeping with flowers under the pillow or holding a silent vigil (T. Wall 2007). Most of these practices have been eclipsed by the Midsummer pole raising tradition, which, according to Nils-Arvid Bringeus, has enjoyed organized support of various societies and governmental units and has been influenced by tourism (Bringéus 1976, 202–3). Also enjoying official support is the idea of the day as a national holiday. In 1935, Midsummer Eve became a bank holiday, and in 1953, its celebration on the Saturday closest to St. John's Day was established (16).

Pole raisings, bonfires, and other Midsummer practices have a long lineage that can be traced to Early Modern Europe.[12] Celebrations that included bonfires, praise of civic leaders, and satirical song and dance were identified with St. John's Day in Sweden as early as the sixteenth century and may have been a German import (Billington 2008, 50). Many of these customs were expressed regionally; for example, the practice of kindling celebratory bonfires at Midsummer has been documented as limited to the southern region of Skåne, Bohuslän (Gothenburg's region) and the western Swedish-speaking region of Finland. Elsewhere, bonfires were set instead at Valborgsmässafton (Walpurgis Night, April 30), the first of May, Easter, or other spring holidays (Campbell and Nyman 1976, 46–47, 104).

The Midsummer pole, now distinctive to the Scandinavian countries, is also credited to contact with the northern German Hanseatic League and, in Sweden, can be dated perhaps as early as the late fifteenth century, with widespread popularity by the seventeenth century (Bringéus 1976, 202; Klein 1996, 14; Swahn 1997, 27). Midsummer celebrations flourished in Sweden during the seventeenth, eighteenth and early nineteenth centuries in spite of resistance from the most Pietistic of Lutheran pastors, who disapproved of dancing and excess (Bringéus 1976, 203–4; Klein 1996, 14). The tradition received even more opprobrium somewhat later and from another religious sector. In the middle of the nineteenth century, the tradition waned with the increasing popularity of the free religious movements that broke away from the national Lutheran church. With their chosen religious practices repressed by the national church, the members of many of these free churches eventually emigrated, taking their resistance to Midsummer with them. Consequently, according to folklorist Barbro Klein, "relatively few reports from early Scandinavian immigrant communities in the United States mention midsummer celebrations and maypoles" (Klein 1996, 15).

Klein's conclusion is verified in the diaries extant from mid-nineteenth-century Swedish America. The Swedish writer Albin Widén examined an Illinois farmer's *dagbok* (diary) for 1865 for documentation of holiday celebrations. According to his diary, Johan Peter Lindstrom's days during June were occupied with outdoor farm chores—plowing and planting—and Midsummer passed without mention. Yet Lindstrom's workdays paused for Sundays, on which only the weather was noted (Widén 1966, 116–23). We see a similar pattern in the diaries that Peter S. Nelson kept for 1860–79 while he was working in logging and establishing a farmstead near Galesburg, Illinois. In the spring-to-summer season, the Fourth of July was the one day other than Sundays when he took a break from logging and planting to celebrate during this mid-century period.[13] In the case of farm laborer Lars Andersson Dahlquist, even time off for the American observances of Decoration Day and Independence Day are missing from his account book for work in Peoria, Illinois, during the 1885 spring-to-summer season.[14]

Swedish folklorists point out that Midsummer is one of the few holidays in Sweden with national significance, especially given that the Swedish Flag Day has generally had a low profile in Swedish national mentality (Bringéus 1976, 195; Gustavsson 2007, 199; Klein 1996), a pattern that may be shifting at the turn of the twenty-first century with increased immigration into Sweden. According to Klein, "as a symbol of Swedishness, the maypole becomes a guard against ideals and values that are not Swedish" (Klein 1996, 21). But Klein also notes that "the maypole appears capable of embracing a wide spectrum of meanings" that are oriented toward place and nature (20). Thus, the Swedish American holiday's association with national values and its ability to reflect varied and complex meanings have analogues in the Old Country.

In Swedish America, Midsummer emerged as a popular Swedish American custom during the same late-nineteenth-century era in which the tradition experienced a renewal in public celebrations in Sweden. This emergence can be tracked in Swedish American almanacs, in which the listing of Midsummer first occurs in the late 1880s or even later, depending upon the publication. In almanacs published by *Amerikanska Emigrant Kompaniet* [the American Emigrant Company] in New York, a listing for Midsummer appeared between 1884 and 1888, when it was noted as a holiday celebrated in Sweden. *Svensk-Amerikansk Almanacka och Kalendar* [Swedish-American almanac and calendar], also published in New York, noted numerous sacred and secular holidays in 1898 but not Midsummer. By 1901, Midsummer did appear, again noted as a Sweden-only observance, but from 1904 onward this almanac was silent about Midsummer. The Chicago newspaper *Svenska Amerikanaren* published an almanac focusing on the Lutheran church year; in this series, Midsummer didn't appear until 1919.[15]

Transatlantic contact was a major influence (Barton 1992, 10–11). According to H. Arnold Barton, Swedish Americans returning to visit relatives in Sweden during the 1890s came into contact with local and private Midsummer celebrations in their home districts and with large, public celebrations at sites such as Skansen, the outdoor folk arts museum on the Stockholm outskirts that had begun development in 1891. Several commented that the public celebrations outshone smaller and more private events in the districts, suggesting that the practice was becoming a more public, sponsored event during this period (Barton 1997). Visits to America by Swedes were also a factor, as with the East Coast and midwestern tour of a Skansen folk dance troupe during 1906–1907, after which many of the dancers remained in America to teach folk dance (Liman 1983).

Peter S. Nelson's diaries provide an excellent example of this transatlantic influence. Beginning in 1869, Nelson made periodic spring and summer trips to his homeland, visiting relatives there but also visiting a health resort where he took the waters, both bathing and drinking, in an attempt to treat chronic health problems, apparently arthritis. His first mention of Midsummer occurs during one of these trips, when he wrote on June 22, 1900, a Friday, "tomorrow is the midsummer Holiday Eve in Sweden; people are making great preparations to celebrate." During the weekend his observations continued. On June 23:

> Today I went to the springs; had breakfast early; a bath at 9 o clock so as to be ready for the afternoon celebration; the children with flags marched from the society building to the [word indistinct] hall, then danced around the may pole; the children's bicycle club also made a nice display of flowers.

And on Sunday, June 24, "This has been midsummer day; the young people of all classes has been out in their best attire, gay and happy. Yesterday I got acquainted with two young American ladies from St. Paul, Minnesota, who are here for their health and pleasure."[16]

This and subsequent visits in 1905 and 1907 appear to have revived Midsummer for Nelson. Prior to 1900, the ideas of celebration, outdoor recreation, and connection to Sweden in the late June season appeared only implicitly in his diaries. In 1879 he went fishing; in 1882, attended a Good Templars' sociable; in 1884, entertained visiting Swedish relatives with tours of the Galesburg area; in 1896, attended a concert presented by singers from Moline, Illinois; in 1897, read and fished.[17] If these days of leisure represented ethnic content, he leaves that meaning implicit in the diary. But in 1911, Nelson began to note Midsummer explicitly even when in America. On Saturday, June 24, 1911 he wrote, "this was midsummer day in Sweden. It is one day of great event," but it was the following Wednesday, June 28, when he attended a gathering and visited Swedish American friends, writing in an uncharacteristically reflective tone:

> This has been one of the days when you feel like life was worth living. Weather cool and pleasant. I went this forenoon to Knoxville to a picnic. I was over to see Swan Peterson. Although he is feeble his head is clear and he likes to talk. I seen a few other old friends and had a good time generally. Got back home at 8:45 p.m.[18]

The following year he was again reflective: "Yesterday [Sunday, June 24] was midsummer day. I did not think of it until today. As a boy in Sweden I enjoyed midsummer Eve immensely." And on June 26, he again attended a Swedish American picnic held by a Lutheran Sunday School.[19]

What had changed for Nelson? Born in 1835, he had emigrated to Illinois in 1853, during the first major wave of Swedish immigration to the American Midwest.[20] By 1900, at the same time that ethnic renewal was occurring on both sides of the Atlantic, Nelson and his fellow mid-century immigrants were entering a new phase of life in which they could hand over to a second generation the hard labor required to maintain their farms or businesses. Nelson's diary becomes a record of visitations, with many of his visits to Swedish American men and their families. This also became his pattern for Decoration Day and Independence Day, which had been important holidays throughout Nelson's diaries. As we will see in the ensuing chapters, these patterns of ethnic renewal and increased participation in old age are factors that affect celebration of Midsummer as a part of the spring-to-summer holiday season among the Swedish Americans of the Rockies.

MIDSUMMER IN NORTH AMERICA

Our knowledge of Midsummer traditions in North America is fragmentary, as scholarly documentation of the holiday has been sporadic and often limited to local studies. Even so, it is possible to conclude that the tradition is long-lived, widespread, and continuous in some localities. Most of our information comes from the fieldwork of Swedish scholars who visited North American during the twentieth century and the work of historians of Swedish America who have retrieved descriptions of Midsummer from Swedish language newspapers and contemporary documents like Nelson's diaries. These scholars have identified Midsummer traditions in the main concentrations of Swedish settlement—the Midwest, the northern plains, the Pacific Northwest, Utah, the Colorado Front Range, the Canadian plains, and the Northeast. Mentions of Midsummer in these documents date to the 1890s and continue throughout the twentieth century to the current day, even through periods of substantial change. Midsummer weathered the Lutheran Augustana Synod's gradual early twentieth-century shift from Swedish to English (also a pattern in other Swedish American churches) and the World War I Nativist movement's antagonism toward Germanic and Scandinavian peoples, which led to a muting of public displays of ethnicity (Blanck 1995, 67; Hanson 1996, 241; Henrichsen et al. 2010; Isaacson 2003, 129; C. Johnson 1982; N. Johnson 1992, 28; Klein 1989, 47–51; McMahon 1997, 36; Mulder 2000, 257; G. Scott 2005, 236; L. Swanson 1996; Trotzig 1977; Widén 1972, 203–6; Youngquist 2002, 254–55).

As in late-nineteenth-century Sweden, Midsummer in North America enjoyed sponsorship from associations of various sorts as a public event, but in the American setting these events could do double duty as fundraisers (Youngquist 2002, 254–55). The Vasa Order of America, local Swedish clubs, and other Swedish and Scandinavian American associations were important sponsors, but Lutheran and other Swedish-Protestant churches (having dropped antagonism against the custom) also held Midsummer events. A key feature of these occasions was holding the celebration out of doors, and descriptions include many of the components of the Swedish Midsummer as described by Bringeus, Klein, and others—a Midsummer pole, music, folk dance performance, social dancing, regional Swedish folk costume, games and races, parades, speeches, and an outdoor meal or picnic—but with some American additions and variations: the United States flag placed on the Midsummer pole (Blanck 1995, 67), reports from members who had traveled to Sweden (N. Johnson 1992, 28),[21] and the idea of honoring "royalty" in the guise of a Swedish American of the year or a Swedish American beauty queen (Klein 1989, 48–49).

Figure 1.2. Midsummer Queen (Linnea Osman) for the Phalen Park Midsummer, St. Paul, MN, 1923. Photograph courtesy of the American Swedish Institute.

One Swedish-born observer of celebrations in the heartland of Swedish America, the upper Midwest, during the 1930s and 1940s was Albin Widén, a writer with training in ethnology. He began his study of Swedish America with field trips in 1935 and 1939 (Barton 1984, 179;

Figure 1.3. The Midsummer pole
at Phalen Park, St. Paul, MN, 1915.
Photograph courtesy of the American
Swedish Institute.

Beijbom, 1985). While not attempting a detailed ethnography of Swedish
American practices, Widén did offer some sweeping observations about
how he perceived traditions as being adapted by the Swedish Americans
of the between-the-wars era. During 1941–42, Widén served as director
of an Augustana Institute of Swedish Culture in Rock Island, Illinois,
and during 1942–47, he was director of the Swedish Information Bureau
headquartered in Minneapolis (Barton 1984, 179; Beijbom 1985). In the
latter position, he contacted Swedish Americans around North America
with a request to complete a lengthy questionnaire concerning their immigration and adjustments to their new country.[22] The holiday section of
Widén's questionnaire prompted some interesting responses from the
ninety-one immigrants who took time to complete it, most of them men

and nearly all from the upper Midwest. Few responded that they celebrated only American or only Swedish holidays; rather, most displayed an
inclusive attitude toward holiday celebrations, saying that they preserved
and sometimes mixed traditions from both nations. One respondent
wrote that he and his family were "American at Easter and Swedish at
Midsummer."[23] Most important to the respondents were *jul* (Christmas)
and *påsk* (Easter), the former usually celebrated with Swedish customs and
the latter sometimes so. New Year's Day, Independence Day, Midsummer,
and Thanksgiving were also volunteered as regularly celebrated holidays,
although by fewer respondents.

Respondents' comments provide clues as to why there were limitations on
the development of Midsummer as a North American holiday. One respondent from a small Minnesota community explained that "Midsummer is
seldom celebrated among the Swedes in this area, but in the large Swedish
communities such as the cities of Duluth, Minneapolis, etc., large celebrations are held at Midsummer time."[24] Part of the requirements for a Midsummer celebration, he implied, was a concentration of Swedish population.
Another respondent saw the main problem with Midsummer as conflict
with the American labor schedule: "Midsummer generally speaking [is] a
work day."[25] So, Midsummer does not emerge from Widén's questionnaire
as a holiday consistently practiced throughout Swedish America, but neither
is it absent. And, given the obstacles posed by American society, its practice
is revealed as especially important to those who did so.

One possibility that cannot be dismissed is that Widén's own interest in Swedish American traditions could have reinvigorated and sustained
their practice, especially in Minnesota. Even though he had received some
ethnological training in his studies at Uppsala and Stockholm, Widén was
scarcely removed from the peoples he studied. On the contrary, he took an
active role as what H. Arnold Barton dubbed "an outstanding ambassador
of goodwill between Sweden and America" (Barton 1984, 179). Today, we
would characterize his activities as "public folklore," his career paralleling
similar efforts by the American folklorist Benjamin Botkin.[26] In addition to
the Augustana Institute of Swedish Culture and the Swedish Information
Bureau, Widén was active in the American Swedish Institute (Minneapolis)
and Sweden's program for selecting a Swedish American of the Year, all
activities promoting the continuity of Swedish tradition in the United States
(Barton 1984, 179–80; Beijbom 1985).

In *Svenska Som Erövrat Amerika* [Swedes Who "Conquered" America],
Widén made clear his position as an ethnic culture advocate:

In [the periodical] *Svenska Nybyggaren* [the Swedish Settlers] of June 12th, 1873, we find an illuminating notice, an appeal to Scandinavians to celebrate the 4th of July, the big American holiday. Today, no appeals are needed to observe the American days of celebration; they are obvious to the Swedish Americans, as for other groups of Americans. Rather, one must work for a common Swedish American Day, because there now is great confusion. One celebrates "Vasa-Day" in connection with John Ericsson's memory, local Scandinavian days, etc., and in the fall of 1935 for the first time Leif Eriksson Day was celebrated, since it has been officially admitted that he was America's actual discoverer—that day naturally took care of the Norwegians, although it might be regarded as a general Scandinavian or Icelandic celebration. Norwegian Americans generally celebrate the 17th of May [Norwegian Constitution Day, celebrated as a day of independence]; perhaps the three-hundred year jubilee in Delaware will give rise to the beginnings of a special Swedish American day. (Widén 1937, 122)

Widén's comments are significant in light of earlier efforts in Chicago, following on the New Sweden, Delaware, 1888 jubilee—the 250-year anniversary of Swedish colonial presence in North America—to create a day on which Swedish Americans would regularly assemble to recognize their common heritage. Lars Wendelius (1990) described "Our Forefathers' Day" in Rockford, Illinois, 1890 as a festivity inspired by Chicago's celebration, which was timed for the third Sunday in September. But this was an abortive effort, as Wendelius noted, "not tied to any particular Swedish celebration. This may have meant that the reasons for the event appeared to be vague and obscure—unlike, for example November 6 and midsummer—and that the fine idea never took root among the Swedish Americans" (Wendelius 1990, 60–61).[27]

The much later emergence of a Swedish American Day, located on or near Midsummer and especially in the Twin Cities, was in part Widén's doing, making his later writings as much reports of his success as they are descriptions of Swedish America. Widén generalized that it was typical for Swedish Americans to celebrate a *sommarfest* (summer celebration) of some kind and compared the practice to those of other American ethnic groups with their own celebratory days, such as St. Patrick's Day (Widén 1972, 203). The Americanized tradition of Midsummer, though, was sometimes celebrated at the solstice, sometimes shifted to the 4th of July, sometimes consolidated with a local pioneer recognition festival, and sometimes tied to June 6, the Swedish National Day (Widén 1972, 203–6). Widén wrote in 1948 that "during recent years there has been a notable tendency to arrange a *midsommarfest* as a sort of Swedish day or 'Svenskarnasdag,' in which all of an area's groups and organizations take part, the largest being the one celebrated in Minneapolis the last Sunday in June and bringing together around 50,000 people" (Widén 1948, 18). In chapter 8, we will examine this pattern as it was followed in Denver.

In addition to the continuities in tradition that have been observed in the American Midwest, early- to mid-century continuities in Swedish American Midsummer celebrations have been documented in the Northeast, specifically in Worcester, Massachusetts, and Huntington, New York, on Long Island. For Worcester, photographic evidence exists from 1912, 1945, and throughout the 1950s. While the annual celebration at Worcester included many activities in the ordinary inventory for Midsummer—national flags, sports competitions, music, dance—it also incorporated a less usual parade. Distinctive features of the Midsummer parade in 1912 were floats depicting the Monitor (Swedish American John Ericsson's ship) and a Viking ship (Salomonsson, Hultgren, and Becker 2005, 85, 116). These float designs dated much earlier, to a Viking float created by the Swedish American organization Svea Gille for an 1892 Independence Day parade and an 1898 Monitor float created by Svea Gille for a parade celebrating the fiftieth anniversary of Worcester's founding.[28] The latter parade was held near Midsummer, on June 22 (Nilsson and Knutson 1898, 53–54). According to Salomonsson, Hultgren, and Becker, "parades . . . were staples of the Midsummer celebration until the 1920s. Midsummer is still celebrated by Scandinavian American organizations throughout the region" (Salomonsson, Hultgren, and Becker 2005, 85).

The Long Island Midsummer event may represent a continuous tradition from the late 1930s through the late 1970s, when a Long Island celebration was observed by Barbro Klein (described in her later publication "Den Gamla Hembygden," Klein 1989), although it is unclear whether this was the same community observed by Albin Widén in the mid-1930s. Widén wrote *Svenskar Som Erövrat Amerika* after his first trip to America. In it, he briefly refers to observations of Midsummer celebrations in Detroit, Michigan; New Jersey; and New York during the mid-1930s. He photographed Swedish Americans in New York dancing in folk costume around a somewhat diminutive Midsummer pole (Widén 1937, 96ff, 122, 132ff). As described by Klein, the Long Island celebration of the 1970s, held the last Sunday in June, was organized by the combined Swedish American associations of the larger New York area as an outing to Lindbergh Park near Huntington, on land owned by the Vasa Order. Huntington's proximity to New York City drew an unusually large attendance to this event, including in addition to the older generation of Swedish immigrants a cosmopolitan crowd accustomed to the festive ethnic celebrations of the city. This made

Midsummer in Huntington "multifaceted" (Klein 1989, 47). The celebration included a short Lutheran service, performance of Swedish songs, singing of the Swedish and American national anthems, sales of Swedish foods, picnicking, folk dance performance, and presentation of the Swedish American of the year, but not the erection of the Midsummer pole nor dancing around it; the pole had been put in place before attendees arrived. Instead of the Midsummer pole as the day's high point, the focuses of the day on Long Island, as observed by Klein, were a Miss Sweden beauty contest and an evening social dance (Klein 1989, 47–51).

MID-TWENTIETH-CENTURY ETHNIC RENEWAL

Whether or not continuously practiced, Midsummer has been identified in several other mid-twentieth-century communities, and there appears to have been a second mid-to-late-twentieth century Swedish renewal of interest in ethnicity that informed the celebration. Dave Sealander's New Sweden pole raising is an example. There is very limited evidence for an old Midsummer tradition in New Sweden, Idaho: people remember Midsummer picnics dating back to 1904, and there is a Midsummer photograph from 1910, but there is also a lack of evidence after that time. The 1910 photograph records an annual Fourth of July picnic at which a Midsummer pole was present. However, Dave Sealander's father Clause never mentioned having seen a Midsummer pole raising during his lifetime (he died in 1982), suggesting a break in the tradition.

The owner of the 1910 photograph, Anna Margaret Nygaard Cobb, who was a young girl when it was taken, characterized the picnic as a secular event, not supported by members of the New Sweden (Mission) church. But, she said, the church members who were uninterested in Midsummer as a tradition did hold summer picnics. The New Sweden settlement began in 1894 with creation of an irrigation and land improvement company by Swedish Americans from the Midwest. Families from Nebraska and Iowa made up the first trainloads of settlers, and they very soon after began holding Mission services in private homes, building a church in 1895 (Attebery 1995). The community eventually formed a New Sweden Pioneer Association that held an annual picnic in early July, beginning in 1919. Sealander Park has been its location since 1954. In the 1950s, Dave's father Clause built a stage at the park to accommodate the programs for the picnic. Musical performances became the expected tradition at the picnics, with Clause and Dave playing accordion duets and other musicians performing as well (Cannon 1985).

Figure 1.4. A 1910 photograph depicts an Independence Day picnic at New Sweden, Idaho, at which a Midsummer pole was present. Photograph courtesy of David A. Sealander; preserved and gifted to Sealander by Anna Margaret Nygaard Cobb.

In comparison to this long tradition of pioneer picnics in New Sweden, the Midsummer pole raising at Sealander Park is quite recent. As Dave Sealander tells the story, he became aware of the national folk music and folk dance movements when folklorist Hal Cannon invited Clause and Dave to play at the Northern Rockies Folk Festival in 1979. From fellow musicians at the festival, Dave learned about the Poulsbo Skandia Folk Dance Society in Seattle, where he attended a festival in 1981. Since then, he has returned many times over the years to the Seattle area to play and meet with fellow musicians at Midsummer and the Skandia Ball.

In 1983, Dave attended his first local Midsummer event when he was invited to a backyard pole raising in Idaho Falls hosted by an American couple who had lived in Sweden. Two years later, Dave and a Swedish immigrant joined forces to invite friends to Sealander Park for the first pole raising there. The local Sons of Norway chapter was one source of attendees. About a hundred people attended that first year, most of them invited directly by phone calls. Dave has since maintained the Midsummer pole raising tradition in New Sweden, accommodating his own continued travels to national events by holding the local event a week earlier or later than Midsummer proper (Sealander 2001).

This story of ethnic renewal at New Sweden has mid-twentieth-century counterparts throughout the United States, part of a larger trend toward increased interest in ethnicity among European Americans, as noted by Matthew Frye Jacobson in *Roots Too* (Jacobson 2006).[29] This renewal included a turn toward public demonstration of ethnic heritage through organizing festivals. Larry Danielson identifies "the 1960s as a decade of Swedish American cultural revivalism in Lindsborg," the particularly well-studied Swedish American community in Kansas' Smoky Valley (Danielson 1972, 296). Ethnic activities included the highly publicized and nationally imitated Hyllnings Fest, a festival celebrating the Swedish American pioneers, held biennially in October, to which we will return in chapter 8. Lindsborg also publically observed St. Lucia, a King Knut (after Christmas) celebration, and Valborgsmässoafton. Midsummer, though, is described by Danielson, and later by Lizette Gradén, who did fieldwork in Lindsborg in 1997–98 with follow-up visits in 1999 and 2001, as remaining a more inward-directed, community event. According to Danielson and Gradén, Midsummer was observed in the nineteenth century, allowed to languish in the 1950s, and revived in the 1970s, somewhat after the institution of the other festivals in Lindsborg. Today it is overshadowed by the festivals organized for public audiences and intended to promote the town's economy (Danielson 1972, 293–96; 1974, 13–14; Gradén 2003, 4).

Other regions and localities with renewed, revived, or invented mid-twentieth-century Swedish celebrations include multiple towns in Nebraska; Turlock, California; Junction City, Oregon; and Denver, Colorado. Henrik Tallgren mentions that the Turlock Skandi-Fest, a festival very similar to Hyllnings Fest and also held in the autumn, was patterned after a Scandinavian festival held since 1961 in Junction City, Oregon (Tallgren 1999, 34). In the Nebraska towns visited by Swedish dialectologist Folke Hedblom during his 1964 tour recording Swedish speakers, Hedblom noted Midsummer celebrations (Hedblom 1965, 150). In Denver, the annual Midsummer celebration held by the Vasa, Valhalla, and Vikings lodges was given renewed life by the Swedish Club of Denver in 1962—a renewal of an event with a continuous history but now for a larger, more public audience.[30]

Survey work by the Swedish sociologist Carl-Erik Måwe places these scattered mid-century observations in some perspective. Måwe traveled throughout twenty-eight states and two Canadian provinces during 1960, interviewing Swedish Americans with connections to the region of Värmland concerning a number of topics that he considered indicative of their cultural adjustments to life in America. Both Memorial (formerly Decoration) Day and Midsummer appeared in his survey, with the interesting result that Memorial Day was ordinarily celebrated by more of his informants (80 percent) than was Midsummer (32 percent). One of the "key people among his interviewees" explained the American milieu for the holiday: "Most Americans do not know what one means by Midsummer Day" (Måwe 1971, 299). Måwe's anecdotal evidence suggests that Midsummer was a stronger practice among first-generation Swedish Americans and in communities that experienced waves of renewed Swedish contact through ongoing immigration.[31] In addition, we should note that Memorial Day would have received heightened attention in this post-World War II era.

Carl Isaacson sees Swedish American ethnic practices like Midsummer as having become "codified" and "frozen in time" by the middle of the twentieth century through their promotion via organizations, which in addition to sponsoring events also published instructive books laying out ethnic traditions (Isaacson 2003, 130). Nonetheless, in the many practices described by folklorists and historians we do see variations linked to the specific historical contexts within which each celebration emerged. Måwe interprets these changes as "Americanization" that could take different forms: "private Midsummer celebrations among friends and acquaintances," "Midsummer celebrations organized by churches," and "large, public celebrations" (Måwe 1971, 300). But Måwe's categories are a bit too neat. The late twentieth-century/early twenty-first-century Sealander Park celebration, for example, fits somewhere midway on the private-to-public continuum. It reflects not just the history of New Sweden but also the Sealander family's enthusiasm for heritage music and in particular Dave Sealander's inclusivity—his ability to reach across the perceived barriers of ethnicity, religion, and locality to include a wide spectrum of participants.

Toward the end of the twentieth century, especially with the sesquicentennial of Bishop Hill, Illinois, in 1996, and the centennial of the Vasa Order in the same year, many Midsummer celebrations also commemorated the history of Swedish immigration to localities across the country. This was the case in Bishop Hill itself as well as Chicago, several Washington state communities, and communities with a heavy Swedish imprint in Maine, Kansas, Minnesota, and South Dakota (Jarvi 1996, 43–47). Similarly, the Historical Society of Stanton, Iowa, chose Midsummer 1995 as the vehicle for launching its Halland project, a study and series of interpretive displays regarding Swedish settlement in southwestern Iowa ("News" 1995, 155).

PATTERNS IN THE SWEDISH AMERICAN CALENDAR

Significant patterns emerge in the evidence we have for the North American practice of Midsummer. Midsummer celebrations existed on a pubic-to-private continuum, with public displays elaborating on the symbols of at least two phases of ethnic renewal, at the turn of and in the middle of the twentieth century. The popularity of celebrating Midsummer waned and then waxed in response to immigration patterns, American Nativism, religious ideas, and contact with Sweden. And, while networks throughout Swedish America helped develop some practices that can be regarded as standardizations, regional and local communities did develop their own patterns for Midsummer.

One overarching trend is that the spring-to-summer passage was celebrated by Swedish Americans with abundance and redundancy, evident in the way the seasonal passage was celebrated in multiple events in which traditional practices were freely intermingled and conflated. This occurred as the Swedish import of Midsummer became amalgamated with the series of extant American holidays and holidays being established during the late nineteenth-century period.[32] American observances in the spring-to-summer season included the Anglo-influenced May Day, Decoration Day (now Memorial Day), Flag Day, Independence Day, and, for the Latter-day Saints of Utah and southeastern Idaho, Pioneer Day (July 24), and other closely contiguous spring/summer days marking points in LDS history. As we shall see in the chapters to come, the pull of these mainly patriotic holidays may have influenced the ways in which the seasonal connotations of Midsummer merged with celebration of Swedish American heritage. In the West, this merging was also expressed as the Swedes' part in settlement— that is, the Swedes as pioneers.

In mapping out the yearly cycle of American holidays, folklorist Jack Santino distinguishes cultural perceptions from the more precise markers of equinox and solstice. Americans perceive the beginning of a long season called summertime not with the solstice in June but with the "transitional month" of May (Santino 1994, 118). Summertime, according to Santino, is a single long season that begins on Memorial Day, at the end of May, and extends through August to Labor Day, at the beginning of another transitional month, September. Throughout May, June, July, and August, then, Americans express a welcoming of sunshine and warmth, marking their many celebrations with flowers as a key symbol and with activities that "celebrate *being* outside" (140). Many of the American holidays are, additionally, civic, expressing national patriotism with the predominant symbol, the American flag (112–41).

A recurring theme in the scholarship concerning both the American Christmas season and the spring-to-summer American holidays is the idea of paired secularization and sacralization.[33] Several recent studies of

Christmas tend to agree with the common wisdom that the holiday has been secularized through commercialization (Lavin 2004; Schmidt 1995). Even the interpretation of Thanksgiving has been pulled into this secularization theory. In her study of Thanksgiving over a hundred year span between 1905 and 2005, media scholar Bonnie Brennan identifies a pattern of secularization and commercialization of the originally religious holiday during the latter half of the twentieth century, paired with a "ubiquity of advertising [that] often made it difficult to determine where news ended and advertising began" (Brennen 2008, 32). To this common critique of American holidays, Santino provides a refreshing reminder that commercialized popular culture is still culture with expressive power. He notes that "the common wisdom is that contemporary calendrical celebrations are debased by commercialism," but, he adds, however much embedded within a capitalist society, American holidays, "continu[e] to possess great significance and power" (Santino 1996, 151).

While Brennan and others are able to point to specific evidence from mass media sources, especially advertising, for the influence of commercialism on American celebration of the winter holidays, their focus on secularization-cum-commodification reflects a larger pattern in thinking about American culture, broadly conceiving of the sweep of American history as a "secularization narrative" (Kaufmann 2007) in which Americans have gradually and inevitably shifted away from the religious orientation brought to North America beginning with the seventeenth century Protestant Separatists and toward a Capitalist-influenced secular society. This secularization narrative has been questioned by numerous scholars who see religious ideas as persistent throughout American history.[34]

Ideas embedded in this secularization theory have also been important in shaping the interpretation of the patriotic American holidays of the spring-to-summer season: Memorial Day, Independence Day, and the Confederate Memorial Day (variable, but held on May 10 in many places). But while Christmas has been seen as secularized, these holidays have been seen as sacralized, revering and ritualizing national symbols such as the flag. Robert N. Bellah saw Memorial Day, Independence Day, Veterans Day, Thanksgiving, and Washington's and Lincoln's birthdays as "an annual ritual calendar for the civil religion" of America, basing his interpretation in part on W. Lloyd Warner's interpretation of Memorial Day and other national days such as Veteran's Day as "rituals of a sacred symbol system which functions periodically to unify the whole community," which is otherwise divided into religious groups and affiliations with various social organizations (Bellah 1967, 11; Warner 1962 [1953], 8).[35]

But as we will see in the chapters to come, the story of Midsummer and other spring-to-summer holidays is more complex than is accounted for by a simple sacralization narrative.

In the chapters that follow, I will examine Midsummer and the nearby holidays in the spring-to-summer season as they were celebrated in four nodes of Swedish settlement in the northern Rockies and the communities for which they became cultural centers: Denver in the Front Range of Colorado, Salt Lake City in the Mormon-influenced culture area that includes southeastern Idaho, Butte-Helena and the Montana communities for which they were centers in the late nineteenth-century mining/ smelting era, and the northern Washington/Idaho Palouse farming country. In addition to describing how the spring-to-summer transition was marked by the Swedes in these communities, I will explore a series of contexts within which the meaning of Midsummer and its season can be understood: the contexts of nineteenth century rhetorical culture, sacralization and secularization, Scandinavianism, and modalities of holiday expression. At several points in our story, the study necessarily broadens to include the other Scandinavian groups that immigrated to this region. Evidence from these Scandinavian groups may include some Swedish-speaking Finns who were involved in Swedish settlement but did not self-identify as Finno-Swedes. However, this study does not otherwise seek to include all of the Nordic and Baltic immigrants to the Rocky Mountain area.

METHODS

Reaching back to the turn-of-the-century period to describe and interpret holiday practices requires an interdisciplinary method that incorporates historical sources and methods within a folkloristic understanding of the structures and meaning-making strategies of celebratory activities. Many sources exist to document the practice of holidays during 1880–1917. Lacking observations by ethnographers (to date, I have not discovered a Rocky Mountain ethnographer who turned his/her attention to groups other than the American Indian groups during this period), the most direct source is the diary. During this period many people regularly recorded a few lines per day in pocket books designed for this purpose. As Jennifer Sinor notes in her study of diaries, it was typical to record the weather, one's daily work, and contacts with friends and family members (Sinor 2002). A typical entry reads like this one from Carl Otto Holm's diary of June 23, 1914, written at his farm in Ammon, near Idaho Falls, Idaho: "I watering wheat and lucern. Henry gone to the hills."[36] This typically terse entry leaves us wondering whether the trip "to the hills" was in any way a Midsummer observance.

A second category similar to the diary is the memorandum book, kept by working men for whom recording the number of hours that they labored was critically important, even though they might ultimately be disappointed by not receiving full pay for the recorded work. Even though these records are more numeric than verbal, they nonetheless provide some monthly tracking throughout the year. For example, in Axel T. Nelson's memorandum book entry for July 4, 1891, when he was working as a farm laborer in Parma, Idaho, we see two *x*'s, a code he used to indicate a work day.[37] For him, Independence Day was not a holiday.

Longer prose manuscript sources such as letters occasionally provide direct evidence of the spring-to-summer season, although typically they do not note specific holidays but rather describe the season more generally. One example is John Swanson's letter to his parents, written in July 1906, in which he describes his summer outdoor activities when given a week free from his work at the Argo smelter.[38] Rarely, we find longer manuscripts devoted more fully to holidays. An especially valuable manuscript, for example, is the 1912 Midsummer speech delivered by Dr. Charles E. Bundsen at a Vasa Order-sponsored Midsummer celebration in Denver, which will be discussed in chapters 4 and 5.

The popular press is also a good source for documentation of the many celebrations that were sponsored by social and religious groups. In the Rockies, several Swedish and Scandinavian newspapers served the Swedish American population. In them we find advertisements for upcoming events and correspondents' columns in which events are described and critiqued. Direct sources also include occasional photographic documentation, although photographs are nearly as rare as speech scripts like Bundsen's. Photographs are ambiguous sources, as they are typically posed rather than candid. For example, a Salt Lake City area photograph depicts Scandinavians at a celebration labeled as Swedish and ostensibly performing an old Swedish bridal custom, leaving us many questions about the nature of the celebration (Henrichsen et al. 2010, 19). Was this an actual wedding in which the couple attempted to recapture Old World custom, or was it merely an enactment? If the latter, are we seeing a tableau or a still representation of a longer performance? Reminiscences and oral histories recorded in the mid-twentieth century also help us reach back to the turn-of-the-century period, although these sources are less direct in the sense that they present memories, often generalized and nostalgic.

We can bring to these historical sources perspectives from folkloristics. Folklorists look at holiday customs as devised by and shared among people to express identifications with abstractions of importance to them, abstract ideals such as "individualism" that may connote for them their common nationality, regional heritage, or ethnic heritage. Folklorists attempt to fathom this *emic* point of view—that is, the view of the custom from within the folk group or community that shares the practice—in addition to the perspectives offered by the complementary *etic* comparative study of cultures from an external view. Also from folkloristics and other fields studying cultural phenomena comes the idea that cultural practice is not just "constructed" by people but also "performed" by them. Performance theory uses the not-so-metaphorical analogy of performing for an audience in a "performance arena," whether one is studying a fiddler literally on the stage at the Weiser, Idaho, Fiddle Festival or a log cabin builder whose "audience" may be remote both in place and time. The celebratory behaviors exhibited in holidays naturally suggest performance in contemporary examples where the celebration is public and publicized. Lisa Gabbert's (2011) study of the annual McCall, Idaho, Winter Carnival examines one example in which local participants can be seen as performing for outsiders who visit specifically to admire the ice sculptures and observe the carnival's parades. Yet, even in this example performance is complicated, Gabbert demonstrates, by the many ways in which local participants perform for each other throughout the carnival (Gabbert 2011). As we shall see throughout our analysis of the spring-to-summer celebrations in the Rockies, an event such as a Midsummer pole raising allows participants to assume both performer and audience roles. After the pole is raised, those raising it can assume the roles of speech maker, singer, or dancer. Singing, orating, or dancing, they can admire their handiwork and observe their fellow participants as they fill their chosen roles.

In interpreting folk custom with this mutual process of performance and audience observation, folklorists have, in recent scholarship, typically shied away from asking whether replications and variations of culture for which performance is a vehicle are also unconscious processes. The notion that folklore resides in the unconscious mind and is therefore both deeply significant and inaccessible to rational analysis, has seemed unverifiable and therefore has been treated as yielding no enlightenment. But the hands-off approach to consciousness is being critiqued by social science scholars inspired by the new neurosciences. Writing from the perspective of *neuropolitics*, a political science that takes into account new discoveries about the brain, William E. Connolly argues that, "it is not only pertinent to see that life is culturally constituted, it is also important to come to terms with the *layered* character of culture itself" (Connolly 2002, 6–7). Culture can be observed, outwardly, but where does culture reside inwardly, in the body? Based on his understanding of neuroscience, Connolly answers, "at several levels of being, with each level both interacting with the others and marked by different speeds, capacities, and degrees of linguistic sophistication" (Connolly 2002, 6–7). What a folklorist observes as she joins Midsummer participants to dismantle, decorate, and assemble the Midsummer pole, debating the process, conversing as they share a meal, singing, and dancing, involves these many layers of bodily engagement. This engagement goes beyond the merely linguistic to incorporate multiple modes of expression. It is perhaps the combination of parallel and redundant layers, conscious and unconscious, incorporating the multimodality of movement, taste, smell, sound, and sight with conscious thought that creates our sense of a festival's deep meaning.

As I've participated in Midsummer at Sealander Park, I have been struck by its contrast to the workaday world: I've already noted that on entering the park one leaves behind day planners and even, if one is willing, timepieces. Also left behind are hierarchical structures of command and supervision. The pole decorating would not happen were it not for coop-eration among the participants. The work has to be negotiated. Around one at the pole raising, one hears, "I'll do [this task]." "Can you help with [that task]." "Perhaps you could do this." No one in particular is in charge, although Dave Sealander is available for advice. The shape of the event—its structuring of human relationships—is that of a rural work party. The workers come together for a set task, often one that can be broken down into components in which workers form teams, and when the task is com-pleted, the workers dance and eat together. This is the structure of barn raisings, harvest crews, and quilting bees.

Work parties exist in the rural West into the twenty-first century, but the opportunities that most Westerners have to participate in them have shrunk considerably. As a girl in the late 1950s, I visited my grandfather's farm in eastern Oregon for the potato harvest. My arduous task at age five was to ride on the wagon, observing as the men loaded gunny sacks of potatoes onto the wagon bed. But as a town girl, I had only this brief glimpse into the kind of work parties that were common experience a generation before mine and that continued among those who still had family farms. At Midsummer, this pattern is reconstructed for me nostalgically. Participants come to the pole raising for the satisfaction of cooperative labor, they dance around the pole once it is erected, and they join in a meal together, although the male/female and age-specific roles have been shattered—or at least bent. The Midsummer pole raising at New Sweden is, in fact, very much like the contra and other folk dancing practiced by many Midsummer participants throughout the remainder of the year, requiring cooperative movement in patterns that are associated in the participants' minds either with older times or with internationalism: as Amy Brunvand notes, such events are an alternative to American popular culture (Brunvand 2000a; 2000b).

In the chapters to come, we will see Midsummer and the other spring-to-summer holidays in various garb. In the Rockies, the spring-to-summer holidays function as multiply meaningful observances. They represent and reconsider ethnicity and panethnicity, sacred and secular relationships, and the rural and the urban. These interpretations of the season's significance might seem contradictory on first blush, but we can regard them, rather, as demonstrating how very flexible and complex traditional celebrations can be.

NOTES

1. I have been a participant observer of the Sealander midsummer celebration in 1994, 2001, and 2007. This description focuses on 2001 but is also informed by observations in other years and interviews with Dave Sealander in July 2001.

2. In describing this late-twentieth century example of Midsummer, I use the term *Nordic* rather than *Scandinavian* because the broad community of participants invited by Dave Sealander included Finns as well as Scandinavians, making this particular celebration pan-Nordic.

3. I use the terms *Mormon*, *LDS*, and *Latter-day Saint* interchangeably to refer to the Church of Jesus Christ of Latter-day Saints and its members.

4. Here I use *ritual* in the sense used by Jack Santino, "dramatic social enactments that are thought by the participants to have some transformational or confirmatory agency" (Santino 2004, 364).

5. A historical context for Swedish settlement in the northern Rockies is established in my *Up in the Rocky Mountains: Writing the Swedish Immigrant Experience* (Attebery 2007, chapter 3).

6. For more recent thoughtful reconsiderations of whiteness, see also Kolchin 2002 and Guglielmo 2003, 8–9, 73–74, concerning Italians in the turn of the twentieth century, but also addressing the larger population of immigrants.

7. Swedish dialectologist Folke Hedblum, visiting Utah to record spoken American Swedish in 1966 was astonished to encounter Utahans who were fully fluent in a contemporary Swedish that had been reinforced through recent immigration and on-going contact via the missions to Scandinavia (Hedblom 1967, 88–89).

8. An excellent example is the mid-twentieth century creation of a Swedish Club of Denver, which is well documented in the club's minutes and scrapbooks, deposited in the Denver Public Library, WH1976 (Swedish Club of Denver Papers).

9. Välkommen to Lindsborg, Kansas (2012); Bethlehem Lutheran Church ("Sancta Lucia Festival" 2014); and Gustavus Adolphus College ("The Festival of Saint Lucia" 2014).

10. Dag Blanck places Christmas annuals in the context of the Augustana Book Concern's "creation of a sense of Swedishness" (Blanck 2006, 137–39). Franklin Scott includes the

Swedish American Christmas annual as part of the ordinary literature against which socialist Swedish American periodicals defined themselves (Scott 1965, 194).

11. Widén collection (Beijbom 1985), boxes 15: 7: 10–13.

12. This parallels the Early Modern emergence of customs such as mumming in England (Hutton 1994).

13. P. Nelson Papers, box 1. Diaries extant from 1860–79 are 1860, 1861, 1862, 1863, 1869, and 1879. Nelson records celebrating the Fourth of July all of those years except 1860. The 1869 diary is the first extant in which he wrote in English.

14. Dahlquist, Lars Andersson Collection, account book entries for 1885.

15. The Swedish American almanacs consulted for this study are deposited at the Swenson Swedish Immigration Center, Augustana College, Rock Island, Illinois. The Swedish Emigrant Company's publication was *Svensk Almanack för År* (1883, 1884, 1888–93, 1895). Other almanacs included *Svensk-Amerikanska Kalendern* (1911, 1912), published in Worchester, Massachusetts, in which Midsummer did not appear in 1911 and 1912; *Svenska Monitorens Almanacka* (1911–15), published in Sioux City, Iowa, in which the summer solstice was noted, 1911–15; and *Svenska Postens Almanack och Kalender* (1912), published in Rockford, Illinois, in which the summer solstice was noted, 1912.

16. P. Nelson Papers, box 2. Nelson observed Midsummer during visits to Sweden again in 1905 and 1907, mentioning especially that the young people danced; boxes 2 and 3.

17. Ibid., boxes 1 and 2.

18. Ibid., box 3.

19. Ibid., box 3. A subsequent mention of an old-timers' picnic at Midsummer appears in 1914. Nelson died in 1916.

20. Ibid., box 1; Peter S. Nelson was born on February 15, 1835, in Gammalstorp parish, Blekinge, Sweden. He emigrated on July 15, 1853. In Illinois he worked as a logger, a flour merchant, a ditch digger, a farmer-rancher, and an assessor, and he was active in local politics. Nelson married Nellie Gibson in Chicago in 1863. Demographics of the Swedish emigration are set forth by Norman and Runblom 1988.

21. In chapters 4 and 5 we will see an excellent example of one such report delivered as a 1912 speech by Charles A. Bundsen of Denver.

22. The questionnaires are preserved in the Widén Collection (Beijbom 1985), boxes 10–13.

23. Widén Collection (Beijbom 1985), box 10, response from a male immigrant of 1891 who had lived in Genoa, Nebraska. At the time of answering the questionnaire this respondent was in his mid-seventies, living in Spokane, Washington. "Americanskt om påsk, Svenskt om Midsommar."

24. Widén Collection (Beijbom 1985), box 13, response from a male immigrant of 1902 who lived in Worthington, Minnesota. At the time of answering the questionnaire this respondent was in his mid-sixties. "midsommar firas sällan bland svenskarna I dessa trakter, men i store svenska samhällen såsom städerna Duluth, Minneapolis m.fl. avhållas stora festligheter vid midsommartiden."

25. Widén Collection (Beijbom 1985), box 13, response from a male immigrant of 1896 who had lived in Minnesota, California, and Canada. At the time of answering the questionnaire this respondent was in his late sixties. "midsommar i allmänhet en arbetsdag."

26. See Rodgers and Hirsch 2010 for Botkin's career.

27. Swedish King Gustavus Adolphus died on November 6, 1632. The day is now Finnish Swedish Heritage Day, established in 1908.

28. *Svea*, referring to the central Swedish region of Svealand, was also used in this era to refer to the nation as *Moder Svea*, Mother Sweden. *Gille* translates as guild.

29. See my comments in chapter 8 regarding the inappropriateness of "revival" in a context that included many continuities of practice.

30. Denver *Westerns Nyheter* and *Western News* issues from 1924 through 1961 document the continuity of the Denver Midsummer celebrations. For more on the Swedish Club of Denver and its activities in relationship to Midsummer, see chapter 8.

31. Måwe's fieldnotes and taped interviews, deposited at The Swedish American Center, Karlstad, Sweden, are well worth further exploration for their documentation of mid-twentieth-century Swedish American culture and the Swedish study of Swedish America. http://www.swedenamerica.se/index-en.htm.

32. Ellen M. Litwicki describes the period 1865 to 1917 as characterized by a "tremendous rush of holiday invention," (Litwicki 2003, 2).

33. Selected studies of Christmas include Davison 1964; Gaudet 1990; Kimball 2001; Monnett 1987; Nissenbaum 1997; Restad 1995; Waits 1993. Of the spring-to-summer holidays, Barrows 1986; Cohn 1976; Cohn 1977; Dennis 2002; Gowers 2001; 2005; Kinney 1998; and Lamm 1983.

34. According to Fessenden (2007), *Culture and Redemption*, America only gives the appearance of secularization through religion's having been restricted to sacred physical and social spaces, but its implicit and pervasive influence in public and everyday life still exists, however unremarked. European historians also question this secularization narrative, maintaining that in America, religion has remained important while Europe is a region of secularization. See Lehmann 1998; and Lenhammar 1998 (critiqued by Hutchison 1998). According to Milich 2004, Europeans stand out worldwide for their secularism (424).

35. Warner also influenced Måwe's work with Swedish American celebration of Memorial Day (Måwe 1971, 293–94). The idea of civil religion also appears in Cohn 1976; Kinney 1998; and Bitton's (1975) interpretation of Mormon history-related celebrations, "The Ritualization of Mormon History."

36. Holm Papers, box 4, folder 15.

37. A. Nelson Papers, box 2. The doubling of the *x* may have indicated overtime work on a holiday.

38. Swanson Papers, Letter C17, 28 July 1906.

2

Midsummer in the Rockies

It is 1891. Which Midsummer celebration in Denver should one attend: Skandia's Midsommarfest planned for Sunday, June 7, in Military Park? The Knights of Pythias, Linne Lodge's Midsommarutflygt (Midsummer outing) to Sanitarium Park in Morrison on June 21? Or near Salt Lake City: the large excursion to Draper's Park, planned for June 24? The smaller gathering in Ogden's Lorin Farr Grove planned for the same day? The gathering at Pleasant Grove, planned for June 23? And, having chosen one of these festive events, would one also have time to attend other celebrations held near Midsummer: the picnic of the Red Cloud Tribe of the Improved Order of Red Men[1] (IORM), planned for June 14 in Denver's Rosendale Park, for example, where one could hear music from the Swedish Military Band?

Denver and Salt Lake City, the Rocky Mountain region's two largest cities at the turn of the twentieth century, served as important nodes for the region's Swedish and, more broadly, Scandinavian populations.[2] Because both cities had Swedish newspapers during the 1890s and after, we have good evidence about the publicly celebrated festivities in their environs. Combining this documentation with evidence from throughout the region, we can reconstruct a sense of the strategies used by Swedes coming into the West. Folklorist Barre Toelken identifies "selection and intensification" as strategies of ethnic groups in the midst of culture contact in the United States, and these approaches were employed by the Swedish Americans (Toelken 1991, 154). But more was required; beyond selecting and intensifying some of their imported traditions, the Swedish Americans attempted to balance the many influences on those practices in the Western American social-cultural environment. A main strategy was additive. Rather than severely winnowing out their former practices or limiting their adoptive ones, the Swedish Americans added celebrations to their calendar.

DOI: 10.7330/9780874219999.c002

In this strategy alone, the practice of holiday traditions reveals itself as an intentional—willful even—expression of orientation toward various positions within American society and their associated clusters of value-laden meaning. Denver and Salt Lake City provide excellent representative examples of the intentional development of a crowded celebrations calendar within the Swedish and Scandinavian communities. The pairing of Denver–Salt Lake City is of interest, also, as it reflects cultures in which, as we will see in succeeding chapters and especially chapter 5, the secular and sacred significance of celebrations was differently oriented.

In Denver, a Swedish population developed sufficient to support events like Midsummer. By 1910, with slightly more than 4,500 people of Swedish birth in the city-county of Denver, 36 percent of the state's Swedish-born population (*Historical Census Browser* 2004),[3] there were social, religious, and political organizations that were specifically Swedish American. Browsing through the city's Swedish language newspaper, *Svenska Korrespondenten*, one senses an active ethnic community engaged in organizing numerous events, even to the point of conflicting with each other. The spring-to-summer season was observed with celebrations for Decoration Day, the American Flag Day, Midsummer, and Independence Day; with Sunday school and old-folks picnics; and with private events. Often these celebrations were labeled as Swedish.

By contrast, in Salt Lake City the Swedish immigrants were swept up in a larger process of cultural consolidation as Mormon converts flowed into Utah from many parts of western and northern Europe. The LDS church had established the Scandinavian Mission based in Copenhagen in 1850. By 1905, Danish immigrants outnumbered Swedes and Norwegians in the state of Utah, but Salt Lake City became a center for Mormons of Swedish heritage, having a slightly greater Swedish-born population than Danish by 1910 (Jenson 1927, 2–3, 411; Mulder 2000 [1957], 31–39, 107). In fact, a "Swede Town" developed in the northern part of Salt Lake City (*Historical Census Browser* 2004).[4]

There was a tendency for these religious converts of Scandinavian heritage to find common cause. They had converted to Mormonism as families, emigrated as families, and once in Utah, unless assigned to mixed communities, tended to settle together (Mulder 2000 [1957], 107–8, 194; Henrichsen et al. 2010, 3). While the dominant mix was Danish/Swedish, with significant Danish and Swedish settlement in two counties south of Salt Lake City, Sanpete and Sevier, Swedes and Norwegians also settled alongside each other, with the largest numbers in the Salt Lake City area and in Cache County, its population center in Logan just eighty miles north of Salt Lake

City. These enclaves of Swedish, Danish, and Norwegian converts organized events that tended to be labeled with the panethnic term *Scandinavian*.

Immigrants of the Denver and Salt Lake City regions added to their celebratory calendar through at least four means. First, they selectively continued and intensified some of their imported holidays; and second, they adopted existing American days of celebration, sometimes celebrating them in ethnic or panethnic versions. Immigrants also added to their calendar by adopting celebrations from or creating joint celebrations with other ethnicities. And, in Utah, immigrant LDS converts joined with American-born Mormons in the ongoing creation of LDS days of observance. Hence, the consolidated calendar of Utah's Scandinavians was especially crowded and complex. The spring-to-summer season included the Scandinavian Midsummer/St. John's Day, the American Decoration Day and Independence Day, the English May Day, and the LDS Pioneer Day, with scattered additional celebrations, such as Old Folks Day and the anniversary of the creation of the LDS Scandinavian Mission, further vying for attention during the busy three months stretching from May 1 through late July. In this chapter, I will focus on Midsummer as the chief holiday selected and intensified by the Swedish Americans. Chapter 3 takes up the other spring-to-summer holidays as they represent other ways in which the calendar expanded for the Swedish Americans, and in chapter 7, I return to holidays such as May 17, for which Scandinavianism posed a problem.

For Swedish Americans in Denver and Salt Lake City, celebration at Midsummer was the chief observance continued from Sweden. We have the first solid evidence of celebration of Midsummer in Denver and in Utah's Wasatch Valley as early as the 1890s, but the immigrants may have had an earlier awareness of Midsummer that was reinforced through transatlantic contact.[5] As mentioned in chapter 1, during the 1890s, transatlantic contact and the establishment of Skansen in 1891 as a tourist attraction in the Stockholm area were important influences in the development of a Swedish American sense of Midsummer and other traditions. But there were at least two other means of contact besides recreational travel to Scandinavia: correspondence and LDS missionary work. Many Swedish immigrants chose Midsummer as a time to write to their relatives and friends at home. This practice, which parallels the practice of Christmastime letters, will be looked at further in chapter 4, as one of the many ways in which Midsummer and other holidays were embedded in a rhetorical culture. Letter writing sustained the idea of the holiday in American life even when specific practices were not continued.

Through the Scandinavian Mission, the Mormons had a form of contact that brought them directly into contexts in which they were exposed to the emerging cultures of Scandinavia. LDS members of Scandinavian descent were encouraged to maintain their home language skills and were called to travel to Scandinavia, often to their home regions, to establish LDS congregations and to foster and support emigration to Utah. This idea was explicitly expressed by Scandinavian LDS leaders like Anton H. Lund, who for example addressed the Scandinavian Meeting in Elsinore, Utah, at its June 19–20, 1892, gathering. According to the Salt Lake City *Utah Korrespondenten,* Lund used his speech to encourage "parents to teach their children the mother tongue, so that they might be capable of becoming missionaries in their fathers' country, where many would embrace the truth [of the understanding of the gospels presented in Mormonism]" (*Utah Korrespondenten* 1892, 8).[6]

The missionary experience put these returnees into a quasi-ethnographic role. Already incorporated into the society of Mormon Utah and fluent in at least two languages, whether or not they actually participated in the celebrations in the Old Country, they observed them with an awareness of cultural differences. Ole Christian Tellefsen returned to Norway as a missionary in 1880–82. In his diary entry for June 23, 1880, Tellefsen noted his observations at Skien as though an ethnographer, and like the antiquarian folklorists of his day, he assumed pagan antiquity for the customs that he observed:

> This day is called Saint Hans Evening, in Norway [St. John's Eve]. It is celebrated by drinking and dancing, and the burning of old boats and tarred barrels on the mountain sides. There were a great commotion among the people this day—celebrations from old pagan times.[7]

Others were less removed from the local population and took part in some form of Midsummer observance. Anders Gustaf Johnson of Grantsville, Utah, served a mission in Sweden during 1880–82. He mentioned Midsummer only briefly in his journal entry for June 24, 1881, and then not by name: "went with the saints to Fiskeby, was out in the Green all day, had a very good time" (Johnson 2002, 77).[8]

These missionary Midsummer observances could do double duty as they provided opportunities for contact and conversations with potential converts. Theo Tobiason, a missionary posted in Gothenburg, Sweden, noted in his correspondence with fellow missionary John A. Carlson that he expected a visit from another Mormon, a Brother Backman, on Midsummer Day, 1895, and thus would not be able to attend a celebration that Carlson was planning.[9] Peter Matson's diary entry of June 24, 1885, similarly reflects this double purpose:

> On Midsummer day, we visited Brother Ekstrangs where we had a long
> discussion with the ropemaster Lovek [regarding Mormonism] . . . . In the
> afternoon, almost all the saints were gathered in Nasby [Näsby] where we
> had a fun time together. (Matson 1979, 54)

To these missionary contacts we can add childhood memories of
Midsummer-time in Sweden. Carlson's wife Anna Lundstrom Carlson, for
example, had emigrated from Vingåker, Sweden, a small Södermanland
village. According to a biography prepared by her descendants, Anna
remembered having attended many celebrations during her childhood in
Sweden, 1866–85, including Midsummer festivals.[10] Accounts like these
are vague, however, documenting awareness more than actual practices.
Detailed evidence of Midsummer in the Rockies begins in 1890 with
newspaper coverage.[11]

Midsummer in the Rockies existed on a continuum between public-
formal and private-informal celebrations. The public-formal, more characteristic of urban areas like Denver and Salt Lake City, will be our main
focus here (private-informal celebrations will receive more attention in
chapter 6). These urban events were large. According to newspaper coverage, several hundred people traveled to them. However, they are distin-
guishable from the kinds of public festivities celebrated at the turn of the
twenty-first century, in which ethnicity is on display to outsiders, folk foods
are for sale, and the erection of a Midsummer pole and dancing around
it are a form of staged performance for which there is prior rehearsal.
We can also distinguish these events from the more public displays of
some turn of the twentieth-century ethnic festivities. For example, when
the members of German American turner (gymnastic) groups paraded
through the streets of Milwaukee in July 1893, their intended audience
included a broader public, and according to historian Heike Bungert, they
were successful in attracting the notice of the English language press
(Bungert 2001, 180). The Swedish American Midsummer planners did
not seek this kind of public audience.

In sum, the Midsummer celebrations in the Rockies fall short of
being fully "public" in the sense used by Jack Santino of "performative
commemoratives"—"an undifferentiated public that can become partici-
patory if it so chooses" (Santino 2004, 364). These turn of the twentieth-
century events were more like very large extended family picnics—reunions
based on common heritage rather than blood relation. Their sense of "public" was a limited public. Seeing the celebrations in this light helps explain
the nature of the activities that cohered around them. Extended families

get together to narrate and perform their common heritage, express their common values, and enable generations to playfully intermix.

Large events such as those planned in 1891 were the work of organizations and committees. In Denver, these were mainly the fraternal and benevolent organizations. 1891 saw the main involvement from Skandia (a Scandinavian group), from a Swedish "tribe" of the IORM, and from a Swedish lodge of the Knights of Pythias.[12] Other 1890s Midsummer celebrations in Denver were the work of the fraternal and benevolent societies Enighet & Vänskap (a Swedish organization whose name translates as Unity and Friendship), the Odd Fellows (a Scandinavian lodge), and the Knights of Sherwood Forest (a Swedish lodge); the culture oriented Svenska Klubben (the Swedish Club); at least one religious group, the Swedish Baptists; and at least one set of private entrepreneurs, Johnson and Lundin, who maintained one of the parks, Sheridan Park, in what we can see as an early phase of the recreation industry.[13]

We can see the attempt to organize through committees as, in part, a matter of social control. For some communities there was a perceived need to control the lines among ethnic groups, an issue that emerged in Denver at the 1891 Knights of Pythias Linne Lodge picnic, where fights occurred between Swedish and Irish youth (an incident described more fully later in this chapter). But the issue could also be with Scandinavian youth themselves. At the logging camp of Big Bear, close to Nora, Idaho, an incident broke out at a dance in 1905:

> A social hop was held at the Big Bear cook house last Saturday night; given by two young sports of Nora. They have given several parties in our neighborhood which have proved successful, but this one was a failure, on account of too many young men who were used to attending parties in the land of the midnight sun, but that will not work in this part of the country.[14]

Here the editor of the *Troy Weekly News* wrote from a normative, non-ethnic position as the chiding voice of the larger community. This was typical of his stance elsewhere in commenting from a distance on ethnic events and boosting all-community celebrations of Independence Day, the product of much committee organization.

During 1891 in Salt Lake City, rather than leave planning to a variety of organizations, the Scandinavians attempted a more centralized, cooperative effort. A city-county committee was created to organize a series of summer excursions, including a large Midsummer celebration, for the Scandinavian population throughout the Wasatch Valley. The committee's efforts produced an apparently successful and well-attended celebration for Midsummer at Draper's Park. But establishing one central event did not discourage smaller, localized events, at least two of which were held that year in Pleasant Grove and Ogden.[15] The city-county committee had been an attempt to resolve issues about "the complex question of 'Who had the right to organize excursions,'" which had apparently caused some strife.[16] Committee members included religious leaders, leaders from the "the old Scandinavian political club," and members of a main performing group, Norden, a band frequently called upon to provide music for Scandinavian events.[17] Unfortunately, it was an incomplete solution. The committee disbanded, and some of its former members involved themselves in organizing events—with poor coordination and results. On July 29, 1891, *Utah Korrespondenten* reported,

> The Board of Directors of "the political club" retired from the [events] committee, and some of the remaining members organized a new excursion, publicized it, and promised that the band would be part of it; this was without the band's knowledge or consent, and consequently they became frustrated, those who took part in the excursion, which took place in Syracuse yesterday.[18]

There were also apparently political divisions within the Scandinavian population that had distracted from the earlier Draper Midsummer event. This was the gist of the correspondent "Karin's" "Letter from Draper" in the *Utah Korrespondenten*, encouraging her "dear cousin Calle" to attend—"you must be with us"—thus casting divisions within the Scandinavian population as though they were family squabbles.[19]

In both Denver and Salt Lake City. these public celebrations of Midsummer were organized as picnics, outings (*utflygter*), or excursions (*lustresor*). Participants traveled out from the city to enjoy the greenery provided by a park setting or the climate, scenery, and facilities provided by a resort. The importance of excursions is apparent in the immigrants' letters. In a June 19, 1891, letter written to her parents, Emma Hallberg reported that people in Denver traveled out to the surrounding parks on Sundays and for holidays.[20] Writing a year later on June 15, Jacob Lundquist described excursions into the outskirts of Denver, which he wished he could share with his sister: "We are now in the midst of [a] beautiful summer . . . I like very much to go on a Sunday to lively Elichs Garden [Elitch Gardens] and beautiful Manhattan Beach by Sloans lake and 3 other summer resorts near by."[21]

Lundquist mentioned Elitch Gardens as one of what he called "resorts" and what Emma Hallberg called "parks" in the Denver area. In the Salt

Lake City area, most towns had a park-like "grove," and there were several resorts dotted along the lake's beaches. These developments, combined with the streetcar and railway systems, played an important role in the promotion of outdoor recreation and celebrations throughout the spring-to-summer months. Denver's Elitch Gardens had been established in 1890 in the Highland neighborhood, the section where Emma Hallberg, her brother John M. Swanson, and their sister Ida Sandberg had households close to each other. Beginning as a zoological garden, the park gradually broadened its appeal with the addition of a summer stock theater, a roller coaster, a carousel, and eventually a dance pavilion. In Hallberg and Lundquist's era, however, the main attraction was simply gardened park lands available for picnicking (Hull 2003, 11). In the Salt Lake City area, several resorts were developed along the southern shore of the Great Salt Lake. Saltair, established in 1893, became the most popular of these, but its predecessor Garfield Beach and a freshwater resort north of the city at Farmington, called Lagoon, were also very popular for picnics, swimming, concerts, athletic competitions, and excursions throughout the summer season beginning on Decoration Day (Gadd 1968, 198–202, 214).

In 1891, Hallberg, Lundquist, and their fellow Swedish Americans of Denver had several choices for their Sunday outings. Beginning on June 7, Skandia's "Stor Midsommarfest" (big Midsummer celebration) was held at Military Park for a more broadly Scandinavian population. Rail transportation had been arranged. In their large advertisement posted in the Denver *Svenska Korrespondenten*, embellished with the United States flag and the Swedish version of the Swedish-Norwegian Union flag, organizers assured attendees that "this excursion to the countryside promises to be the high point among all of the Scandinavian folk festivals during the summer."[22] The advertising and newspaper notices highlighted band music and a variety of "folk-games" and competitions in which men and women would "run, dance, shoot, and strike," to win prizes from local merchants. These competitions included races, a tug of war, and social dancing. A sewing machine was the lottery prize. Six hundred people were reported to have attended. In describing the event, the newspaper correspondent focused on the beauty of the setting and weather and on the competitions, describing the gracefulness of the women runners and listing the winners. Of the setting, the newspaper wrote, "Warm summer winds played in the brush, butterflies kissed the bowls of flowers, and the mountain tops glittered gold and crystal."[23]

The two following Sundays in June also offered the Swedes of Denver an opportunity to attend excursions. The Red Cloud Tribe of the IORM

Figure 2.1. Elitch Gardens, an amusement park in Denver, was a popular picnic and excursion destination. This image dates from 1900 to 1910. Photograph courtesy of the Denver Public Library Western History Collection; MCC–1235.

planned its picnic at Rosendale Park with "good music by the Scandinavian Band!" Races for the all-male Red Cloud members and attending women and children included footraces, a "free for all," and a sack race. Railway transportation was provided for a relatively low fee of fifty cents. About six hundred people were reported to have attended. *Svenska Korrespondenten* again emphasized the setting, weather, and competitions in its report on this event:

> The weather was beautiful, the birds sang, anemones [*sipporna*] wafted their fragrance, and members of the fair sex wore fresh roses both on their cheeks and in their hats. . . . The park had been adorned by Flora in the summer's sweetest beauty. Everything seemed like a paradise, and mild winds were playing in the bushes and shrubs.[24]

The "anemones" of this correspondent's report seem more metonymic of Sweden's early blooming spring flowers, *blåsippor,* which are signs that spring has arrived, than real. In the United States, the anemone hypatica is distributed only in the eastern woodlands. Similar species of anemones do

appear in June in the higher elevations of the Rockies, but none of these flowers are particularly fragrant. The reporter appears to be writing not empiri-
cally but from imagination, casting the Rockies as an extension of Sweden.[25]

At the Knights of Pythias' excursion to Sanitarium Park on June 21,
1891, picnicking with a view of the Front Range of the Rockies and the high
quality of the dance band were emphasized in advertising, along with the
park's mineral springs. The rather grumpy *Svenska Korrespondenten* reporter
who attended provided a lengthy description of the outing that gives us a
mixed sense of the excursion experience, from morning exertions through
midday picnicking, to dancing and train transportation back to the city. The
correspondent had enjoyed a morning climb in the mountains but, contrary
to the park's reputation as the "most beautiful and best organized Park in
Colorado with arbors and large shady trees and seating,"[26] the venue didn't
offer enough lawns and tables for good picnicking. The correspondent was
pleased, though, with the dance and the band, which was a high point of
this particular picnic:

> Most of the guests were . . . gathered together already at noon in and
> around the dance floor, the best [dance] we've seen so far in the neigh-
> borhood of Denver. The dance lasted there until the train was departing
> without any interruption, other than those quite necessary to catch one's
> breath. The band deserves particular recognition for its courtesy in playing
> several pieces by special request and changing its own program to satisfy
> the public taste.[27]

Rail transportation, such an important part of these excursions, also
was described by the correspondent. It included a long wait at the Morrison
station and then a train car full of boisterous people, when all the reporter
desired was to sleep on the way back to Denver.

Midsummer received a great deal of attention in Utah during 1891
as well. The Draper's Park Midsummer was characterized in newspaper
reports and advertising as an "outing"; the celebration took urbanites out
from Salt Lake City on June 24 to a more rural setting in the village of
Draper, located about twenty miles south of the city. "The place chosen for
the excursion was excellent," the paper reported after the event, "both large
and well shaded." The location had been vetted by committee members,
who also arranged rail transportation from as far north as Ogden, about
forty miles north of Salt Lake City, and as far south as Ephraim, about one
hundred miles south of Draper.

Midsummer was on the minds of the Utah organizers well before
the event. Advertising with a full program commenced on June 10. The

program was planned to include raising a Midsummer pole, after which there would be dancing around the pole "in the old Nordic way."[28] After the pole raising there was to be a performance by the band Norden, dressed in Swedish colors: "the pride of the Scandinavians . . . in their blue and gold glittering uniforms."[29] The published program of presentations planned for the afternoon included two musical groups in addition to Norden—the Sandy Glee Club and the Scandinavian Men's Quartet—and a number of speeches and declamations, unfortunately not indicated by name. According to *Utah Korrespondenten*, the program included presentations representing Scandinavians from all over Utah. The paper highlighted the celebratory poem delivered by John Bohn, "the old songwriter."[30] In all, seven musical presentations, six speeches, one declamation, one lecture, a poem, an opening prayer, and concluding thank yous were planned, a program that would have lasted at least one and a half hours, and possibly as many as three. This Midsummer celebration concluded with an evening dance, for which the park was lit with colored lights.

With railway transportation arranged to this large and centrally located celebration, did a Scandinavian need to do anything else for Midsummer? Yet, the Draper celebration was not the only one that took place in the Salt Lake City area in 1891. Scandinavians at Pleasant Grove, twenty miles southeast of Draper, arranged their own local celebration on June 23 with a program of music by the Pleasant Grove Brass Band, songs, speeches, declamations, and poetry written especially for the occasion by Charles J. Sundberg. The date was selected so that those desiring also to attend the Draper celebration could do so.[31]

Ogden, too, held its own celebration at Midsummer, probably on June 24, as the day was referred to as Saint John's Day by one of the event's orators, C. J. Renström. The celebration was held at Lorin Farr's Grove on the Ogden River (now Lorin Farr Park) for a crowd, reportedly, of four hundred, who gathered from Ogden and nearby populated places. Conflating the intent of the gathering with a uniquely Utahan celebration, Old Folks Day, the celebration honored the elderly with prizes—rocking chairs—given to the oldest attending woman and man, aged seventy-five and seventy-seven, respectively. Cash prizes also were given out in a drawing and to winners of footraces.[32]

Even though the 1891 city-county excursions committee of the Salt Lake City region had had difficulties that led to its disbandment, in 1892 another city-county committee came together on May 8, to plan events for the ensuing summer.[33] The 1892 Midsummer Day celebration was announced in *Utah Korrespondenten* on June 5, the intended venue being Garfield Beach,

Figure 2.2. A group poses at the base of a Midsummer pole, Pleasant Grove, Utah, sometime during 1880–1920. The "Union is Strength" sign quotes the proverb used by the American labor movement and here may be associated with a day of rest from labor, shifted from Labor Day to Midsummer. Photograph courtesy of the L. Tom Perry Special Collections, Harold B. Lee Library, Brigham Young University, Provo, UT 84602; MSS P–1 #4416.

which according to the newspaper had "undergone many improvements."[34] Not a grove or a park, Garfield Beach was located on the southern shore of the Great Salt Lake. Garfield Beach and nearby Lake Point had been established as resorts in 1881, and Garfield Beach was improved with a dance pavilion by the Union Pacific, which served the resort with excursion trains, in 1887.[35] By 1892, Garfield Beach was facing competition from newer resorts on the lake's east shore, including Saltair.

Garfield Beach offered a very different setting from a shaded park. Plans for the "big excursion" included a program at noon, music throughout the day, and men's and women's footraces with generous prizes. Excursion trains were scheduled as far north as Ogden and as far south as Draper. According to the newspaper, "the committee promises . . . that no one will go and find himself idle at the celebration."[36] But the chief entertainments at the resort would be in the dance pavilion and in the lake itself, where there were boat rentals and a beach for swimmers. After the event, the *Utah Korrespondenten* reported that an estimated two thousand people had

Figure 2.3. Garfield Beach, resort near Salt Lake City, Utah, ca. 1889. Photograph by C.R. Savage. Courtesy Church History Collections, The Church of Jesus Christ of Latter-day Saints and Intellectual Reserve, Inc.; PH 500 27 2.

attended; food sales had been good, but liquor sales poor, which the LDS-friendly *Utah Korrespondenten* saw as not surprising in a Mormon-dominated community.[37] But the celebration had been affected by poor weather. Editor Otto Rydman wrote in his column "Krönika" (Chronicle) in response to the heat wave that hit at Midsummer, "Pooh! So everyone says in this heat." Rather than reporting the Midsummer event, which he had not attended, Rydman called into question the value of large Midsummer events in general, sorting their attendees into gluttonous materialists, overly avid dancers who would ache the next day, vain egoists who attended to be seen, and the sanguine who enjoyed the day as a break from mundane things.[38]

Planned, public Midsummer celebrations in Denver and the Salt Lake City area continued throughout the 1890s and into the next century. We can see the abundance of celebrations as symptomatic of a nationwide movement among Swedish Americans to come together in various kinds of celebrations expressing their shared sense of cultural and historical heritage, spurred by the 1888 New Sweden Jubilee (Blanck 1988, 6). With additional evidence from similar events elsewhere in the Rockies, we can sketch an inventory of typical components for the region's public-formal Midsummer events during this period: their timing, duration, location, activities, objects, and participants, components that together made up a formula for Midsummer as a vernacular event.[39] The inventory reveals that the strategy of adding Midsummer to the calendar was not the only strategic move by the Swedish Americans. In adding the holiday, they also syncretized it with existing American holidays.

The timing of Midsummer celebrations in the Rockies demonstrates at most a weak and implicit link to the summer solstice and to the Christian-informed tradition of celebration on St. John's (John the Baptist's) Eve or Day, June 23 or 24.[40] We can point instead to two patterns in timing: during the first half of the 1890s, the timing of Midsummer excursions in Denver was arranged to be convenient for workers and their families. Sunday was the preferred day, when workers had time to travel out from their cities or towns. In addition, the organizations sponsoring these excursions seem to have attempted not to compete with each other directly. So, an excursion labeled as *Midsommar,* while still held during June, could appear on the calendar as early as the first Sunday or as late as the last Sunday in June. One way to intensify a practice is to repeat it. In the Denver area, particularly, we can speak not of Midsummer, but of Midsummers. The general practice constituted more of a Midsummer season than a celebration timed for the solstice or for St. John's Eve or Day. We see a gradual shift away from this practice as the decade continued. By 1897, the Midsummer celebration held by Court Walhalla of the Foresters of America was scheduled for June 24, 1897, a Thursday, in Elitch Gardens, and celebrations throughout the 1900s and 1910s were held more closely to St. John's Day—June 23, 24, 25, or 26—as though an Americanized practice had been pulled back more closely to Old World tradition.

In LDS Utah, there was a stronger tendency to time Midsummer on June 24, whenever it fell in the week, but Mormon conventions concerning the avoidance of holiday celebrations on Sunday shifted this timing during certain years. Both Independence Day and Pioneer Day celebrations were shifted to Monday in years when July 4 or July 24 fell on a Sunday, a pattern we see clearly reflected in entries in Carl Otto Holm's and Anders Gustaf Johnson's diaries and John A. Carlson's memorandum book, for example, as well as in newspaper coverage.[41] Similarly then, in 1894 when June 24 fell on a Sunday, the Salt Lake City organizers followed this principle, scheduling their Midsummer excursion to Bountiful for June 25.[42] But Midsummer could also be shifted one day earlier, to a Saturday, as was done in 1900 for the excursion to Lagoon.[43]

In both cases, Americanizations and secularizations of the timing of Midsummer had occurred. The Denverites' concern for accommodating workers was an attempt to shoehorn a Midsummer celebration into a calendar where there was neither recognition of Midsummer Day nor of saints' days. Hence, the American workers' day off, Sunday, had to be used for these Midsummer events. The Wasatch Valley dwellers shifted the holiday away from the Swedish pattern of holding the more important celebration on the eve of a holiday, a pattern followed for Christmas as well as Walpurgis and St. John's Day. They fixed their idea of Midsummer on St. John's Day proper, but calling it Midsummer, even though the Mormon and the Lutheran idea of sainthood differed markedly enough that the image of St. John the Baptist was not as strong an association for the Mormons as was Latter-day Sainthood.

Multiplicity of celebrations was another overarching pattern. In Salt Lake City, as much as its residents may have desired cooperation and attempted to create it through a single committee, multiple celebrations were held. In 1891, as we've seen, there were at least three celebrations in the Wasatch Valley, two of them on the same day. In 1893, a Midsummer excursion to Saltair was arranged for June 24, a Saturday, with rail transport extending southward to Draper. On Monday, June 26, another celebration labeled as a Midsummer for the Scandinavians of the region was offered by the Western Shoe and Dry Goods Company in Salt Lake City, this one in Calder Park with free round trip tickets.[44] Still, the number of conflicting Midsummer celebrations in Salt Lake City was generally fewer than in Denver and these celebrations were consistently clustered around June 24 from the beginning.

As apparent from the 1891 and 1892 events in Salt Lake City, Midsummer took form in participants' minds well before the event itself. Planning could begin as early as the first week of April, twelve weeks before the event, and public announcements in the form of advertisements and notices in the newspaper preceded the occasion by as much as four weeks beforehand. The event's duration also included post-Midsummer Day summaries, accounting, and evaluations of success. Some of these lagged after the event itself as late as the end of July, making for a window of time in which organizers were engaged with the idea of Midsummer that extended from beginning to end as long as seventeen weeks.[45]

The seasonal duration of Midsummer also bled over into generic English language usages of the term *midsummer* as the middle or height of summer. This was the common meaning of *midsummer* in turn of the century American English ("midsummer, n." 2011). It turned up in advertising, for example, of midsummer clearance sales held during June and July.[46] In Salt Lake City a "Mid-summer Carnival" was held July 2, 3, and 4, 1896, in celebration of Utah's having been granted statehood earlier that year. All of Utah's cities and counties were invited and asked to elect county queens, who would in turn vie for carnival queen. Bands would also compete for prizes, and a parade was planned.[47] This already existing English usage for the middle of the summer season may have been influenced and intensified as the English-speaking population became aware of the Scandinavians' selection and intensification of Midsummer as their particular holiday. The *Box Elder News* wrote on Decoration Day in 1906 that "[t]he Scandinavians are known as top notchers in the fun making specialty and Mid-summer day has been particularly selected by them as a day of festivity."[48] In localities like Salt Lake City, where English-as-a-first-language speakers interacted with the multilingual Scandinavian population, the generic term could have reso-nated with the Swedish *Midsommar* and its connotations of festivity. Subtly, this correlation between Swedish and American English pulled the holiday toward its secular connotations, as Midsummer rather than St. John's Day.

In the locations used for Midsummer events of the Rockies we find a combination of Swedish and American customs. As we've seen in the examples from 1891, the idea of Midsummer as an excursion or outing for a picnic to a developed park or resort in the countryside was at the heart of Midsummer celebrations. In part, this pattern stemmed from midwestern precedents ultimately based on Swedish tradition. The Swedish professor Jules Mauritzson of Augustana College, Rock Island, Illinois, commented on excursions in a 1903–1904 lecture tour of Sweden, telling the Swedes that in America Midsummer was "observed everywhere in outings to open air events, with maypole and bonfire."[49] More broadly, he also observed that excursions in general were a summer pattern for Swedish Americans, often used to raise money:

> One kind of festival much liked is the summer picnic or party in wooded areas. Such events are arranged by single groups—the clubs [listed earlier in his lecture] have at least one such event each year—or by the congrega-tion as a whole, the Sunday School, or one of the societies. Sometimes the participants are satisfied with an excursion to a city park or to some gardens in the vicinity, other times it's out in the country by extra train. (Mauritzson 1994, 11)

As will be developed further in chapter 6, the appropriate location for Midsummer was out of doors, whether one was involved in a public or pri-vate celebration. For the public events, this was usually a park or resort—a location that could absorb several hundred people for a variety of activi-ties. In the Denver area, in addition to Elitch Gardens there were Garfield, Military, Sanitarium, Sheridan, and Jefferson parks, Rocky Mountain Lake, and the Manhattan Beach resort. In Salt Lake City, in addition to the sev-eral resorts along the lake, small towns close to the city had parks that were used for excursions. In all of these locations, urbanites could retire to a pastoral idyll.

Part of the significance of an outing is that it included picnicking, the act of eating out of doors, *i det gröna*. Also important were the foods consumed. These, however, turn out to be very difficult to document. In letters and diary entries, foods are rarely mentioned specifically even when they are appreciated, and additionally, the main food preparers, women immigrants, left us fewer letter and diary texts as evidence, and even in those sources specific foods are rarely mentioned.[50] Also rarely mentioned—and then mainly when it had been the source of altercations—is alcohol. While we have evidence that alcohol was present as a Midsummer beverage, its type and quantity are simply impossible to gauge.

A second Midsummer activity that intensified the significance of the holiday was a program that combined music and oration. This was an earlier and more prominent part of Midsummer activities in Utah than elsewhere in the Rockies. Programs for Midsummer appear in Denver by 1905, when the Midsummer celebration at Manhattan Beach included song, music, and theater performance; in Salt Lake City they were evident by the 1890s, as in the Draper's Park celebration in 1891.[51] We can assess the Utahan's devotion to Midsummer Day through the sheer duration of these programs. The key roles of oration and musical repertoire and the many kinds of texts surrounding Midsummer and other spring-summer celebrations, will be taken up in chapter 4.

In addition to music in the program, music was central to one of the main attractions, social dancing. In Utah, an afternoon dance was held for children. There and elsewhere, the highlight for adults was a dance held in the evening, sometimes lasting well into the night. Advertising frequently pointed to the presence of a Swedish or a Scandinavian band as an enticement to attend. This suggests that at least some of the repertoire would include social dances from the Old Country, such as the *polska*. As with the food shared at Midsummer, specific information about dance music and formats is decidedly lacking from the documentation available, perhaps a sign that these were so embedded within Swedish American culture as to be taken for granted.

We can also point to competition as an activity that was intensified in these American Midsummer celebrations. Advertising and newspaper notices highlighted the generous prizes provided by merchants from the Scandinavian community. Races organized for men, women, married people of one gender, single people of one gender, and children were a common form of competition. These appeared in Denver and Salt Lake

City by 1890 and continued into the twentieth century as significant components of Midsummer. Scandia's Midsummer at Military Park in Denver, 1891, for example, featured men's and women's races and tug of war competitions.[52] Other celebrations mention dance competitions. Alongside these competitive activities, there were lottery drawings for substantial merchandise. After the event, several inches of newspaper copy were devoted to listing the winners.

Did these Midsummer celebrations include the iconic object identified today with Midsummer on both sides of the Atlantic—the Midsummer pole? Not necessarily. The Salt Lake City excursion to Draper in 1891 stands out as a celebration at which there was a Midsummer pole raising.[53] When Scandinavians gathered at Garfield Beach the following summer, they experienced a hot, dry environment with no shade except that provided by the dance pavilion, and June 24, 1892, was a hot day after a long mild spell of weather. No Midsummer pole was mentioned in the program, and indeed a Midsummer pole would have been an odd object on that arid lake shore.[54] In Denver, it was also the case that few of the Midsummer events during the 1890s evidence a pole raising. Tracking Midsummer announcements through *Svenska Korrespondenten* in the 1890s, it is not until 1895 that we encounter the statement "the Midsummer pole and other enticements will make the excursion genuinely old-Swedish."[55] This was a Svenska Klubben outing to a park within the city, Sheridan Park. The logistics of many excursion locations in the Denver and Salt Lake City areas may have discouraged the raising of Midsummer poles. And, too, the Midsummer pole may have gradually grown in importance as American Swedes were affected by the renewal in Sweden and Swedish America of activities perceived as "genuinely old-Swedish."

Who participated in these events? The evidence that we can glean points to participation across gender, age, and socio-economic groupings. The prize categories for races, for example, suggest that organizers hoped to attract both genders and all ages. And what we know about some attendees points to participation by both middle class business owners and their families, who were involved as sponsors as well as attendees, and working class families. John Swanson, Emma Hallberg, and Jacob Lundquist, who wrote of excursions to Denver's parks in the 1890s and the first decade of the twentieth century, were working class. Swanson worked at the Argo smelter, Hallberg was married to a railroad crew worker, and Lundquist was a farm laborer (Attebery 2007, 74–75, 189, 210, 236). The fraternal groups organizing these events, especially the Knights of Pythias, the Improved Order of Red Men, and the Independent Order of Odd Fellows, were nineteenth

too much blood, can become obstreperous. Perhaps, too, the "bitter pill" would counter an imbalance of humors. "En mot en i ställdes, och det var årligt spel. Men busarne— irländarne—tjugo mot en—förtjenade ovett, men förstå ej, när man talar på svenska med dem" "en bittermandel och en åderlåtning, innan i gån på nästa picknick."

3

A Crowded Celebrations Calendar

IMMIGRANTS TO THE ROCKIES ALTERED THEIR celebratory calendars in a number of ways. As explored in chapter 2, they were affected by the late nineteenth-century renewal of interest in folk culture, selecting and intensifying Midsummer as a practice with multiple meanings, including Swedish Americanness or Scandinavian Americanness. In this chapter we will explore three further ways through which their celebratory calendars became not just altered but also crowded. First, the Swedish Americans reinforced the American side of their combined ethnic and national identities through participation in Independence Day and Decoration Day (now Memorial Day), sometimes emphasizing the ethnic side of this identity through separate observances. Second, finding themselves in a region of ethnic and racial convergence, they joined in celebrations held by other groups within the Protestant northern and western European spectrum of immigrants. And third, they also joined with their neighbors in the creation of new holidays such as the LDS Pioneer Day. The result was a celebratory season in which events came to resemble each other in their expressive formulas, always with the potential, not always fully exploited, of expressing a hyphenated American identity.

Participation in Independence Day and Decoration Day marks the perceptual boundaries of Americanness. Jack Santino calls these dominant holidays of summertime "civic holidays," aligning them with Robert N. Bellah's "civil religion," (Santino 1994, 125) a point we will address more completely in chapter 5. Suffice it to say here that Swedish participation in Independence Day and Decoration Day—the choices made by Swedes in various locales—marked the perceptual boundaries not just of their Americanness but also their Swedish Americanness. This was true not just of the Swedes but also of America's growing number of ethnic groups during the turn of the century period. In Chicago, for example, Ellen M.

DOI: 10.7330/9780874219999.c003

Litwicki explains American holidays as celebrated by the city's ethnic groups as "not simply about becoming Americans but about becoming ethnic Americans" (Litwicki 2000, 6).

For the Rocky Mountain Swedes, the choices were as follows: Should one celebrate these patriotic American holidays publicly with one's fellow citizens of all origins? Were Decoration Day and Independence Day mainly occasions for whole-town assembly? In that case, one might not know fellow celebrants as intimately nor would one speak Swedish with them. Or perhaps, should one celebrate privately or publically with one's fellow ethnics? Were these days for gathering with a more private, smaller group of family and close friends? Were these days for an organized Swedish American event sponsored by one's church or by a fraternal organization? In either of these latter scenarios one chose to gather in a reunion-like way for interactions with a group that could speak Swedish together and assume a common set of traditional expectations. All of these patterns existed, but in the Rocky Mountain West the last was rarest and mainly restricted to the larger cities.

Like the respondent quoted by Widén who said his family was "American at Easter and Swedish at Midsummer,"[1] the Swedish population generally tended to be Swedish at Midsummer and American at Independence Day and Decoration Day. A number of factors were at work here. While celebrations for the general population were readily available both in cities and in rural locations, only in urban locations such as Denver or Salt Lake City were people and organizations concentrated enough to enable separate celebrations. In outlying villages Swedish Americans were drawn instead to civic involvement with the varied groups with whom they interacted on a daily basis in public life. Some of these locations also did not have an organized Midsummer celebration, suggesting a general lack of recognition of Swedish or Scandinavian ethnicity in those locales. We should not forget that this period, 1890 through 1917, was an era in which the term *ethnic* retained some of its connotations of heathen otherness in its association with race as well as language and nation.[2] The goal of many immigrants was to blend in.

For the Mormons of Utah Territory, a further complication arose from their historically strained relationship with the federal government. In 1880, the United States imposed a governor on Utah, deposing LDS church president Brigham Young as territorial governor. Independence Day was used as a way of excluding Mormons when the new government held a large celebration without inviting the LDS (Dennis 2002, 48–51).[3] The residents of Salt Lake City responded the following year with a celebration organized after last-minute deliberation about its meaning for the Mormons. High-ranking church official George Q. Cannon, appointed to head the organizing committee, mused that "I think there is no people on this broad continent of ours who have so much interest in the celebrating of the 4th of July and the maintaining of everything connected with the Declaration . . . as the people of this Territory."[4]

On July 4, 1885, the Mormons themselves used the Fourth as a means of protest. Salt Lake City Zion's Cooperative Mercantile Institution and other prominent buildings flew the United States flag at half-mast as a statement against the federal Edmunds Act, under which polygamous men were being jailed. As *The Deseret News* put it,

> Who could rejoice on the 4th of July, and make it a day of revelry and mirth, and indulge in gratulations over liberty when some of our best men are languishing in prison, committed there, as we believe, in gross violation of law and of every right that belongs to citizens of this Republic?[5]

Throughout the 1880s, therefore, Independence Day was a matter for reflection on Utah's and the Mormons' place in American society. A rhetoric of inclusiveness emerged in the press: "No man's religion or politics should be taken into account" in the selection of committees and speakers, the *Deseret News* declared in 1888, and a letter to the editor describing the celebration at Eureka, Utah, claimed that "all shades of opinion with regard to politics or religion were for the time being laid aside."[6] The tensions over Utah's relationship with the United States were resolved somewhat by 1896, when the territory became a state, prompting "massive celebrations of localism and nationalism on both July 4 and 24" (Dennis 2002, 48–51).

One rural locale in Utah with a substantial Scandinavian population was Grantsville, located thirty-seven miles from Salt Lake City, just south of the southern tip of the Great Salt Lake. Grantsville held no Midsummer celebration identified as such, although a June 23, 1885, "Old Folk's Excursion" did take some of the townspeople on a picnic to Garfield Beach about fifteen miles northeast on the southern edge of the Great Salt Lake. According to Anders Gustaf Johnson (2002, 139), "Grand Mother got a Dress patern for being the Oldest Lady present from Tooele County." Whether this excursion doubled in people's minds as a recognition of Swedish heritage as well is unclear. The timing suggests at least an unconsciously held residue of Swedish practice.

In Grantsville, not only did the Scandinavians not hold their own Decoration, Independence, or Pioneer Day celebrations, but the village itself chose not to regularly recognize all of these patriotic American days with town sponsored celebrations. We can get a good sense of when and what the townspeople did celebrate from diaries kept from 1878 through 1900 by Johnson, who had emigrated from Sweden in 1861 as a Mormon convert. Because Johnson played in the city band, he was a regular participant at celebrations of all sorts.

In 1884, 1885, and 1886, Grantsville did not hold its own Independence Day celebration. Instead, townsfolk went to Garfield Beach or the nearby town of Lake Point. Johnson comments on this pattern, noting that he stayed home in 1885 and, in 1886, went to the Lake Point celebration to perform with the band (Johnson 2002, 112, 168). Again, in 1887, he wrote that Grantsville was not planning to hold an Independence Day celebration. Evidently, though, he and two others felt this was wrong. On Sunday, June 26, Johnson wrote that this small delegation went from the LDS meeting to "Confer with City Council" to encourage the council to sponsor a celebration. Initially they met with a refusal, but two days later the council reversed its decision. Johnson was then involved in the planning for what he called "a pretty good programe." On July 4, the brass band met to rehearse in the morning. Johnson wrote:

> In the afternoon People assembled on the Block house Square where we had built a bowery [a structure built of willows, with a domed roof[7]] for the ocation, there was a Base ball match and games, foot racings & some horse racings and other amusements & Fire works in the evening & a dance in the Hall. (Johnson 2002, 188–89)

The town council's hesitation over sponsoring Independence Day festivities may have been affected by the Utah/Federal tensions noted above. But Grantsville's situation also reflects a pattern found elsewhere in the Mormon region; facing two closely contiguous holidays with similar patterns of activities, towns chose one or the other. The day competing for attention was Pioneer Day.

Pioneer Day, on July 24, marks the entry of the Mormons into the Wasatch Valley in 1847 and was therefore a significant celebration of regional and religious identity. According to folklorist Eric A. Eliason, in spite of its religious associations, the holiday was celebrated in nearly identical fashion to Independence Day. Because the two holidays were so closely contiguous, towns in Utah became known as Fourth of July towns or Pioneer Day towns depending upon whether they emphasized one or the other day with city sponsored activities (Eliason 2002). That a city would sponsor Pioneer Day was fully in line with the early LDS church's establishment of a theocracy in nineteenth century Utah. It is not surprising, then, to see Grantsvillagers

Figures 3.1 and 3.2. Boweries provided shade where little was otherwise available. They had religious connotations and uses as well as secular. The photographs depict an 1854 bowery on what would eventually be Temple Square, Salt Lake City, and a bowery at a Midway, Utah, Pioneer Day celebration in 1883. Used by permission, Utah State Historical Society, all rights reserved; #06421 and #24518.

sponsoring Pioneer Day in 1884–1886, 1888–1894, and 1896, as tracked by Johnson, and traveling to nearby Lake Fork and elsewhere for Independence Day celebrations rather than sponsoring their own festivities (Johnson 2002, 112, 139, 170, 216, 236, 264, 291, 309, 324, 338, 369).

Other localities, where the mixed population included a significant portion of Swedes and other Scandinavians, but where they joined in celebrations with the general population, were Gunnison and Logan, Utah; St. David, Arizona; and Troy, Idaho. The comments on these occasions reflect the ways children, women, and men could experience festivities very differently. Gunnison's celebrations during 1879–81 were remembered by Hannah Christenson as requiring a period of preparation during which her mother busily sewed new summer clothes for the children. The celebration itself began at dawn with the men shooting firearms and the town band serenading the town's prominent families (Hartley 1983, 120–21). In Logan, Utah, Anna Carlson took her children to the town's Fourth of July parade in 1898, writing to her husband John, who was stationed in Sweden as a missionary, that there wasn't much to see, that it was terribly hot, and that it was a strain to look after the children at the festivities.[8] St. David, Arizona, was a southern extension of the Mormon settlement area. There, the Swedish convert Peter Anderson Lofgreen, a town and church leader, was honored with requests to deliver the orations for the town's celebrations of both Independence Day and Pioneer Day in 1896.[9] None of these LDS Swedes made note of Midsummer celebrations.

The Troy, Idaho, Independence Day pulled together the better part of the population in a town celebration in which the Swedes and Norwegians were major participants. Thirteen miles east of Moscow, Idaho, Troy had begun in 1890 as a railroad stop called Huff's Gulch and later Vollmer. In the 1890s, Swedish and Norwegian settlers came into the area, some settling three miles east of Troy at Nora, a hilly agricultural area. The populations at both Troy and Nora established churches with an ethnic base: Swedish Lutheran, Swedish Baptist, Swedish Mission, Norwegian Lutheran, and Scandinavian Methodist (Stella Johnson 1992, 15–21; "History of Latah County" 2012).

As we will see in chapter 6, Troy and Nora's Swedes spent their Midsummers at picnics held in groves near town. But unlike the Mormons of Utah, they did not allow Midsummer's proximity to Independence Day nor concerns over the Fourth's political implications to dissuade them from being active in both celebrations. This created overlapping announcements and reports in the Troy newspaper as plans for both observances were being made in late June. Concordia Society's picnic on June 24, 1906, was anticipated alongside the Troy celebration of the Fourth of July in newspaper articles of June 22. In 1907, newspaper readers were encouraged to "Celebrate in Troy," where a bowery, liberty car, races, and prizes—"the tallest lady gets the Christie prize"—were enticements to attend. In the same issue, we read that "the Swedish population of Troy" had observed Midsummer with a picnic.[10] In 1908, the description of the Swedish Lutheran church's Midsummer picnic ran alongside a reminder of the upcoming Independence Day speech.[11]

The Troy Independence Day celebrations were fondly remembered years later for such storyable events as Erick Alfred Peterson's driving "a string of 12 oxen down Main Street in a 4th of July parade" (Stella Johnson 1992, 277). The *Troy Weekly News* editor, boosting the "Glorious Fourth" with many inches of newsprint, sketched the typical components for a small town Independence Day at the turn of the century—parade or procession at 10:00 a.m., a program at a pavilion or bowery at 11:00, a picnic or dinner at noon, baseball game at 1:00 p.m., and races, sports, and prizes. A highlight of the program was the invited speaker of the day. The program also included music and declamations; in 1908, it included a reading of the Declaration of Independence.[12] As remembered by Hannah Christenson, the Gunnison, Utah, celebration followed the same structure with the addition of activities typical in Mormon celebrations: a children's dance in the afternoon and an adult dance in the evening (Hartley 1983, 121).[13]

Processions were means for "marking the separation of the celebrants from ordinary life," according to historian Heike Bungert in her interpretation of German American celebrations of this period (Bungert 2001, 184). Translating this idea into the terms of performance theory, we can point to the way that the simple act of donning a costume, even just a hat, and marching in step with others down the middle of a street keys one's actions as out of the ordinary, and therefore more intentionally meaningful that just an ordinary walk along a sidewalk in street clothes. Even down the few blocks of Main Street, a parade such as that in Troy could accomplish this separation and elevation for its participants by bringing them together at the day's opening and having them march to the bowery or pavilion where speeches and music would deliver a more explicit patriotic message. Drawing upon the iconography of civil religion, towns used their youth to depict Liberty, the states, America and other nations, and the relationships among those entities. In Troy's 1908 parade, the town's girls rode in a "Liberty car . . . beautifully arranged . . . . Each state was represented by the smaller girls who wore crowns with the names of states printed on the crowns. Miss Elsie Larson characterized the Goddess of Liberty, and was a beautiful character in the car."[14] An undated photograph of an early Troy celebration depicts the Goddess of Liberty, Mary Cole, with an Empire waist white gown, and a crown with a single large star. Her court includes

Figure 3.3. Uncle Sam, the Goddess of Liberty, and Idaho depicted at a Troy, Idaho, Independence Day celebration. Photograph courtesy of Latah County Historical Society, item 15–08–02.

Florence Knott, depicting the state of Idaho, garbed in similar gown and crown, and Uncle Sam, Sam Peterson with a theater beard, wearing a star-spangled stovetop hat, striped tunic, and striped and starred slacks. Draped behind these three young dignitaries is the American flag.[15]

Processions or parades and speeches had emerged early in the nation's history as core components of Independence Day (Dennis 2002, 18; Fabre and Heideking 2001, 3). By the end of the nineteenth century, a formula including picnics and competitions and sometimes day-trip railway excursions had emerged. Litwicki identifies two trends in the late nineteenth-century period: fragmentation into separate celebrations—"a plethora of picnics, dinners, military parades, and bombastic oratory"— and commercialism—"commercial excursions, amusements, and sporting events increasingly penetrated the holidays, offering attractive alternatives to what official celebrations existed" (Litwicki 2003, 151).

As Swedish and Scandinavian Americans celebrated Independence Day in towns like Grantsville, Logan, St. David, and Troy, they absorbed these well-established conventions, and as we have seen in chapter 2, they especially fit Midsummer into the excursion pattern. That they also used the idea of excursions as a framework for their expressly Swedish or Scandinavian Independence and Decoration days testifies to their fondness for the idea of going out to the countryside to enjoy special spring-summer occasions.

In organizing ethnic Independence and Decoration days, they participated in patterns elsewhere in the United States. As early as the 1850s, reacting to both increased immigration and concerns about the unsafe nature of Independence Day, middle class Anglo Americans withdrew somewhat from participation in public patriotic festivals. In Chicago, for example, according to Litwicki, rather than participating in city organized programs, "[m]any deserted the city for lake excursions and picnics, while others took in baseball games or horse races" (Litwicki 2000, 4). Excursions of various sorts—small or large, private or public—also became a common pattern for the Fourth of July in the urban West, as witnessed in numerous newspaper announcements and advertisements. When Dr. Rollin L. Thorp retreated to Orchard, Colorado, northeast of Denver, to enjoy the Fourth in 1897, his retreat location was disturbed by "two excursion trains" that "came through this morning [July 4]."[16] Whether joining an excursion or making a solitary retreat, these urbanites were beginning to use the holiday for leisure rather than civic observance.

Traces of the other pattern fueling an Anglo middle class withdrawal from public celebrations—concern for safety—also appear in the West, in newspaper reports from Colorado and Utah in the 1880s through the turn of the century era in which the "safe and sane" movement began in earnest. In 1888 fireworks injuries in Ouray, Colorado, made the state news, as did injuries to children in 1889 at Leadville; newspapers also regularly reprinted news of distant disastrous results of carelessness with fireworks especially.[17] One observer in Denver, a volunteer firefighter, wrote in his 1881 diary that there were fire alarms throughout the day on July 4, including the early morning, and "drunken men without number. . . . This has been one of the liveliest days Denver has seen."[18] Independence Day mishaps also received attention in the Swedish American press, as for example in *Utah Korrespondenten* of July 15, 1891; an article entitled "Fourth of July Mischief" reprinted reports of accidents from other Swedish American newspapers across the United States.[19]

At the same time that the Anglo American middle class withdrew, immigrant groups began organizing "their own 'ethnic' parades and festivals" (Fabre and Heideking 2001, 6). Litwicki points to this pattern among Chicago's ethnic groups in the period 1876–1918 (Litwicki 2000, 4). Examining the Swedes in particular, Roy Rosenzweig (1983) notes separate Independence Day celebrations during the late 1880s through the 1890s held by the Swedish immigrants of Worcester, Massachusetts. The Swedish American churches of Worcester organized teetotaler events with church services, a procession to a picnic location, speeches with religious and patriotic content, prayers and hymn singing, a picnic lunch, and competitive sporting events. Swedish American secular organizations organized similar events that included additional, more potentially dangerous or frivolous components, such as fireworks, alcohol, secular music, and social dancing (Rosenzweig 1983, 82–85).[20]

This was the context in which Swedes and Scandinavians of the Rocky Mountain region crafted their Independence Day events. They pulled together the ideas of excursion into natural surroundings; civic, patriotic observance; and ethnic-derived leisure activity. They didn't elide the day's patriotic connotation, but they did conflate it with the high value they also placed on nature, ethnic culture, and sometimes religion. The lineup of activities—an excursion to a grove, park, or resort enabled by railway travel; a midday picnic; a program of music, speeches, and sometimes prayer; competitive games with prizes; and afternoon and evening dances—made their Swedish or Scandinavian Independence days nearly identical to their Midsummers.

This pattern occurred, for example, in Denver for sporadic Independence Day celebrations planned by various Swedish and Scandinavian groups. For most years, we do not find documentation of ethnic Fourth of July celebrations. In 1890, for example, Denver's Swedes gathered with their fellow citizens to march in the large city parade, as an estimated Swedish contingent of five hundred people (those named were male),[21] and in 1891 and 1892, the Swedish population was involved in Midsummer and other outings bracketing July 4, although apparently no specifically Swedish celebration of the Fourth.

In 1893, though, also in the midst of numerous other organizations' plans for Midsummer and other spring-summer outings, the Ancient Order of Foresters' Valhalla lodge planned an Independence Day picnic excursion to "the picturesque Medow park, Lyons," a site forty-four miles northwest on the edge of the Rocky Mountain foothills. This excursion combined the ideas of procession and outing by having participants gather at 7:00 a.m. to march roughly seven blocks to the Union depot, from which the excursion train was to depart at 8:00 a.m. "Music, dance, sports, and games" were promised to attendees.[22]

One of the advantages of excursions from the Swedish Americans' point of view was that it removed families from the excesses of city celebrations, as they took participants away from saloons and carousers with firecrackers. These events were clearly designed for whole families, as for example the racing competition categories included men and women, married and single, adults and children. But the same ends were sometimes satisfied much closer to home. The same year of the first Valhalla event, the Swedish Evangelical Free Church of Denver took its Sunday School to the city's Arlington Park for a gathering at which children would enjoy candy and lemonade.[23] The Valhalla lodge similarly visited the much closer location of Denver's Sheridan Park in 1894, peppering the Swedish population with more numerous advertisements leading up to the event than in 1893, beginning on June 14. Again planned as both excursion and picnic, this event did away with the idea of an early morning procession but did provide railway transportation. In addition to men's and women's races for which generous prizes were promised, the event was to include a tug of war between two teams: one of United States soldiers and one of state militia.[24] Again in 1897, Swedish Denverites had the opportunity to celebrate as a heritage group at the July 4 picnic arranged by the Knights of Sherwood Forest. Railway cars took excursioners directly to Berkeley Lake six miles northwest of the city, where the competitions included both footraces and boat races. Music was provided by Swedish and Svea bands.

In Salt Lake City, Fourth of July celebrations expressly for Scandinavians pre-dated documentable Midsummer celebrations; there were Scandinavian Independence days in 1885, 1886, and 1895. The first of these was held at the farm of a "Brother" (that is, a fellow Mormon) Lövendahl at South Cottonwood, probably the Cottonwood Heights area that has since been incorporated into the city's southeastern metropolitan zone. This gathering brought together Scandinavians from throughout the Wasatch Valley. The days' components, covered at length in the Salt Lake City *Svenska Härolden*, began with a 10:00 a.m. program that included speeches, prayers, songs, and music. The speeches clearly were inflected with the Mormon participants' awareness of the pressure being brought to bear on Utah's polygamists by the federal government. Reflecting the kind of rhetoric seen in contemporary English-language newspapers, the speakers "hoped to see the day soon dawn when the freedom, for whom the nation's patriots fought, should be enjoyed by all, when tyrants should not have the power to oppress or hinder a free people to enjoy all the blessings bestowed by the Constitution."[25]

Those enforcing the 1882 Edmunds Act were seen by these Scandinavian Mormons as violating the Constitutional protection of religious freedom which they had traveled to the United States to enjoy: "We have chosen this country, far from the north, that the freedom we have here [we may] enjoy," they sang in the opening program.[26]

But in addition to these concerns for religious freedom, the proceedings were equally infused with hyphenated Scandinavian Americanism and enthusiasm for nature, both also expressed in Midsummer celebrations. In fact, much of the day's activities and sentiments, to which we will return in chapter 5, are nearly indistinguishable from the Utahans' Scandinavian Midsummer celebrations. Especially interesting in this respect is a flagpole that received the kind of attention reserved for a decorated Midsummer pole: "the big liberty-pole, 50 feet tall, was decorated with Scandinavian flags over which flew the American," a reporter wrote, bringing to mind the practice of topping Midsummer poles with both Swedish and United States flags.[27]

The excursion to Lövendahl's place included a span of time between the morning program and activities scheduled for 3:00 p.m. During this time, attendees probably ate a picnic dinner, but this was not described by *Svenska Härolden*'s correspondent. The writer did describe participants' seeking shade for the hot midday sun under the grove's trees and under bowers that had been erected for the event. The activities at 3:00 p.m. included more speeches and then games and dances from the nations assembled, Swedish, Danish, and Norwegian. At 7:00 p.m. the evening social dancing began in the local schoolhouse, and those who wished to depart for Salt Lake City took a 10:00 p.m. train home, sent off "with joy and cheers from those who stayed behind,"[28] presumably to continue the dance.

Wasatch Valley Scandinavians assembled again the following year for a similar outing to the Moses place in Cottonwood, on July 5 as Independence Day proper was a Sunday.[29] For the late 1880s and early

1890s, we have no evidence of specifically Scandinavian gatherings until 1895, when Norden, a literary society, and the singing group Svea planned a Scandinavian Independence Day outing at Lake Park, a location between Salt Lake City and Ogden. As with the Cottonwood excursions, the outing hoped to gather attendees from throughout the valley: "Come, all Scandinavians, and meet old acquaintances from south and north."[30] Planned for the program were songs by Svea and the Swedish Men's Quartet, speeches by John C. Sandberg, C.A. Carlquist, and August Carlson, declamations, and footraces.

Traditional Midsummer is bracketed on both sides by important patriotic American holidays, with Independence Day falling only ten days after Midsummer and Decoration Day falling twenty-four days before. Originally memorializing fallen soldiers with the simple practice of strewing flowers over their graves and lacking a fixed point on the calendar, Decoration days emerged soon after the Civil War in both the North and South through the efforts of women's groups. By the 1880s, Decoration Day had expanded in scope to include processions to local cemeteries, where speeches and graveside ceremonies, including decorating, could take place. This celebratory space was usually in a major city cemetery, within city limits, and the focus was on military veterans and those who had died in American wars. Sometimes the day also included military parades and drills, but overall a somber, sacralizing tone was appropriate (Litwicki 2003, 11–33; Warner 1962 [1953], 15–16).

Much to the chagrin of organizers, however, in the 1880s, some Americans began to use the day for leisure activities such as competitive games, picnics, and excursions (Litwicki 2003, 32). For the Swedish Americans of Denver and the Scandinavian Americans of Salt Lake City, though, it was not necessarily a cavalierly antipatriotic or sacrilegious stance to consider Decoration Day as one more opportunity for an excursion. These Western Swedes had little connection to the Civil War.[31]

Furthermore, there were no clear parallels to Decoration Day in Swedish custom. For the poorest Swedes, at the turn of the century, burial could have been merely a temporary disposition of the body after death. The Swedish ethnologist Birgitta Skarin Frykman explains that Swedish cemeteries were segregated by class, and grave plots in the workers' sections were crowded: "When they decayed away after twenty years the grave was excavated for another laborer's corpse" (Frykman 1994, 99). For the middle class, Swedish customs for grave tending defined a community wide and year round shared responsibility for maintenance, not a single day for decorating. Nils-Arvid Bringéus notes:

Thinking about death was imbedded in the weekly cycle of activities. Before the Saturday evening ringing in of the Sabbath [by a tolling of church bells] women gathered at the graves of relatives in the churchyard with rakes, watering cans, and flowers. Sunday's visit to church included another gathering in the churchyard. There one stood gathered as a flock and talked together before the church bells rang. (Bringéus 1994, 9)

A Swedish immigrant might not, then, expect that tending graves and commemorating departed loved ones would be circumscribed to a particular day in May.

Even with these striking differences in customs, the Swedish newspaper commentary on the Improved Order of Red Men's attempt to hold a Decoration Day excursion in Denver, 1891, called into question whether the excursion formula should be used for the solemn occasion of Decoration Day. *Svenska Korrespondenten* commented that attendance was sparse, "Decoration Day seems inappropriate for holding a picnic, the restauranteur York [now] knows that with all certainty."[32]

But those in Salt Lake City, 1886, were entirely unembarrassed by treating Decoration Day as an excursion day. The editor of *Svenska Härolden* wrote this announcement on May 20:

Well, now summer has seriously arrived, and it is so hot that you could "fry herring on the roads." But on the 31st of May, Decoration Day nevertheless will be commemorated, and so that "we Scandinavians" shouldn't go entirely without employment, a few enterprising countrymen have arranged a pleasure trip to the Calder Farm. Further notifications to this effect in the next issue. For now, think of this, and prepare yourself![33]

By placing "we Scandinavians" in quotation marks, the editor sets them apart from the rest of the Utah population, implying that Decoration Day isn't relevant to the Scandinavians, who would be left out were an especially Scandinavian excursion not being arranged for their enjoyment. Indeed, it was probably the case that few of the Scandinavians in the Wasatch Valley were related to veterans or to soldiers who had died in an American war.

Decoration Day excursions that included patriotic observances were organized in Denver in 1895 and in Salt Lake City in 1893. The 1895 event in Denver was held by the Swedish Lutherans as an excursion to Dome Rock, "where patriotic speeches and songs will be held and sung."[34] This excursion took attendees to a remote location southwest of the city in the mining country near Cripple Creek, a long journey for holding speeches in the forest. The Decoration Day excursion in 1893 to Smooth's Park, a destination about thirty miles southeast of Salt Lake City, was sponsored by the Scandinavian Democratic Club and the Norden Military Company, who assured readers of their advertisement that "all are kindly invited to participate in this excursion, without regard to political or religious views."[35] The program included a demonstration of military exercises as well as band music, singing, speeches, and an evening social dance at the park's pavilion. After the event *Utah Korrespondenten* reported the excursion's success, barring "a couple of minor exceptions—caused by *spiritus 'bierus.'* "[36] This unusual reference to the presence of beer at an event attended mainly by Mormons suggests that the event may have successfully drawn attendees across religious divisions.

An additional process that multiplied the number of spring-to-summer celebrations in Denver and Salt Lake City was the influence of neighboring ethnic groups. In Denver, the Swedes lived alongside numerous groups. And, while they had bristled at the attendance of drunken Irishmen at the 1891 Knights of Pythias Midsummer celebration, they found it appropriate to join forces with German immigrants in celebrations like the Swedish-German picnic arranged by the Gustaf Adolf and Bismarck Club in Denver's Sheridan Park on June 13, 1897. This excursion event included a German American band, song, dance, and games.[37]

In Salt Lake City and the Watsatch Valley, Swedish immigrants lived among fellow immigrants from throughout western and northern Europe and were influenced by their celebrations. The Norwegian and Danish national days were sometimes observed, and all Scandinavians were invited to attend. Clearly these national days meant something other than national separatism in Scandinavian Utah, where Scandinavianism was actively promoted by the LDS church. Scandinavianism will receive more attention in chapter 7, where Swedish-Norwegian and Swedish-Danish interactions in Montana and Utah will be examined.

Another example of interaction with other immigrant groups is Scandinavian participation in the English May Day.[38] This category provides one of the most interesting examples of festive blending among the Mormons, an 1894 celebration of May 1 by the Scandinavians of Salt Lake City. *Utah Korrespondenten* described the celebration as including a curious combination of activities: a Scandinavian choir, dancing, a May pole, a tableau entitled "Spring," and a Scandinavian national tableau with a representation of the Statue of Liberty. This odd mixture of activities performed for the first of May by Scandinavians has a later counterpart in the use of an apparently British American Maypole dance at the Lindsborg, Kansas, Hyllnings Fest (Klein 1989, 59, 63). May Day is still especially observed by descendants of the English and Scandinavian settlers of Mendon, Utah.[39]

The LDS Scandinavians also joined with their fellow converts to create days of celebration distinctive to the Mormon region, such as Pioneer Day and Old Folks Day. Here is Ole Christian Tellefsen's description of Pioneer Day in Hyrum, Utah, in 1882:

> It being the pioneer day the celebrations started at sunrise. There were gun salutes and the hoisting of the Stars and Stripes. A meeting was held at 10 a.m. Opened with song and I was called upon to open the meeting with prayer. Then there were songs sung and speeches made and readings till 12 noon. Then a dance program for children from 4–6 p.m. and for the grown people from 8 p.m.[40]

Hyrum was a Mormon village mainly settled by Scandinavians, with a strong Swedish presence (Mulder 2000 [1957], 214–20), yet Tellefsen, who was a Norwegian immigrant, described a celebration devoid of explicitly ethnic or nation-of-origin markers. It includes the set of practices that came to be associated with Pioneer Day: a volley of gunshots, raising of the national flag, speeches, songs, readings, and dancing. To this accumulated "repertoire" of Pioneer Day components, folklorist Eric A. Eliason adds the shouting of hurrahs and the "Hosanna Shout," processions, military band music, parades with floats, feasting, games, and contests; and anthropologist Steven L. Olsen adds excursions (Eliason 2002, 146–47; Olsen 1996–97, 160). But these were just the public components of Pioneer Day. Tellefsen's day ended with visiting among the LDS immigrants in their homes, evidence of a private dimension to the celebration of Pioneer Day that paralleled and augmented the public performances.

Another extended account of Pioneer Day in a town with many Scandinavian and Icelandic immigrants, Spanish Fork, Utah, appears in a letter written by an Icelandic immigrant, Þorsteinn Jónsson, in 1884. Like the Hyrum celebration, the day's events at Spanish Fork included components similar to those of the other spring-summer holidays, in this case a parade from city hall to a grove just outside of town, public speech and song, an outdoor meal, and games: "we went just outside of town to a forest, which was planted for pleasure. There were held speeches and singing, then lunch was served and we ate, and there after we played games."[41]

But in contrast to the Hyrum celebration, at Spanish Fork national origin was foregrounded. Participants were chosen to represent their nations of origin and were expressly requested to display representative costumes and artifacts: "they [perhaps church officials; the referent is unclear] call on a few men of every nation to show their national costumes and various traits, to display ones status and crafts, which they brought with them from

home" (Wood 2005, 57)[42] in the Pioneer Day parade. The Icelanders—three
couples including Jónsson and his wife—chose to display "a symbol for
the group from blue linen, with a falcon on one side, and a Viking ship
on the other side" and "a symbol made out of white linen with big blue
inscription, saying: Iceland delights in you, Zion." Þorsteinn's part in the
display was to wear the uniform he had brought with him from his former
post as a policeman in Reykjavik, Iceland; his wife's, to wear "her national
costume, which was considered the most beautiful costume they had ever
seen" (Wood 2005, 58).

The display gave an impression of parity among the ethnic groups
assembled, yet as Jónsson described it, the parade was organized in a
hierarchical fashion. Groupings began with the English, then Americans,
"Swedish, Danish, Icelandic, German, all in wagons, which were
decorated," and riding with the wagons was a court similar to the courts
of Independence Day celebrations: "young men and women on horse-
back, riding side by side, the boys dressed in black on gray horses, but
the girls on brown horses all dressed in white. This was to represent the
24 days of the month [of July leading up to Pioneer Day]" (Wood 2005,
57–58). In this parade's organization, the primacy of English-speaking
Mormons was clearly established, a hierarchy that dovetails with two heritage ideas: English as the first language of translation for the Book of
Mormon and North America as the locus for reestablishment by the LDS
of a Christianity in keeping, according to their theology, with Hebrew/
early Christian times. This reestablishment was further reflected in the
"Hosanna Shout" that was included in early Pioneer Day celebrations.
According to Eliason, the Mormons thought the shout to be an "ancient
Israelite practice reserved for the holiest and happiest of occasions such
as temple dedications" (Eliason 2002, 147).

In the smaller Utah towns such as Hyrum and Spanish Fork, the
Scandinavians were mutual participants in shaping Pioneer Day. In Salt
Lake City, the Scandinavians sometimes organized their own Pioneer Day
celebrations, similarly to their doing so for Independence and Decoration
days.[43] Furthermore, the Mormon culture area's festive calendar included
other distinctively Mormon celebrations throughout the spring-to-summer
season: Brigham Young's birthday, the anniversary of the founding of the
Scandinavian Mission, and Old Folks Day, which is a day recognizing the
elderly that dates to the 1870s and that was sometimes celebrated with separate Scandinavian excursions.[44] For the Swedish converts in Salt Lake City, it
was a very crowded spring-to-summer season, and people had to be selective in which events they attended.

As we sift through the evidence about how Midsummer, Independence Day, Decoration Day, and Pioneer Day were celebrated, a few points of correspondence emerge that are worth further exploration as keys to the season's meanings. Throughout the many descriptions of these holidays we hear repeatedly about programs with speeches and songs, about Swedish Americanness and religious significance, and about excursions to groves or resorts. The following chapters will pick up on each of these patterns as we turn to the many ways Swedish Americans and their fellow Scandinavians spoke and wrote about the spring-summer season emphasizing its secular and sacred significance and its expression of human-ecological connections.

NOTES

1. Widén Collection (Barton 1984), box 10.

2. See for example Brad Evans 2005, and Werner Sollors 1986, chapter 1.

3. Eliason (2002, 150) juxtaposes this territorial Fourth with the large Pioneer Day celebration held the same year to observe the church's jubilee.

4. "Fourth of July Celebration: Citizens' Mass Meeting." *Deseret News* (Salt Lake City), June 22, 1881, page 8.

5. *Deseret News* (Salt Lake City), July 8, 1885, page 9.

6. *Deseret News* (Salt Lake City), June 27, 1888, page 8; July 11, 1888, page 1.

7. Describing the boweries built for the Fourth of July at Gunnison, Utah, Hannah Christenson compares these woven willow structures to tabernacles (Hartley 1983, 121). From the Mormon point of view, a tabernacle—a temporary shelter for outdoor worship—would call to mind both the Jewish Feast of Tabernacles and meetinghouses used for multiple purposes, the most substantial of which is the 1860s tabernacle still standing in Temple Square, Salt Lake City.

8. Carlson Papers, Letter from Anna Carlson to John Carlson, July 6, 1898, box 1, folder 11.

9. Lofgreen 1896–1919 journal, page 42.

10. *Troy Weekly News*, June 28, 1907, page 1, 12. The Christie prize was evidently offered by T. H. Christie, who ran a grocery/dry goods store in Troy.

11. *Troy Weekly News*, June 26, 1908, page 10.

12. *Troy Weekly News*, July 6, 1906, page 1; June 28, 1907, page 1; July 5, 1907, page 1; June 26, 1908, page 6; July 20, 1908, page 1, 10.

13. Strikingly similar was a July 5, 1886, celebration in Lindsborg, Kansas, as described in Tonsing 2000, 222–23.

14. *Troy Weekly News*, July 10, 1908, page 10. Other examples can be found in *Deseret News* (Salt Lake City), July 2, 1884, page 1; July 16, 1884, page 1; July 11, 1888, page 1. The July 16, 1884, article describes a Chester, Utah, celebration in which "thirteen little girls represented the original States, and the same number of boys representing various nations acted as attendants; three young girls represented the rising star of Utah." The July 11, 1888, article describes "the Goddess of Liberty surrounded by 38 young ladies dressed in white to represent each State in the Union."

15. Latah County Historical Society, photograph 15–8–2. Attributed to Henry Erichson, active in Moscow, Idaho, from 1884 to 1908 ("Digital Memories" 2001).

16. Thorp Diary. See for example *Deseret News* (Salt Lake City), July 2, 1884, page 1, where we find that Salt Lake City planned its own celebration with speeches, a reading of the Declaration of Independence, fireworks, and a group of girls depicting the states and territories, but that an excursion train would also be available for those wishing to take an outing on the Fourth to nearby Ogden. Excursions out from Salt Lake City to lake resorts and to Ogden are also mentioned in *Deseret News* July 14, 1886, page 15. *Utah Korrespondenten* (Salt Lake City) regularly reported in the 1890s on Fourth of July excursions to the resorts and parks near Salt Lake City: July 8, 1891, page 6; July 1, 1892, page 8; July 6, 1893, page 8; July 6, 1895, page 4.

17. *Aspen Daily Chronicle*, July 6, 1888, page 1; "Incidents of the Day," *Leadville Herald Democrat*, July 5, 1891, page 5.

18. Diary entry for July 4, 1881, Turner Collection, Denver Public Library.

19. *Utah Korrespondenten* (Salt Lake City), July 15, 1891, page 4.

20. Rosenzweig refers to the withdrawal of middle class Anglos in the context of growing fears about Independence Day safety (Rosenzweig 1983, 154).

21. *Svenska Korrespondenten* (Denver), July 10, 1890, page 1.

22. *Svenska Korrespondenten* (Denver), June 15, 1893, page 4. "den natursköna Medow park, Lyons," "Musik, dans, spel, lekar."

23. Swedish Evangelical Free Church Collection, box A, Minutes of Congregational Meetings, 1893. An identical event appears in the 1908 Minutes of Sunday School Teachers' Meetings, box A.

24. *Svenska Korrespondenten* (Denver), June 14, 1894, page 8; June 21, 1894, page 8; June 28, page 8; July 12, page 8.

25. *Svenska Härolden* (Salt Lake City), July 9, 1885, page 2. "hoppades att se den dag snart randas då den frihet, för hvilken landeta patrioter stredo, skall njutas af alla; då tyranner ej skola hafva magt att förtrycka eller hindra ett fritt folk att njuta alla de välsignelser hvilka Constitutionen gifver."

26. *Svenska Härolden* (Salt Lake City), July 9, 1885, page 1. "Vi valt detta landet, långt ifrån nord, / Att frihet vi har månde njuta."

27. *Svenska Härolden* (Salt Lake City), July 9, 1885, page 1. "Den stora frihets-stången, 50 fot hög, var prydd med skandinaviska flagger öfver hvilka vajade den amerikanska." By using the definite article the author seems to suggest this was a permanent pole decorated for the occasion.

28. *Svenska Härolden* (Salt Lake City), July 9, 1885, page 1. "under jubel- och hurrarop från de, hvilka stannade qvar."

29. *Svenska Korrespondenten* (Salt Lake City), June 24, 1886, page 3.

30. *Utah Korrespondenten* (Salt Lake City), June 22, 1895, page 1. "Kommen, alla skandinaver, och träffen gamla bekanta från syd och nord."

31. It is important to note that this statement is limited to the Swedish immigrants to the Rockies. Swedish and other immigrants had fought in the Civil War, but most Swedish immigrants to the Rocky Mountain West, and especially those dealt with here in a study of the period 1880–1917, came to America after 1864. For Swedish involvement in the Civil War, see Kvist 1999, 21; and Tonsing 2000, 225–26.

32. *Svenska Korrespondenten* (Denver), June 4, 1891, page 4; see also May 28, 1891, page 8. "Dekorationsdagen synes ej lämpa sig för afhållandet af pic-nic. Restauratören York vet det med all säkerhet."

33. *Svenska Härolden* (Salt Lake City), May 20, 1886, page 3. "Jo, nu ha vi fått sommer på allvar, och varmt är det så att man kunde 'steka sill på vägarne' men den 31 maj kommer dock

dekorationsdagen det oaktadt att högtidlighållas, och för att 'vi skandinaver' på den dagen ej skola gå alldeles utan sysselsättning, hafva några företagsamma hrr landmän anordnadt en lustresa till Calders Farm. Närmare underrättelser härom i nästa nr. Dock, tänken på detta, och bereden eder!"

34. *Svenska Korrespondenten* (Denver), May 30, 1895, page 8.

35. (Salt Lake City) *Utah Korrespondenten,* 25 May 1893, page 8. "Alla inbjudas vänligast att deltaga i denna utflygt, utan hänsyn till politiska eller religiösa åsigter."

36. *Utah Korrespondenten* (Salt Lake City), June 1, 1893, page 8. "Med ett par mindre undantag—förorsakade af *spiritus 'bierus'.*"

37. *Svenska Korrespondenten* (Denver), June 25, 1891, page 8; June 10, 1897, page 8.

38. *Utah Korrespondenten* (Salt Lake City), May 11, 1892, page 8; June 1, 1893, page 8; May 3, 1894, page 4; April 17, 1896, page 4.

39. *Utah Korrespondenten* (Salt Lake City), May 3, 1894, page 4. The city of Mendon, Utah, explains its understanding of its May Day history on MendonUtah.net. Accessed 17 January 2012. http://www.mendonutah.net/default.htm.

40. Ole Christian Tellefsen, Diaries, MSS B 87, Utah State Historical Society, Salt Lake City, box 1, folder 5.

41. Þorsteinn Jónsson's letter appears in Wood 2005, 57–59, quotation on page 58.

42. Eliason (2002, 151) mentions a similar event foregrounding nationality in Salt Lake City, 1880.

43. *Utah Korrespondenten* (Salt Lake City), July 27, 1892, page 8; July 12, 1894, page 4; July 19, 1894, page 4; July 26, 1894, page 4; July 20, 1895, page 4.

44. See, for example, the Scandinavian Mission remembrance festival held in 1894: *Utah Korrespondenten* (Salt Lake City), June 14, 1894, page 4; June 21, 1894, pages 1–2.

4

Speaking and Writing Celebration

AT THE DENVER VASA ORDER'S 1912 CELEBRATION OF Midsummer, the honored speaker was Dr. Charles A. Bundsen, well known throughout Swedish America for having founded Denver's Swedish Consumptive Sanatorium. As represented in a typed version filed in his papers, his speech, delivered in Swedish and addressed to "Swedish men and women," encouraging them to reflect on and nurture their love for the fosterland—their country of birth—would have taken slightly over eight minutes to deliver, assuming no elaborate digressions from his text.[1] Bundsen's speech exemplifies an important part of the fabric of celebratory practice during this late nineteenth- to early twentieth-century period, serving as a reminder that these festivities were not identical to those of our own era, the early twenty-first century.

Today celebrations tend toward a combination of kinesthetic and material expressive performance with a focus on, for example, the modalities of folk cuisine, dance, costume, and for Midsummer one main symbolic physical object, the decorated pole that is somewhat ceremoniously raised. A key idea is display to and entertainment of observers. The Swedish Heritage Society of Utah, for example, focuses its Midsummer celebration on folk music and dance, decorating and raising a Midsummer pole, children's games, and a ticketed dinner ("Midsommar 2011" 2011). The contemporary Swedes of the Rocky Mountain Front Range communities of Denver and northward similarly focus on entertaining performances presented in a rotational schedule after a morning Midsummer pole raising. This event retains the idea of an excursion through its scheduling as a two-day event in Estes Park, a destination resort seventy miles into the Rocky Mountains ("Scandinavian Midsummer Festival" 2012). The three-day Midsommar Festival at New Sweden, Maine, also focuses on activities and food, with the use of words constrained to museum text, religious services,

DOI: 10.7330/9780874219999.c004

and informal conversations ("New Sweden, Maine 2012" 2012). It is not that oral and written performances are missing from these contemporary Midsummers, but rather that they are less important than the kinesthetic and material modalities, which lend themselves to a combination of recreational activities, entrepreneurship, and public display of ethnicity for outsiders and spectators.

For Bundsen's era, oral and written genres were more central. Kinesthetic and material expression were surrounded with oral expression, so that the practices and objects of a celebration like Midsummer were amply and redundantly interpreted, often as much for the in-group of a smaller community than for any visitors. Through this use of words, the activities of Midsummer were explicitly interpreted as they unfolded. We can apply Vernon K. Robbins' term "rhetorical culture" to this situation (Robbins 1994, 80). In a rhetorical culture, speaking and writing coexist and reinforce each other, expressing and inscribing an event like Midsummer as meaningful for its participants.

Speeches, recitations, proclamations, poetry, singing, theatrical performance, and prayers were key parts of celebrations. This pattern, which gradually took hold in Bundsen's Colorado by the early twentieth century, was especially prominent in nineteenth-century Mormon Utah. Speech making and prayers were prominent components of the LDS celebrations of Decoration Day, Midsummer, Independence Day, and Pioneer Day, components received and appreciated by participants in the same way that they appreciated the oral genres of LDS Scandinavian meetings. "What is uppermost in my memory are those meetings," A.J. Hansen reminisced: "Those good old songs . . . Bishop [Ole N.] Liljenquist, the illustrious old Bishop of Hyrum, came to talk . . . . [r]eturning missionaries preached the gospel with all sincerity in their native tongue, and brought interesting reports from the old world" (Liljenquist n.d.). Historian Steven L. Olsen comments on the function of oratory and other speech acts as components of Pioneer Day celebrations; speakers "provided the formal sanction to the day's events and provided the official link between the frontier community and its religious heritage" (Olsen 1996–97, 169).[2]

Other literate and oral practices accompanied and surrounded celebrations. Conversations among participants, diary notations, and letters written to relatives in Sweden inscribed and expressed holidays on a personal level. In this way, Midsummer became embedded in Swedish American life as a holiday parallel to the United States' many other patriotic outdoor holidays of the spring-summer season not just through its content but also through its expressive patterns.[3]

Figure 4.1. Decoration Day observation at Mount Olivet Cemetery, Salt Lake City, 1911. Photograph by Harry Shipler. Used by permission, Utah State Historical Society, all rights reserved; Mss C 275 #12048.

The term *rhetorical culture* can be used in many ways, and here I use the term rather narrowly to refer to a culture in which the expressive patterns of orality and literacy are elevated such that group identity, human interaction, and meaning-making through texts are particularly reliant on a mixture of oral and literate genres that are used redundantly. Rhetorical culture, then, can appear in particular circumstances—among particular peoples in certain eras and places—but is not a characteristic of all cultures. This is not, then, the "rhetorical culture" of Thomas B. Farrell's (1995) *Norms of Rhetorical Culture*, nor is it the "rhetoric culture" of Ivo Strecker and Stephen Tyler's International Rhetoric Culture Project (Strecker and Tyler 2009). In both these cases, rhetoric is seen as a universal practice, and its study as useful in understanding all peoples in all times and places. My own narrower use of *rhetorical culture* to characterize the array of verbal practices of Swedish Americans and others in parts of the nineteenth- and twentieth-century West is similar to Robbins' (2006) use of *rhetorical culture* to describe early Christian communities in Judea, in which the texts shared within the Christian community included a combination of oral and literate word use.

Early Christians kept sacred writings—"the writings"—safely stored, and while they might occasionally have read silently, more commonly, the writings were recited or read out to an audience, with the recital dependent upon skills developed through the culture's ongoing use of orality in parallel to literate practices (Robbins 2006, 126–27; 1994, 80–81).

Classical Greek development of the art of rhetoric as an oral practice alongside literature is another example of rhetorical culture, but the term as used by Robbins in no way limits rhetorical culture to Classical rhetoric. Rather, Robbins' formulation of *rhetorical culture* is a refinement of Walter J. Ong's idea of the differences between oral and literate verbal activity and thought processes occurring with the invention of writing (Ong 1982). Ong's work inspired further investigations of genres such as the oral epic, with a focus on how the differences among aural, chirographic (handwritten), print, and digital modes of communication lend themselves to differences not just in the mechanics of expression but also in how words are used to create meaning within cultural and social contexts. John Miles Foley's work, in particular, explores how aural expression relies on metonymic meaning-making, pointing to how sometimes puzzling formulas like "white dwelling," recurrent in Serbo-Croatian epic, access a body of knowledge shared by singers and auditors (Foley 1991, 107).[4]

The work of Robbins and others has broken down the hard line of the "Great Divide" between orality and literacy by examining how orality and literacy can coexist, dynamically reinforcing each other. This idea becomes more comprehensible in our current age of digital communication. As we experience multimodal communications in which blends of aural, visual, and print modes are increasing popular—in Youtube videos, for example— we increasingly realize that competence in oral genres has not just persisted but has flourished well beyond the invention of writing. Robbins points us toward paying attention to the kinds of modal blending and juxtaposition used in particular cultures.

Late nineteenth-century North America had a rich mixture of orality and chirographic and print literacy, as did Sweden and other western and northern European cultural regions. In America, oration had developed as a practice in many venues, not just in more formal urban pulpits and lecterns but also in less formal rural cultural sites, including the celebrations held by small communities for the spring-summer patriotic holidays, especially Decoration Day and Independence Day. Martha E. Kinney notes this expressive richness in Decoration Day observances (Kinney 1998, 239). Laurel Thatcher Ulrich comments on its active power in creating popular mythologies like the "age of homespun" and the "mythical log cabin":

The mythology of household production [developed in Horace Bushnell's speech of 14 August 1851 at a Litchfield, Connecticut, centennial celebration] gave something to everyone. For sentimentalists, spinning and weaving represented the centrality of home and family, for evolutionists the triumph of civilization over savagery, for craft revivalists the harmony of labor and art, for feminists women's untapped productive power, and for antimodernists the virtues of a bygone age. Americans expressed these ideas in local and national celebrations, in family festivals, and in craft demonstrations. (Ulrich 2001, 29)

The Swedish Americans used celebratory oratory and other genres to express meanings relevant to their relationships to nation, ethnicity, region, and religion. However, what was perhaps most distinctive about the texts of their rhetorical culture is an orientation toward the future as much as the present and past, even in examining Sweden as a fosterland that had progressed since their departure. Further, in many of the texts presented at Midsummer, they blurred distinctions between sacred and secular (as will be further explored in chapter 5).

The Swedish Americans' use of oration stemmed as much from Sweden as it did from America. In Sweden, oration was also important as part of festive or memorial occasions, such as funerals, for example. A model was set early in the nineteenth century by Esias Tegnér, best known to Swedish Americans as the poet of *Fritiof's Saga*, whose speeches in Swedish departed from earlier practice by using the vernacular, and influenced later oration through using a compelling and plain style that included rhetorical figures such as antitheses, maxims, and metaphors (Johannesson, Josephson, and Åsard 1998).[5] Traces of Tegnérian style can be detected in some of the immigrants' writing. Leonard Nilsson, for example, an autodidact who labored as a miner in Rocky Bar, Idaho, during 1879–84, and who read widely in the Swedish American and English-language American press, slipped into antithesis (high versus low) as well as maxim and metaphor when he wrote that President James Garfield "was born into poor circumstances. . . . from the ax and plow as well as the planer's bench . . . pulled himself up to the highest achievement in the whole world that you can earn" (Attebery 2007, 35).

Nilsson, who grew up the son of unlanded farm workers, came into contact with the rhetorical turns of oratory through his reading. Bundsen, from a higher class, came into contact with Swedish oratory as a youth. He was the younger son of an estate owner, growing up with the model of a father who, according to Bundsen, "was an orator and often called to make speeches at dinners and other occasions."[6] His speeches used a number of rhetorical patterns. For example, in a speech delivered in May 1904 regarding "Sweden and Its People," he began with a rhetorical question that incorporated a three-part series used for emphasis and rhythm (*hendiatris*): "Where is there a feeling more deep, strong, and noble than patriotism?" Then, Bundsen bifurcated this feeling: it was expressed by men through their strength and lofty thoughts, as juxtaposed to women's sympathy and charity (*distributio*). He continued to describe Sweden through metonymic reference to trolls and wars; Sweden was not a perfect homeland. Softening this judgment (*metanoia*), he reminded his audience that here in a foreign land, they found their thoughts returning to the earth upon which they had first tread as children, using a metaphor common among the immigrants.[7] Finally, he antithetically denied the idea that the Swedish Americans had to feel entirely exiled from Sweden, for they still had an intangible Swedishness, an enduring character that in the second half of his speech he cataloged: honesty, altruism, hospitality, and diligence, all qualities especially useful in immigrant life.[8]

Bundsen's career in America reflected the production of both oral and literate texts that were part of a rhetorical culture—in both Swedish and English. In addition to the twenty-six speech scripts that are extant in his bilingual papers, he produced a handwritten autobiography, scrapbooks, geneologies, and correspondence in the form of letters and postcards. His papers also include a homemade Swedish-language book, "The Poachers [*Tjufskyttarne*]" recounting a hunting trip on Arapahoe Peak taken by Bundsen (called "Doc" in the manuscript) and two friends "Mas" and "Tars." The book's Swedishness is emphasized in the choice of language and also in its hand binding with blue and yellow ribbon. But Western Americanness is also indicated in a hand inserted black and white photograph of "Doc" depicted in a Teddy Roosevelt pose.[9]

At celebrations, oratory was part of a "program," a label so common that we might overlook its significance as a framework for expressive genres. In a program, a series of oral performances, planned for the occasion, were offered to the community members who had assembled. The framework of a program keyed the event as a formal, decorous occasion, but as a whole the program also served a pedagogical function. Remembering these occasions from his youth in Brigham City, Utah, Orlando N. Anderson saw the program as a way of "celebrat[ing holidays] for what they were . . . . in a group and really enjoy[ing] the program. . . . always a program of some sort to show us what the day was for."[10] Programs were parts of the celebration of many days throughout the year. Writing a very regular diary while living in the village of Grantsville, Utah, Anders Gustaf Johnson noted many celebrations in which he took part as a member of the town's brass band. Describing the program for the 1886 LDS Pioneer Day celebration, Johnson wrote, "ceremonies commenced in the Severe's Orchard we had a very good time, listening to singing of songs, and recitations, and speaking, all was tempered with a good spirit" (Johnson 2002, 170).

Elsewhere in Swedish America there were counterparts for the kinds of programs found in the Rockies. Studying the many Swedish American organizations of Rockford, Illinois, at the turn of the twentieth century, Lars Wendelius (1990, 59) describes *körsång aftnarna* (choral evenings) that "were more than concerts" because they included humorous and serious "declamations." Materials were drawn from well-known Swedish writers such as F.A. Dahlgren, author of the popular play *Wermlänningarne* and the song "Jänta och Jag" (a lass and I) and Johan Ludvig Runeberg, author of many poems set to music, including "Vårt Land" (our nation) (Wendelius 1990).

In the Rockies, programs could include declamations, musical performance, poetry, speeches, and theatrical performance. In Utah specifically, they could also include prayer. In 1894, for example, the "Big Scandinavian Midsummer Celebration" in Eden Park, a pleasure garden in Bountiful, Utah, began at noon with a Midsummer pole raising according to Scandinavian custom. Around the pole, there were to be music, dance, and games advertised as old fashioned. At 2:30 in the afternoon the formal program began:

1. Music.
2. Welcoming speech by chairman C. J. Gyllensvan.
3. Song by Svea [literally, "the organization Svea"].
4. Declamation, Mr. John Engbeck.
5. Duet, Mr. Oscar Larson and Mrs. Anna Malqvist.
6. Speech: The day's importance, Mr. F.S. Fernström.
7. Song by a men's quartet.
8. Speech by Editor O.J. Andersen.
9. Song by Svea.
10. Declamation by Mr. Almqvist.
11. Music.[11]

This was a typical arrangement for the programs at Utah's summer celebrations, incorporating an alternation of spoken and sung materials and leaving many of the slots somewhat vague. While the names of specific speakers and singing groups were often cited in publicity, the titles of speeches and names of musical selections typically were not listed and may have been left to the performers to choose—or audiences may have been able to anticipate their usual repertoires.

A program pamphlet from a later era suggests a couple of patterns for the Utah celebrations for which we see traces in the 1890s—multilinguality and wide-ranging (perhaps one could say miscellaneous) tone and topicality. The "Midsummer Celebration at Lagoon" on June 23, 1939, was organized by a committee representing several Swedish organizations in Salt Lake City. The day boasted "amusements for all . . . from Baby to Great-Grandfather." A formal program scheduled for 6:30 p.m. began with the Swedish songs "Vårt Land" and "Sköna Maj" (lovely May), the latter a spring song commonly sung at Midsummer, followed by a celebratory speech by Swedish immigrant Swante Johnson, an LDS convert who served as a Vasa Order president.[12] But it also listed one Norwegian song, "Naar Fjordene Blaaner" (As the fjords turn blue) and several with English titles ("Beautiful Heaven," "Sharp Shooters March") including the originally Czech and eventually panethnic "Beer Barrel Polka."[13] Clearly, not all of these selections focused on a Swedish or a Midsummer message, but they did retain and perpetuate the importance of music, especially choral music, in Scandinavian American culture.

Public oratory in these programs was assigned to community leaders such as Swante Johnson and Charles A. Bundsen—usually male—and the choice of speaker bore some importance and was a matter taken up by program committees. Being chosen as an orator was an honor; the oration was anticipated by attendees and the press and was evaluated after its delivery. Nils C. Flygare of Ogden, Utah, noted proudly in his journal that he had been "selected to speak on the introduction of the [Mormon] Gospel in Sweden [on June 14] which I done in the Swedish language. There was a great gathering of Scandinavians and their descendents."[14] The orator chosen for the Grantsville, Utah, celebration of Pioneer Day in 1898 was William Jefferies, an LDS patriarch who had served as a district president in England and had emigrated in 1861 to live in Utah (Johnson 2002, 409). In Troy, Idaho, the local newspaper editor, anxious to promote the town's Decoration and Independence Day celebrations, provided detailed listings of the programs, lauding the choice of speakers, who were prominent men—lawyers, ministers, and congressmen.[15]

Bundsen himself gently joked about the privileged position of the speaker and the speech when he delivered a brief welcome on behalf of the Orpheus choral association at its banquet on January 4, 1914. Bundsen began by noting that the banquet program listed only one speech for the afternoon's entertainment and hastened to add that his words were not the speech. Nevertheless, he warned his audience, he was going to say a few words entitled "No Speech."[16] This humorous tone ran throughout the evening's printed program: "Inget Tal" (no speech) appeared after "Patriotic tones by the Orpheus [singers]" and before "Now they sing again." The actual speech listed on the program may not have been genuine, either, as it was entitled "When in full steam" (När ångan är oppe) and followed a five-course dinner in which each course was accompanied by a glass of aquavit, beer, or alcoholic punch. Following the speech the crowd was to sing the Swedish national song "Du gamla, du fria" (Thou ancient, thou free), but the program noted it was to be sung standing "if you can."[17]

It was so common to praise public speeches with vague compliments that it is difficult to generalize about quality. In Grantsville, Anders Gustaf Johnson evaluated a Pioneer Day program of 1891 as "quite a celebration . . . the speeches were very short Some good songs. And very good sentiments, every thing passed off very agreeable I thought" (Johnson 2002, 291). For Johnson the sentiment expressed was the key quality for evaluation, and a speech did not have to be long to convey that sentiment. Perhaps, indeed, brevity was a good quality if audience members were restless and if there was no seating. The *Troy* [Idaho] *Weekly* editor also focused on the sentiments offered by speakers in his evaluations of Independence Day speakers: "The oration by Wm. E. Stillinger . . . contained much that was worth remembering, and those who heard it could but feel that there was more to July Fourth than firecrackers"; "every sentence was pregnant with patriotic praise and elegant eulogy . . . his interpretation of American citizenship could not but thrill every patriotic citizen."[18]

Bundsen was evidently a frequent speaker at events organized by the Swedish Americans of Denver. For these he sometimes prepared just notes, but mainly full scripts, some handwritten and some typed. Topics and purposes ranged. His informative lectures reflected his interest in social problems, historical issues, and medical and scientific advancements: evolution, Napoleon's career, vaccination experiments, the levels of plant and animal life, the poverty and unsanitary conditions in Denver when he first arrived there in 1902, and social and political systems ("Sociology and Socialism"). Information blended with persuasion and argument when he addressed groups regarding the Swedish Consumptive Sanatorium (SCS), in a 1905 speech on the laying of the cornerstone of the first SCS building, a speech on the SCS and its good work, addresses at annual meetings and banquets of the SCS, a farewell speech to patients and friends before a trip to Sweden, and a speech of thanks on the hanging of his picture in the SCS parlor. More generally, he prepared speeches that were likely fodder for discussions at a literary society or fraternal association, such as on the "virtue of Selfishness," "Which is to be preferred Richness or poorness?" and "the good that benefit societies do in this country."

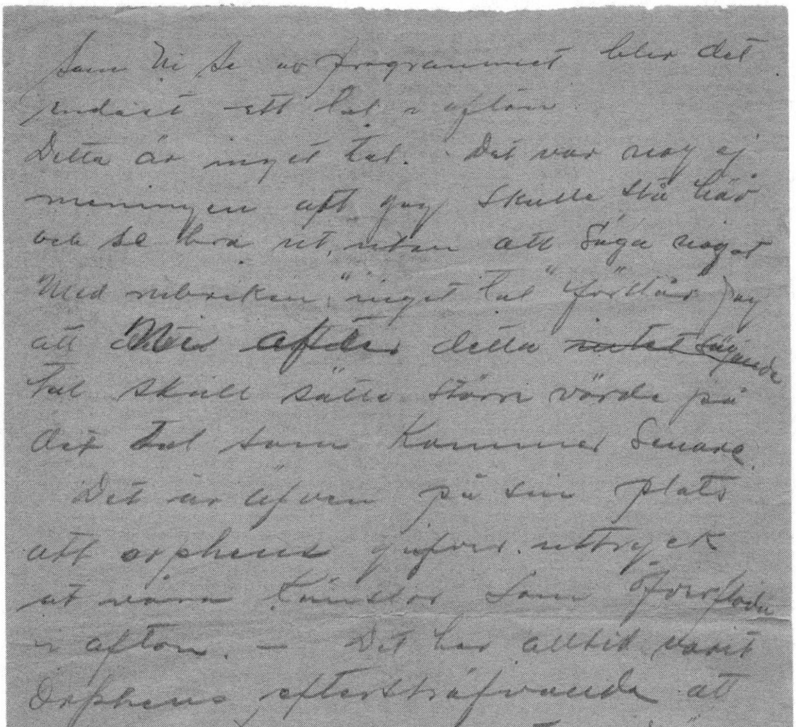
Som Ni se af programmet blir det
undvikt ett tal i afton
Detta är inget tal. Det var nog ej
meningen att jag skulle stå här
och se tvär ut, utan att säga något
Med rubriken "inget tal" förklarar jag
att detta
Tal skall sätta större värde på
det tal som kommer senare.
Det är äfven på sin plats
att Orpheus gifver uttryck
åt våra känslor som förefalla
i afton. — Det har alltid varit
Orpheus eftersträfvande att
genom toner något vidröra
de strängar som vibrera
för svenskhet och fosterlands-
kärlek. Huru våra vackra
strängar åstadkommit i
detta afseende är ofta svårt
att finna, men att döma
från denna stora skara
som kommit hit i afton
synes det som vi lyckats
öfver all förväntan

Figure 4.2. Charles Bundsen's script for "Inget Tal," a brief introduction to a segment of a New Year's program, 1914. Image courtesy of The Denver Public Library Western History Collection; Swedish Medical Center Collection, WH 958.

Bundsen was also asked to speak at many ceremonies and observances within the Swedish American community: the funeral of an SCS nurse, the welcome return to Denver of the Lutheran pastor Brandele, the surprise birthday party of a fellow member of the Orpheus singers, and performances of Orpheus, where his role was to welcome and offer hospitality, as in the "Inget Tal" performance. At many such occasions, and in some of his informative and persuasive speeches, the focus was on Swedishness, as we have seen in "Sweden and Its People" of 1904 and as will be explored further in chapter 5. Public oratory in all these forms served as a binder for the Swedish Americans.

Alongside public oration and the programs of which it was a part, many forms of vernacular speech and writing also expressed and inscribed the meanings of celebrations. Immigrant letters, for example, represented Midsummer both explicitly and indirectly, although the former was rarer. A sample of nineteen letters written from Denver during the 1890s includes one explicit notice of Midsummer. Emma Hallberg noted in a letter to her parents dated June 19, 1891, that she wrote to her sister Ida on Midsummer.[19] Hallberg's brief, explicit mention of Midsummer is similar to the way Christmas was frequently represented in letters very simply with greetings of *god jul.* Anna Carlson of Logan, Utah, similarly noted Midsummer as a time for receiving letters when she wrote to her husband John A. Carlson, then serving an LDS mission in Sweden, that an "old man Larson," whose relatives lived in the area where Carlson was posted, was concerned about not having received a letter from them "since Midsummer."[20] In the letters written by August Wilhelm Carlson of Salt Lake City on June 23 and 24, 1905, to relatives named Augusta and Olga, we see this pattern again as Carlson wrote expressly at Midsummer to note and describe how the holiday could be celebrated in the desert. To Olga, Carlson wrote that "today is Midsummer Eve and even here we celebrate as well as we can."[21]

Midsummer joined Christmas, then, as an appropriate season for writing to relatives in Sweden. While the sample of nineteen letters written from Denver during the 1890s are nearly silent about Midsummer per se, the Swedish Americans wrote many of their letters to relatives and friends near Midsummer Day, just as many correspondents wrote on or around Christmas. In fact, in our sample of 1890s letters from Denver, more than two-thirds of the letters were written during these two seasons, with the higher frequency in May/June. The season was marked by letter writing even when Midsummer was not explicitly cited as the reason for contact. In springtime as well as Christmas time, the Swedish Americans' thoughts turned to home.

Midsummer was inscribed in diary entries as well as letters. One writer who turned from one mode to the other in one sitting was Viktorina Holm of Ammon, Idaho. Writing in her diary in 1936, Holm remembered a celebration of 1900, which she had also just recounted in a letter to an aunt:

> Midsummer Day in Sweden: there one could have fun. Last Midsummer Day or night there we were in Per Kal's arbor and drank coffee at midnight. Aunt Hilda and Uncle Per were with us. Their son, Per Kal's son, sang "På Böljorna de Blå" [On the Waves of Blue[22]] and I was soon going to travel on "the waves of blue" to America. Mamma cried so for my sake. I wrote a letter to Aunt Hilda just now, and reminded her about it.[23]

In this diary entry and in her letter, Holm was not describing a specific Midsummer celebration in her contemporary Ammon, Idaho, of 1936, but rather using the holiday to reestablish her individual sense of connection to Sweden and her relatives there.

As with letter writing, diaries, memorandum books, and journals were genres in which Midsummer and other celebrations were often recognized implicitly more than explicitly. In part, this was a characteristic of these personal and everyday genres, for which the audience did not have to be reminded of important matters that could simply be taken for granted. Often, writers made notations that only labeled the day. On May 30, 1907, Axel T. Nelson of Parma, Idaho, wrote "Decorat." and on July 4 of the same year, "Fourth."[24] Or, they briefly noted an activity peculiar to the day. Keeping diaries from 1898 to 1959, Carl Otto Holm of Ammon, Idaho, began noting memorial and celebratory activities on Decoration Day in 1906 ("I to graveyard"), on Midsummer Day in 1908 ("with Father salabrating"), and on Independence Day in 1908 ("I watering and to town salabrating"). In most of these instances of briefly relating activities that broke with the daily farm schedule, Holm also noted a half-day work. This brevity, though, should not be misread as lack of significance. The notation of "I and family to Anderson's salabrating," as Holm wrote on June 24, 1909, could, for the writer, represent a constellation of personal and cultural associations— signifying family and ethnic relationships and connectedness with the Old Country. This metonymic signification was especially present in the shorthand of letter-writing.[25]

The popular press, too, was a place where words were used to represent and interpret holidays. But in this print venue, Decoration Day, Midsummer, Independence Day, and Pioneer Day appeared represented as much in advertising of events by various groups and businesses as they did in the local news columns. Newspapers placed advertisements for events in the midst of commercial advertising, where visual rhetoric was as important as verbal. Especially in Denver, groups were in competition with each other for Swedish Americans who might be tempted to their particular excursion. In the varied methods used to catch readers' attention, we can sense an entrepreneurial spirit as well as signals to the Swedish Americans as to how one should be thinking about and preparing for the upcoming events.

The Föreningen Enighet och Vänskaps' Midsummer picnic in Denver, 1890, was advertised with a drawing of a bipedal elephant, dressed in suit and hat and bearing a furled umbrella on its shoulder. Hanging from the umbrella, a sign read "I am on my way to Enighets & Vänskaps' Pic Nic in Garfield Park on the 22nd of June." Two weeks later the sign changed: "I will not be late to the Pic Nic this year," and code switching to an English-language Americanism, "That's a sure thing." The advertisement used the visual interest of an elephant in human clothing, gently spoofing the mode of dress of the Swedish American middle class and the "thick and fat" image of substantiality and health current in Swedish thought.[26] The change in the sign's wording was also an attempt to catch the readers' interest anew, and the English language expression would have affected readers not just through its code switching but also through its use of a phrase Swedish immigrants would have heard on the streets of Denver and found amusing as an American vernacular expression.

Typically, advertisements took up a block of three to four column widths. They displayed centered text in large type of varied fonts. Drawings related to the event bracketed or sometimes interrupted this text. Headline-like, the text exclaimed: "Hurrah for 'Military Park'! Big Midsummer Celebration" or "Big! Big! Big! Big! Picnic Decoration Day the 30th of May, '91."[27] Accompanying these two particular headings were, for Midsummer, drawings of the United States flag and the Swedish version of the Swedish-Norwegian Union flag, and for Decoration Day, a drawing of a line of military men marching with rifles in the left shoulder arms position. Other symbols commonly used in advertising for celebrations included pointing hands used as highlighters or text bullets, shining suns, stylized foliage, geometric shapes, and symbols associated with the sponsor, such as the Knights of Pythias shield with a helmeted knight, crossed battle axes, and skull and crossbones.[28] These devices—multiple columns, multiple fonts, large type, exclamatory text, and drawings—were much more common in the advertisements for Denver area events than in the Salt Lake City advertisements, where it was more common simply to label the event, provide its time and location, and focus on listing the planned program and activities.

Newspapers were also venues for sharing poetry about Midsummer and other holidays. Here again, we see a parallel between the Midsummer season and Christmas time, as both seasons were marked with newspaper verse. In both Denver and Salt Lake City, we find verse written by local authors and verse reprinted from other Swedish American and even Swedish sources. In Salt Lake City, *Utah Korrespondenten* ran local writer C. J. Renström's lyrics for a Midsummer song and a poem by Artillus (Nils Forsberg, partial owner of the paper). The paper also picked up work by Swedish poet Octavio Beer and editor of the Sioux City *Skandia*, E. Thimgren. In Denver, *Svenska Korrespondenten* ran work by the popular Swedish American poet and Chicago *Svenska Amerikanaren* editor Magnus Elmblad as well as work by Ninian Waerner, editor at *Svenska Korrespondenten* during 1889–91 and a well-known Swedish American poet and editor in the Midwest.[29]

Many of these poems, even though they celebrated the season in generalities, also localized the holiday season to the newspaper's regional audience. Ninian Waerner's "Summer," for example, began with these lines:

There lie many poems on my desk
About how summer smiles with eyes so clear:
A stem of fair, weak words.

These weak words were juxtaposed with the actuality of "Nature rejoicing so sweet and warm," which was then localized "In Elitchs Garden—oh what joy and delight!"[30]

Similarly, Artillus (Nils Forsberg) of the Salt Lake area localized his song lyrics for a particular 1892 excursion, "Song on Scandia's Excursion to Syracuse," an outing planned to celebrate Pioneer Day:

From dust-shrouded streets and stuffy alleys
"Scandia" directs
Its way to Salt Lake's enchanting beaches
Where waves dance, and the foam is light;
Among the fragrant roses and greenery to spend
One day, separate from the effort and constraint of work;
Swinging women in dance,
And listening to Norden's beautiful, ringing song.

He continued with several similar verses anticipating the day's amusements, through which newspaper readers received a listing of the planned events. The verse was very similar, then, in content and function, to the kind of notices used to announce such events. We learn that the day will include a picnic, ice cream, dancing in the pavilion, singing by Norden, prizes, and railway transportation from Ogden and Salt Lake City.[31]

The newspaper poetry fits squarely into poetic forms of the era, using fairly regular rhythmic feet and rhyme—iambic pentameter with an ABAA rhyme scheme (in the case of Ninian's verse) or dactylic tetrameter with ABAB (in Artillus' verse). Ninian's use of iambic meter sets up his poem initially, at least, with a thoughtful tone, but Artillus' verse is rollicking from the beginning, evoking the polska rhythms that attendees could expect to hear at the event. Both poems use a rhetoric of oppositions that beckon the reader (who is assumed to be male) to an outdoor excursion: inside (a desk covered with poems) versus outside ("Nature . . . so sweet and warm"); urban ("stuffy alleys") versus rural ("enchanting beaches"); and work (Ninian's desk, "constraint of work") versus leisure ("In Elitchs Garden," "swinging women in dance"). In both, passive images in the beginning shift to active images. Ninian's lines ironically suggest that his "weak words" (the more passive modes of chirographic and print text) are not completely sufficient for the season, as much as textual genres were prevalent in spring-summer observances.

In these verses and in the other texts associated with spring and summer celebrations, we see the holidays performed verbally. Through oral and literate means, the holidays were signaled as important, performatively keyed as they commenced and concluded, emphasized through multiple genres, localized to the region, and elaborated as marketing or teaching opportunities. Among the Swedish Americans of the Colorado Front Range these texts were used to express a sense of entrepreneurship as well as Swedish Americanness and seasonal celebration. Among the Utahans, with their focus on programs, a serious engagement with pedagogical purpose is evident. In our next chapter another significant difference emerges in the ways that texts of the spring/summer season also expressed secular and sacred meanings.

NOTES

1. Charles A. Bundsen, Speech to Vasa Order of America, at the Midsommarfest, Jefferson Park, Denver, June 24, 1912, Swedish Medical Center Collection, Folder 1, Item 26.

2. See also pages 163–65, 171, for Olsen's comments on the motifs, themes, and functions of Pioneer Day speech acts.

3. For the importance of speech making, recitations, and other speech acts in American public celebrations of the post-Civil War nineteenth century and twentieth century, see Litwicki 2003, 22–23, 50–52, 107–10, 123–25, and chapter 5; Ulrich 2001, 12–17, 26; and Warner 1962 [1953], 9.

4. Ong's and Foley's work was inspired in part by Milman Parry's idea of oral formula and theme, as discovered in the oral epics of Serbian and Croatian culture, and Albert B. Lord's (2000) idea of the song as a larger unit of expression.

5. For the popularity of Tegnér's poetry in America, see Beijbom 1985. For funeral oratory, see Frykman 2007, 84.

6. Bundsen, manuscript autobiography, n.d., Swedish Medical Center Collection, Folder 12.

7. The metaphorical image of treading on the soil of the Old Country appears in Swedish immigrant letters (Attebery 2007, 95–96).

8. Bundsen, "Sverige & Dess Folk," May 1904, Swedish Medical Center Collection, Folder 1, Item 18. "Hvar finnes der en känska mera djup stark & noble än i patriotism."

9. Bundsen, "Tjufskyttarne," December 1917, Swedish Medical Center Collection, Folder 5. "Tjufskyttarne" is the Swedish translation of the title of Offenbach's 1873 opera *Les Braconniers* (The Poachers). Although Bundsen was not yet present in Denver when the play was performed at the Tabor Grand in 1889 and 1890 (see Ralph 2011), he may have been exposed to it in Sweden, where it was performed in translation, before he emigrated. *Svenskt Porträttgalleri* (1895–1913) lists performers who appeared in the opera in the 1870s, 1880s, and 1890s.

10. Orlando Anderson (1983) interview transcript, 11.

11. *Utah Korrespondenten* (Salt Lake City), June 14, 1894, page 4. "Musik. / Hälsningstal af ordf C. J. Gyllensvan. / Sång af föreningen Svea. / Deklamation, herr John Engbeck. / Duett, herr Occar [probably Oscar] Larson och fru Anna Malqvist. / Tal: Dagens betydelse, hr F.S. Fernström / Sång af en mansqvartett. / Tal af Redaktör O.J. Andersen. / Sång af föreningen Svea. / Deklamation af hr Almqvist. / Musik."

12. *Salt Lake Tribune*, May 26, 1969, 32.

13. "Lagoon Welcomes the Swedish Societies" 1939 pamphlet. PAM 5219, Utah State Historical Society.

14. Flygare Collection. The Jubilee of the LDS Scandinavian Mission was held in Salt Lake City in 1900. June 14, recognized as the establishment day for the mission, was also emerging at the time as the American Flag Day. See Zelinsky 1984, 280.

15. *Troy Weekly News*, May 19, 1905, page 5; June 28, 1907, page 1; June 19, 1908, page 5.

16. Bundsen, Speech for Orpheus Banquet, January 4, 1914, Swedish Medical Center Collection, Folder 1, Item 7. "inget tal."

17. "Nyårs Soiré 1914," Aronson Collection. The program featured drawings of a plump man in a three-piece suit with bowtie and cigar and a hand holding a punch glass. The menu provided for flavored herrings and cold meats with a pilsner and a toast of aquavit shots ("helan går" [the whole thing goes down]), hot meats and fish with a second glass, omelets and hare with a third glass, vegetable relishes and cheeses with "en nubbe [a small or final shot]," followed with desserts and "kaffe me' dopp [coffee with an alcoholic shot added]" with Swedish punch. "Fosterländska toner af Orpheus," "Nu sjonger dom igen," "om ni kan."

18. *Troy Weekly News*, July 6, 1906, page 8; July 10, 1908, page 1.

19. Swanson, John M., Papers, Letter C1. Hallberg's letter had to have been completed after June 19. Even if by "Midsummer," she meant the June 7, 1891, celebration held by Scandia, she also included in her letter a description of an accident in a local park in which a child was killed by an elephant, an incident that was reported in the July 9 *Svenska Korrespondenten*.

20. Carlson, John A., Papers. Letter of January 8, 1895, box 1, folder 1. "han hade ej fått bref sedan midsommar."

21. Carlson, August W., Letterbook. Letter to Olga, June 24, 1905, 23. "I dag är det midsommar-afton och äfven här fira vi den så godt som vi kunna." In this statement *äfven,* usually translated as *also,* may be a bit of Swenglish.

22. Identity of this song is not clear. Many Swedes today would identify the phrase "på böljorna de blå" with a line in the popular summer song "Så Länge Skutan Kan Gå: Vals på Kariben," written by Evert Taube in the 1950s. But the phrase "böljorna de blå" is a formula used in many Swedish broadside ballads.

23. Holm, Carl Otto, Papers, box 4, folder 12, Viktorina Holm diary entry, June 24, 1936. Even at this late date, thirty-six years after she had emigrated from Sweden, Viktorina Holm wrote in Swedish: "Midsommardag i Sverige där man kunda ha roligt. Sista midsommardag eller natt där. Var vi i Per Kals berså och drock kaffe i midnatten. Moster Hilda och Morbror Per var med. Deras son, Per Kals son, sjöng 'På böljorna de blå' och jag skulle snart på 'böljorna de blå' och resa till America, Mamma grät så för mig. Jag skref bref till Moster Hilda just nu, och på minde henna om det. Det är svalt och got i dag. Man männen kan inte köra hö, det är för våtte."

24. Nelson, Axel T., Collection, box 2, memorandum book for 1907.

25. Holm, Carl Otto, Papers, box 1, folder 2; box 5, folder 16. Unfortunately, we do not have diary entries from Carl Otto and his wife Viktorina for the same celebratory days in the same year. For metonymic signification in letters, see Attebery 2007, 14–16.

26. See Attebery 2007, 123, for comments on *tjock och fet* (thick and fat) as a Swedish and Swedish American formula connoting health and wealth. *Svenska Korrespondenten* (Denver), May 29, 1890, page 5; June 12, 1890, page 5. "Jag är på väg till"; "Jag ska inte komma försent till."

27. *Svenska Korrespondenten* (Denver), May 28, 1891, page 8.

28. *Svenska Korrespondenten* (Denver), June 9, 1892, page 8; June 28, 1894, page 8; May 30, 1895, page 8; June 6, 1895, page 8; June 20, 1895, page 8; and *Utah Korrespondenten* (Salt Lake City), June 23, 1892, page 8; June 18, 1900, page 1.

29. Renström's lyrics appeared in *Utah Korrespondenten*, July 1, 1891, page 1; Forsberg's, July 20, 1892, page 1. Artillus is identified as one of Forsberg's pen names by Dahllöf 1980, 52; he is likely the same person as Nels Forsberg, who also used the pen name "Brother Nels" (given as "Broder Nils" by Dahllöf) and who owned stock in *Utah Korrespondenten* (Olson 1949, 70). Thimgren is identified as editor of *Skandia* in *N.W. Ayer & Son's American Newspaper Annual* 1894, 244. Ninian Waerner's spring-summer poems appeared in *Svenska Korrespondenten* on June 12, 1890, page 1, and July 10, 1890, page 1. He was one of the *Svenska Korrespondenten* editors from November 1889 to November 1891; see Skarstedt 1879, *Våra Penn-Fäktare*, 186–93. Magnus Elmblad's poetry appeared in *Svenska Korrespondenten* on July 3, 1890, page 1. His career is discussed by Skarstedt 1879, *Våra Penn-Fäktare*, 45; and Williams 1991, 94–97.

30. *Svenska Korrespondenten* (Denver), June 12, 1890, page 1. "Der ligga många qväden på mitt bord / Om huru sommarn ler med blick så klar; / En blomsterskaft [literally flower stem] af fagra, veka ord" "I Elitchs Garden—ack hvad lust och fröjd!"

31. *Utah Korrespondenten* (Salt Lake City), July 20, 1892, page 1. "Från dammhöljda gator och qvalmiga gränder / Föreningen "Scandia" brådakande styr / Sin kosa till saltsjöns förtjusande stränder / Der vägorna dansa och skummet det yr; / Bland doftande rosor och grönska tillbringa / En dag, skild från arbetets möda och tvång; / I hvirflande dansen med damernasvinga, / Och lyssna till Nordens skönt klingande sång."

5

Midsummer Blendings of Sacred and Secular

In Scandinavia, the spring-into-summer season is anxiously awaited and gratefully celebrated when it arrives with Walpurgis Eve and Day (the last day of April and May 1) and continues through Ascension Day, Pentecost, and St. John's Eve and Day, or Midsummer. At the height of this season, Midsummer anchors a turning point in the year for a culture that closely watches how much daylight wanes and then waxes from day to day during October through March. On or around May first, warm weather first occurs, and by Midsummer, the long, light days already begin to shorten. So, it is with bittersweet feelings that the Scandinavians erect greenery-bedecked poles or light bonfires at Midsummer.

Spring-to-summer traditions in Sweden include singing spring and summer songs out of doors, such as the nineteenth-century song "*Sköna Maj, Välkommen*," meaning "Welcome Lovely May," sung both for Walpurgis Eve celebrations and for Midsummer. A setting by Lars Magnus Béen of Johan Ludvig Runeberg's poem, "*Sköna Maj, Välkommen*" describes winter's ravages over the landscape and the triumphant return of spring flowers, ending with a self-referential description of the choir itself, out in the grove singing praises to spring: "with thankful tongues a thousand birds sing, like us: Welcome, lovely May!" (Runeberg 1870).[1] Redolent with physical sensations of spring and summer, the lyrics celebrate the season's warmth, colors, sounds, and sunlight.

But compare these sentiments with the lyrics written for a Midsummer celebration by a Swedish American Mormon missionary, John A. Carlson, who was stationed in Vingåker, Sweden, in 1895:

> We meet here to hold a celebration
> And rejoice together today;

DOI: 10.7330/9780874219999.c005

With speeches and songs and with innocent games,
Every heart is happy.

. . .

God has revealed to us
So well what displeases
Him. Let us, therefore, seek with
Gravity and diligence to do what the Word teaches us.
We will get to meet together
Once again throughout a thousand years rest
And peace. And shout jubileum
At Sabaoth's Throne. And ended
Will be our trial and strife.[2]

We are surprised at this Midsummer song in which, instead of physical sensations of springtime, sacred Christian ideas are foregrounded. Certainly, we have numerous examples of Scandinavian Americans' reshaping their celebratory practices (as developed throughout chapters 2 and 3). Celebrations comprise a very fluid vernacular genre. But in Scandinavia today, Midsummer is regarded as a secularized festival. Encountering such explicitly stated sacred Christian connotations in this Americanized example is therefore startling.

Swedish tradition associates Midsummer with the supernatural and magical ways of knowing. Bringeus and other Swedish folklorists point to magical practices, such as picking a bouquet of wildflowers to be placed under one's pillow with the intended result that one would dream of a future mate, or looking into a spring in which one would see the visage of a future spouse. Springs and spring water, associated with John the Baptist, whose birth was noted in the church calendar as June 24, were visited at this time of year and seen to be efficacious in various ways (Bringéus 1976, 211–14; Tidholm and Lilja 2004, 22; and Wall 2007). In popular and academic mentality, Midsummer also has sacred associations, having been assumed to have ancient, pre-Christian roots in sun worship, although this association turns out to be difficult to document. Nevertheless, the will to believe in the connection runs deep, according to Sandra Billington, affecting assumptions about Scandinavian tradition from Wilhelm Mannhardt to J. G. Frazer, who influenced a host of twentieth-century writers and scholars (Billington 2008, 41–42).[3]

These traces of sacred connotation attached to Midsummer suggest that a further consideration of the meanings of spring-into-summer celebrations with an eye toward their sacred and secular meanings may prove fruitful. To do so requires a close examination of both celebratory practices and the texts surrounding celebrations, the texts of the turn-of-the-century rhetorical culture described in chapter 4. But before we get to that exploration, it is important to explain how I am using the terms *sacred* and *secular* and the closely related term *ritual*. In what follows, I adapt the ideas of Talal Asad (2003, 25), whose discussion of sacred and secular have had considerable impact throughout the humanities and social sciences. Asad proposes "that the 'religious' and the 'secular' are not essentially fixed categories," that is, that our understanding of whether a practice, a text, or a discourse is sacred or secular is contingent upon particular uses in cultural context.

For Asad, sacred and secular are not stable terms even though he conceives of them as a binary—each dependent upon the other. He maintains that "there is nothing *essentially* religious, nor any universal essence that defines 'sacred language' or 'sacred experience'" (Asad 2003, 25). There can be, rather, a set of cultural expectations that interprets a particular family story—the coming of the Charles Rich families to Paris, Idaho, for example—as recounting sacred experience or that interprets a particular practice—assembling family genealogies—as a sacred practice. Treating sacred and secular as contingent categories is consistent with folklorists' interest in understanding the emic, or insider, worldview of a culture group like the Swedish Americans.

One of the issues with any binary is the way in which the activities on each side of the imagined divide are simplified through lumping. We can label as "secular" activities and artifacts from a number of spheres that range from everyday to commercial to governmental, yet often the commercial is emphasized in the popularly imagined secular. Activities such as shopping on so-called Black Friday (the day after Thanksgiving) for Christmas presents and purchasing new clothes for Easter can be figured as secular rather than sacred because they are seen as evidence of commercialism in contemporary America. Similarly, we can label as "sacred" activities and artifacts from everyday to celebratory, from private to public, and from informal to official. Yet, activities in the second part of each binary, overseen by officially ordained religious authorities and located within spaces designated as religious, are most readily perceived as sacred. "The sacred," especially in contemporary American life, becomes a sequestered zone—limited within the walls of religious institutions—and everything outside of it is "secular." When we speak in this way we fail to define sacred sufficiently, conflating it with institutionalized religion, and we fail to define secular at all.

But how can we avoid lapsing into treating sacred and secular as empty of meaning? This is a crucial question in light of the evidence from human history: the practices and language seen as sacred, and even the practices and language seen as secular, have deep significance for those possessing them. I'd like to shift our focus, ethnographically and semiotically, to the sacred or secular *significance* of a practice or discourse. This allows us to ask, "what is the field of reference within which sacred or secular meaning is created?" These are not necessarily the institutionalized realms of government and religion but rather are realms within which a relationship is being established.

Here are my own provisional definitions: We can define practices and discourse seen within a culture as sacred, for instance, a practice like meditation, as signifiers within a field that establishes a response to transcendental issues of human relationship to spirit, cosmos, the numinous. These practices and discourse may include creeds, tenets, maxims, and other forms of spiritual language that encapsulate beliefs and attempt to explain the transcendent. Yet, meditation can be shifted toward secular meaning in particular contexts, as in medical prescription of meditative techniques.

We can define practices and discourse seen within a culture as secular, a practice like placing Swedish and American flags on a Midsummer advertisement, as signifiers within a field that examines and may establish a human relationship to the physical, including human-to-human and human-to-nature relationships. These may include ethical or identity statements. Yet, the use of flags can be sacralized in particular contexts, such as in an American military burial ritual. Here, I am using the idea of *sacralization* developed by folklorist Susan J. Ritchie, as a process parallel to secularization. According to Ritchie, the countertrend of "sacralization" occurs when "that which was profane takes on sacred qualities" (Ritchie 2002, 444).[4]

One form of sacralization has been famously identified by Robert N. Bellah (1967) in his article "Civil Religion in America." Bellah explains how Americans have come to sacralize the nation, its symbols, and its values in a manner similar to sacred practice and ritual. Decoration Day developed to include speeches that Martha E. Kinney compares to liturgy (Kinney 1998, 239). The other major "red, white, and blue day," Independence Day, also developed a "sacred status," according to historian Matthew Dennis (2002, 23). Thus, Midsummer was imported into a setting in which the spring and summer holidays already skirted a blurred borderland between secularization and sacralization.

Asad adds an important clarification, though, to the idea of civil religion. He specifies that he does not "claim that if one stripped appearances one would see that some apparently secular institutions were *really* religious" (Asad 2003, 25). In dealing with the practices and texts of Utah's Mormon population, for example, it is indeed tempting to identify everything—the service of Brigham Young as territorial governor, folk medical practices, family settlement stories—as religion in disguise. Much of LDS culture can be seen as "ritualizing" Mormon history, for example.[5] Presumably, however, one could also maintain the opposite, that if one stripped appearance one would see that some apparently sacred institutions were really secular. This is the approach we can easily fall into if we approach a culture, one that is suffused with practices emically understood as sacred, as an unbelieving outsider. To this Jack Santino offers a well-stated warning: we must remember that for believers *ritual* is emically "efficacious," seen as effecting a changed state of being that is transcendent. Santino offers the alternative term *ritualesque* for ritual-like performances that attempt to effect a changed state that is not transcendent but rather situated in social concerns. This is where we might place LDS ritualizing of history (Santino 2009, 10, 24).

Asad's and Santino's clarifications help us distinguish between two sacralizations that are apparent in the rhetoric and practice of celebration of these turn-of-the-century immigrants. The first is a sacralization of hyphenated ethnicity which parallels the trend in America at large toward "civil religion," in which matters ordinarily considered secular are treated as if sacred, a form of the ritualesque. The second is an explicit and implicit sacralization concerned with the numinous. We can also identify at least two secularizations, one of the marketplace and another converging on civil religion in the form of hyphenated ethnicity. With these distinctions in mind, let's examine a few of the texts and practices that emerged from Swedish American celebrations in the Rockies. What do they tell us about areas of secular and sacred significance in immigrants' lives?

Examining the inventory of Midsummer activities developed in chapter 2, we can ask whether sacred and secular fields of reference provided frames for the event. Timing reflected both sacred and secular significance. As we've seen, Midsummer celebrations in Utah generally were scheduled on St. John's Day, June 24, but the Mormons were careful to avoid the Sunday celebration of Midsummer. This shift to avoid celebrating Midsummer on a Sunday aligned the holiday with the standard practice of shifting Independence Day and Pioneer Day to a Monday when July 4 or 24 fell on a Sunday. This points to a mainly secular orientation for Midsummer, as well; although all three holidays could contain sacred content such as prayers and sacred language in songs and speeches, they were ultimately dissonant with the setting aside of Sunday for sacred observances, apparently not so imbued with sacred significance that they could be actually celebrated on a Sunday.

While locating Midsummer on or close to June 24 reflects the holiday's connection to the Lutheran church calendar, the extended seasonal duration of Midsummer, especially in 1890s Colorado, points to the holiday's secular connotations, as does the generic use of the idea of the Midsummer and Independence Day season as a marketing tool. For example, A. Anderson of Denver wished his patrons "a pleasant picnic" in an 1893 advertisement:

> Summer excursions often become tedious and embarrassing, especially when you have improper footwear on your feet. To really enjoy yourself and feel good, you should immediately visit A. Anderson of 811 15th street and buy a pair of his first-rate and strong footwear, and you will find you are out in front on the running track.[6]

Carlson's Ice Cream of Denver similarly used the Midsummer season to advertise: "Now is the time for ice cream and picnics."[7] Photographer G. R. Appel of Denver used June 23, 1898, as a day to label a special offer as "Svenskarnas Dag!" (Swedish Day). The offer actually had begun June 10 and extended through July 1—a reduced price to the first two hundred new customers for his best "cabinet cards."[8] Midsummer was clearance sale time for many establishments. The Oscar Larson mercantile of Troy, Idaho, advertised in May 1906, "You can't celebrate the Glorious Fourth right unless you are well dressed," following up with a clearance sale that began on June 23 and ran through July 3.[9]

Some towns and cities expanded the idea of middle of the summer celebrations to multi-day events, and businesses, recognizing that the event would draw people from out of town, used this idea in marketing. In Moscow, Idaho, Independence Day was a two-day series of activities in the period 1905–10.[10] In 1910, the typical line-up of parade, program, prizes, competitions, and baseball game on Independence Day was followed on July 5 with a horse show, horse races, baseball game, and "bucking broncho contest." Merchants advertising in the "Official Program" enticed town visitors to purchase headache medication and firecrackers at Hodgins Drug Store, watches and jewelry at Wallace and Griffin, and groceries at a 20 percent discount at O.C. Carssow's grocery store. The Crystal Theatre was showing "The Waif" and "Roanoke," while the Idaho National Harvester factory was open for tours.[11]

We can see this dovetailing of marketing, multi-day events, event sponsorship by organizations vying for attendees, newspaper editor boostership, and the event advertising strategies described in chapter 4 as one phase of spring-to-summer holiday secularization, in which middle class business owners didn't need to make fine distinctions between their entrepreneurial interests and their involvement in ethnic fraternal and social organizations. But it was not the only phase. A strong focus for Midsummer in particular and the other holidays as well was the idea of hyphenated ethnicity.

Charles Bundsen's 1912 Midsummer speech cited in chapter 4, for example, began explaining the purpose of the holiday. Midsummer was an opportunity for "the native land's lost sons and daughters to gather around the blue-gold flag, not to oppose and criticize living conditions, laws, and institutions in America, but to awaken and maintain love for the Fatherland."[12] Bundsen continued to describe with considerable emotion the occasion of visiting Sweden in 1910:

> I'll never forget the day, just two years ago, when I, in company with the Swedish American singers, arrived in the fatherland. . . . When we approached the harbor and saw before us a city adorned in blue and yellow, mixed with "The Stars and Stripes," and over ten thousand compatriots who were there to receive us, and, when 150 Swedish singers standing on the shore began singing "Vårt Land, Vårt Land, Vårt Fosterland," [Our Nation, Our Nation, Our Fatherland] then our tears could not be held back. Choked with tears we replied "Jag vet ett land långt upp i höga Nord." [I know a land in the far North]. That song came from my heart, I assure you and the next moment we were surrounded and embraced both by people we knew and by strangers.[13]

Bundsen's speech assembled potent icons, indexes, and symbols of hyphenated Swedish Americanness. They include the immigrants figured as lost children, the Swedish and the United States flags, particular songs from the Swedish and Swedish American repertoire, and the image of embarking and disembarking at the Swedish shore. These are powerful pointers in a field of reference that we can say is secular in its alignment of the individual with a heritage group but that in its elevation of these signifiers shifts toward a ritualesque sacralization. Bundsen celebrated the presence of an ethnic community in his region of America and the ability to gather its members together at Midsummer, which was a substitute for return to the Old Country. He also celebrated that community's potential in America as a political interest group, albeit from his perspective a mainly contented one patriotic to both Sweden and America. Through his words, he attempted to charge his listeners with a sense of connection to both Sweden and America.

The Swedes of his day might have thought of the summer solstice holiday of Midsummer mainly as a seasonal marker, but Bundsen's words make it apparent how the Swedish Americans expanded and reshaped the holiday to examine and celebrate many facets of hyphenated American life. The holiday's contiguity with Decoration Day and Independence Day provided examples for expressing this multivalent significance. As we have seen in chapter 2, American Midsummer imitated components of those already existing celebrations. Their ritualesque sacralization of American patriotism rubbed off, shifting to a hyphenated Americanism, waving both the American and the blue and gold flags. Both insiders and observers came to see Midsummer as a national day for Swedish American celebration. Advertisements in the Denver *Svenska Amerikanska Western* in 1905 labeled the Midsummer celebration at Manhattan Beach as "Swedish National Day."[14] The *Troy Weekly News* noted local Swedes celebrating Midsummer in 1908, not quite accurately calling the day "a national holiday in the old country."[15] More broadly, and reinforcing the idea of Midsummer as a specifically Swedish festival, in Swedish America, Midsummer day became regarded as Svenskarnas Dag (Swedish Day). At the Omaha exposition of 1898, for example, Svenskarnas Dag was on June 24, and railway tickets were available to and from Denver for the occasion.[16]

Bundsen self-consciously and explicitly confronted and embraced his own sense of ethnicity and of living with dual identities and allegiances. When he first reached Denver to study medicine, as he related in his autobiography,

> the students found that I was Swedish so one of them drew a picture on the blackboard of Ole Olson with his knapsack [an image of the unassimilated Swedish peasant newly arrived in America]. This was a play in the theaters at that time. As I was proud of my nationality, I pinned a small Swedish flag on my coat lapel and wore it all through my college years.[17]

This ethnicity-on-sleeve response was evident throughout Bundsen's later speeches to the Swedish American community of Denver, in which he proudly espoused his loyalty to Sweden and America. He also, simply as an exemplar, rebutted the Swedish stereotype of the male Swedish immigrant as an uneducated, unlettered country bumpkin. His career as a physician, founder of a hospital, solicitor of funding, orator, and choral singer stood in contrast to every part of the stereotype.

A February 12, 1906, toast handwritten in English and titled "Swedish Am. Swedish Patriotism" offers an excellent example of one of Bundsen's public and explicit statements about hyphenated ethnicity. In it, Bundsen expressed the idea that one could "worship" one's native land, seemingly elevating heritage to sacred status, but in this part of his text he waffled, considering an alternative wording, "love," which would place the relationship to heritage not within the sacred but rather in the realm of affect.

> It is a feeling of great pleasure to be present at a banquet given by the Swedes at which so many of us are present. The patriotism to one[']s own

country & the love for its people should not be critisized or denied us. We cannot help, no matter how fortunate we have been in this country, that we still worship (love) the soil our fathers trod. That we love the language our mothers taught us, that we like the sports of our youth, the habits of manhood our traditions & sagas history & our melodious songs. That is only natural gentlemen & you find it amongst all nationalities abroad from the American to the Chinese[.] I will therefore take this opportunity to ask you to lift your glasses & drink this toast to our dear old Sweden the land of the midnight sun.[18]

We are at times critisized by our Ame. brothers of being to[o] clanish. They are right we are clanish & we stick together like sticking plaster when necessary[.] This is the [word indecipherable] of our successes both for our self & of the small services we endeavor to render our adopted country America[.][19]

In the toast Bundsen expressed the value of gathering together based on common heritage. He specified that heritage as including a sense of homeland, language, culturally specific pastimes, customs, literature, the arts, and a common history. Even though in his era he did not yet have the term *ethnicity* available, he clearly outlined its components and expressed its emic value. He used two assertions and comparisons to illuminate ethnicity. One assertion is that people who have left their nations share a universal, "natural" tendency to love the land they have left and its culture. Interestingly, in supporting this assertion, he refers to Americans and Chinese as others who have experienced migration. In both cases, these would have been surprising references, as emigration from America was light during his era and there was significant prejudice against the Chinese as immigrants to America.[20] A second assertion was that Swedish Americans should be "clannish" even though they were criticized for being so. Describing this quality with a medical metaphor that implies its healing quality—"we stick together like sticking plaster"—Bundsen defended clannishness as the key to Swedish American success both within the ethnic community and outside of it. Within a decade of the delivery of this toast, he might have found this message less viable, at least to an outsider audience, in the midst of a Nativist point of view that ethnic celebrations were not American.[21]

The concern over heritage also appeared in the spring-to-summer celebrations of the Utah Scandinavians, but the ostensible common thread in Utah was not Swedishness but rather a secular Scandinavianness. But as Midsummer programs were shaped by participants, this attempt at secular Scandinavian Americanness blurred into both civil religion and explicitly sacred concerns. The public celebrations held in the Salt Lake City area represented efforts not only to cut across ethnic boundaries within the broad category "Scandinavian," but also (as mentioned in chapter 2) to ally religious, political, and arts-oriented segments of the Scandinavian population. The city-county committee's multiethnic membership was one means of assuring parity among the Scandinavian countries of origin in the activities presented at the Midsummer celebration. The attempt at Scandinavianness was simultaneously undercut and augmented, though. For example, however Scandinavian in intent, the 1891 Midsummer celebration at Draper hinted strongly of Swedishness in the pole raising, folk dancing around the pole, and the Swedish national colors. Perhaps this was why the Swedish-language newspaper *Utah Korrespondenten* called it a "real *national* celebration."[22] The newspaper's editor Otto Rydman was a staunch supporter of maintaining Swedish culture as distinct from Scandinavianness (Olson 1949, 3–6). Scandinavianness is a topic that we will revisit in chapter 7 in a comparison of Scandinavianness in Montana and Utah. Here, it will suffice to say that within Utah's Mormon population, Scandinavianness was a programmatic choice enabled by formal mechanisms such as lay committees, the LDS mission, LDS Scandinavian meetings, and the church's encouragement of immigrant assimilation.

We can compare the Denverite Bundsen's sentiments, in which he pulled back from the idea of worshipping, with a number of texts from the spring-to-summer celebrations of the Utahans, in which both sacralization of ethnicity as if a civil religion and sacralization through explicitly sacred language frequently emerged. C.J. Renström wrote a speech and lyrics for the Ogden, Utah, Midsummer celebration in 1891.[23] Like Bundsen, Renström expressed hyphenated Scandinavianism when he drew on a field of reference strongly inflected with the Romantic Nationalist reinvention of Scandinavian mythology, of which Tegnér's *Fritiof's Saga* was the prime example and well known among Swedish Americans. But unlike Bundsen, he mixed explicitly Christian ideas with these non-Christian references (Beijbom 2004, 163–66). Renström's speech text as published in the newspaper begins by referring to the Viking past. Those attending possessed, Renström said, a heritage from "konung Ring." This is Tegnér's character King Ring, who was associated with Mimir, god of wisdom and knowledge, and who is depicted by Tegnér as having a long, peaceful reign. These references to Tegnér would have resonated especially with the Swedish attendees. Renström's poetic speech shifted interestingly, though, from the Viking past to the present struggles of the immigrants in Utah, in which their goals could become tainted, and then to the promise of a future afterlife:

Welcome therefore everyone here,
Who are descended from these heroes—
From courageous King Ring,
From the hero Frithiof, pious and good—
However we struggle in the world;
We may, over time, follow them!
Many are constantly looking for happiness with vain toil and trouble.
We strive here in "the Western desert" like ants crawling on each other,
As if satisfied by clouds and haze;
Toward our aims, however, we strive forward,
To the land beyond the veil of death
Our languishing spirits yearning.
Oh,
May we follow these good ones to bliss in the land of peace![24]

Very much like Carlson's song laden with references to an afterlife, Renström's speech reminded his audience of their mortality and the promise of "land beyond the veil of death," pulling his speech into the realm of sacred concerns, the relationship of individuals to spirit, to an essentialized good and evil, and to the question of life after death. But Renström's language was less specifically Christian and LDS than Carlson's and informed instead by mythology. The references to the Scandinavian pantheon, which was after all not living myth, could evoke a sense of Scandinavian patriotism and were often used in this way during Renström's era, having already been secularized by Tegnér and other Scandinavian writers.

The "Western desert" and the ant-like struggles in which Renström depicted the settlers in his speech contrast with the more positive image of his song lyrics. In the lyrics, references to "nature so beautiful" run throughout. Nature was beautiful specifically in the grove where the Scandinavians were gathered for Midsummer, Lorin Farr's Grove, and nature was beautiful in the Scandinavian countries from which the emigrants came. As Renström said in his lyrics, "I see here today, as I look around / A crowd from various nations." To the "Midsummer celebration in the greenery" Renström's lyrics welcomed, in turn, those "from Dannebrog's land . . . where the beech stands green," "from Norway's scenic seashore," and finally "from the Svear's beloved land with blooming fields so green."[25] Mentioned last in the lyrics, the Swedes were positioned as hosts to the other two major Scandinavian nations from which the Utahans had emigrated.

The celebration planned by John A. Carlson in 1895 was an interesting adaptation of Midsummer that conflated sacred and secular, with sacred significance explicitly stated as the more important meaning. It was to take place in Vingåker, Sweden, the small Södermanland village from which Carlson's wife Anna had emigrated and where she remembered having attended many celebrations during her childhood, including Midsummer fests.[26] Anna Lundstrom was among a group of families that created a chain of migration from Vingåker to Logan, Utah (Rhodes 1988). Her husband John A. and later their son John W. used Vingåker as a base for mission work.[27] The June 24, 1895, celebration was called a "Sunday School Celebration." According to Carlson's lyrics, its activities were to include speeches, songs, and games, not unusual in the inventory of activities associated with Midsummer in Utah. These activities were listed in the song's first stanza. In the second stanza, though, the gathering's mixed intent was clearly established:

> Both old and young here have a part
> And thank and laud our god.
> And do his will and hear his Word
> And hearken unto his holy commandments.[28]

The song continued with the somewhat sobering thought that the children assembled to celebrate, while enjoying their youthful vigor, should remember that old age approaches fast. Hence, they should think of their Creator while celebrating. And the Creator, referred to in the poem as "Sebaot," or Jehovah Sabaoth—the Hebrew Lord of Hosts who has some wrathful moments in the Old Testament—was presented both as a father who could be displeased and as an enthroned deity who could ultimately provide a happy afterlife.

The tone was solemn, and the message was focused on how comportment in this world was perceived by the LDS to be directly connected to an afterlife. Their comportment at Midsummer, then, could be truly performative, effecting a changed state. Joy in this world was forward-looking, to the afterlife where the real "jubileum shouts" would occur. The song's lines dwelled on interiorized sentiments rather than the externalized physical sensations of spring and summer so well expressed in Swedish songs of the season. This distance, solemnity, and sacred substance was a dramatic departure from the Midsummer celebrations of the Swedes during this same period, and there was certainly no hint of pre-Christian sacred meanings; this was a Mormon-inflected Christianity in which the role of "Heavenly Father," the LDS term for deity, was focal. And it was a departure from the "fun," a meaning we might take as secular, remembered by Viktorina Holm from her childhood. The effects of missionary contact in renewing

Midsummer were seemingly tempered by the primary importance that the LDS Scandinavian Americans placed upon sacred meaning in everyday life.

This sacralization of the spring-to-summer holidays by the LDS reached back at least to the 1880s. In the 1882 celebration of Pioneer Day in Hyrum, described by Ole Christian Tellefsen in a diary entry (see chapter 3), a number of practices signaled sacred connotations. Tellefsen called the public assembly a "meeting" rather than a program, employing a term typically used among the Mormons for their religious services, and he noted that the meeting opened with prayer. He also employed the term commonly used by the Mormons as a self ascription, the "saints," signifying their presence near the millennium as a people informed by a renewed understanding of the Christian gospels.

But many other components listed by Tellefsen point to patriotic secular content: a volley of gunshots, raising of the national flag, speeches, songs, readings, and social dancing. In many ways, the Pioneer Day experienced by Tellefsen was very similar to Independence Day celebrations. And, indeed, Eliason (2002, 144) notes a "similarity in timing and style of celebration" for Independence and Pioneer days, and Olsen (1996–97, 163) agrees that "Pioneer Day served as an independence day for the Latter-day Saints." Yet, both scholars also draw parallels to Thanksgiving, a day with originally sacred connotations.

If we attempt to pigeonhole celebratory practices as secular or sacred, a holiday like Pioneer Day defeats us. In LDS Utah, there was no clear separation of religion from the realms of everyday life, commerce, and government; rather, the categories secular and sacred were regularly blended. We find this repeatedly in the evidence for LDS celebrations. An 1885 Scandinavian Independence Day excursion featured a choir singing in praise of not just "the Constitution from the sons of liberty" but also the "Creator" responsible for the natural beauty of a green valley surrounded by mountains and the "freedom of religion, here worshipping God as we please."[29] We find, as well, the Salt Lake City *Svenska Härolden* publishing a poem to Pioneer Day in which "soon God's power will show you . . . the earth free from tyranny . . . and a home for those who obey the Lord's commandments."[30] Even in rejecting the idea of attending large public Midsummers when he wrote about the Garfield Beach Midsummer celebration of 1892, editor of *Utah Korrespondenten* Otto Rydman situated the meaning of Midsummer in the sense of spiritual renewal that can come with an excursion to the countryside to be in a natural environment with close friends and literally and figuratively imbibing its fruits. These sacralized festivities became emically efficacious—rituals.[31]

The celebrations of these Swedish Americans offer us a significant pool of primary evidence of vernacular practices in cultural context. It is just the sort of data that William R. Hutchinson calls for when critiquing historians' treatments of the secularization or sacralization of society: "When historians discuss secularization or dechristianization they are nearly always referring to the views of intellectuals, political leaders, and ideologically articulate socialists." We need instead, he argues, to seek evidence of "the religiosity of ordinary people" before making generalizations about the secularization of society (Hutchison 1998, 140, 141).

The degree to which America has or has not become secularized over the centuries since British, Spanish, and other nations converged here— bringing Christianity, Islam, Buddhism, and many other religions—to encounter American Indians with their own sacred practices, is a contested issue. Susan J. Ritchie (2002) sees this relationship as an engagement along "the boundary between the sacred and the profane" (444). While much scholarship has focused on the "profane" side of this boundary— explaining the trajectory of American culture as secularization that occurs when "that which was sacred enters everyday life," presumably losing its sacred significance along the way—sacralization has received less attention (Ritchie 2002, 444).

This complex relationship between perceptions of the sacred and secular is attracting new scrutiny in a number of disciplines. In American studies, the so-called secularization narrative through which the development of nineteenth- and twentieth-century America has been imagined is being questioned by scholars such as Michael J. Kaufmann and Tracy Fessenden. Kaufmann critiques "traditional secularization narratives," stories that imagine American culture as progressing from religious roots to a rational, current day secularism and calls for history "that instead restores the dynamic relationship between the secular and the religious as a formative element in that history" (Kaufmann 2007, 622). This "dynamic relationship" was at work in many sectors of nineteenth-century society. In American literature, Fessenden sees the development of a generalized Protestant Christianity into the unmarked case, a norm for an unlabeled American ethos that could masquerade as secular, for example in the sentimental nineteenth-century novel. Sarah Barrington Gordon similarly traces this generalized Protestantism in the trials of alleged blasphemers and Mormon polygamists. Nineteenth-century American law was imbued with the ideas of a generalized Christianity that condemned blasphemy and polygamy: "the moral difference of Mormonism was evidence of the perversion of [a localized] democracy" that attempted to subvert the Christian ethics of the majority. Gordon sums up the nineteenth-century trajectory as follows: "The hardening moral lines of constitutional jurisprudence translated the prescriptive nature of 'general Christianity' from a basic fact of American legal culture before the Civil War, into a constitutional code by 1890" (Gordon 2000, 709).

In these legal debates, however, the laws regarding blasphemers and polygamists were explicitly examined vis-a-vis religious terms. And in that debate, Mormon society was viewed from without. Viewed from within, Mormon society constructed a union of religion and structures ordinarily assumed to represent the secular, including government as well as law, and expressed this union in language such as that used by Tellefsen and many other LDS celebrants.

The blending of secular and sacred may simply be more apparent to us in the Mormon materials, as the LDS are not hesitant to explicitly embrace the possibility of sacred meanings embedded within seemingly secular contexts. As Eliason points out, the LDS religion is materialistic and its system for sacred signifiers can be seen as both having material (secular) importance and pointing to important theological ideas. Utah society at the turn of the century still bore traces of the theocracy with which Deseret had been established. Hence, celebration of mainly secular holidays like Midsummer could incorporate traces of the sacred, and vice versa.

By first examining how the Swedish immigrants altered their celebratory patterns and then paying attention to the rhetoric of celebration, we come to a deeper understanding of the immigrant worldview of this turn of the century period. Swedish Americans in the Rockies were strongly aligned with American nationhood at the same time that they considered themselves as possessing what Bundsen labels as *Svenskhet*, or Swedishness. The groves where they assembled for Midsummer briefly became Swedish soil during a Midsummer program, a place to perform hyphenated ethnicity.

At the same time, an explicit and implicit sacralization runs throughout the rhetoric used at these celebrations. As we've seen in several examples, the nineteenth-century Mormons in particular created multivalent artifacts, activities, and discourse signifying within sacred and secular fields of reference simultaneously. For them, Midsummer became a time for a turn in the soul, not just a turn in the year. In this context, John A. Carlson's Midsummer lyrics are part of a broader pattern of sacralized festivals and secularized rituals.

In the American Rockies, the spring-to-summer holidays have functioned as multiply meaningful observances, but in a very complex social and cultural environment in which nationalistic, ethnic, and sacred ideas were at stake. The season was used to represent and reconsider human relationships to heritage groups, to nations, to nature, and to the numinous. These multiple facets of the season's significance might seem contradictory on first blush, but we can regard them, rather, as demonstrating that America's celebratory traditions are richly expressive of cultural tensions; they give voice to and embody a blurring of sacred and secular that runs throughout American culture.

NOTES

1. "Sköna Maj, Välkommen!" "med tacksam tunga / tusen fåglar sjunga / liksom vi: Välkommen, sköna maj!"

2. "Sjungen på Sondags Skolfesten i Wingåker den 24 Juni 1895," Carlson, John A., Papers, MS26, box 2, folder 10. I've attempted to translate the original Swedish into a literal English equivalent, so this is not a poetic rendering. "Wi mötas nu här till att hålla en fest. / Ock glädjas tillsamman i dag; / I tal ock med sång. Ock i oskyldig lek / En hvar utaf hjertatt är glad. / Då får vi mötas tillsamman / Engång i Tusen års hvila / Ock frid. Ock jubla så glade / Vid Sebaots Tron ock slut / Är vår pröfning ock strid."

3. See also Billington 2007, in which she traces and interprets the absence of evidence for summer solstice rituals and festivities in the Nordic regions during pre-Christian times.

4. Secularization—and to a much lesser extent sacralization—are explored as historical social processes in sociology of religion; a schema and critique of theories of secularization is offered by Tschannen 1991. Kenneth Thompson (1991) focuses on "boundary disputes" at the boundary between sacred and secular. Here, I am intentionally drawing rather upon folkloristics, as a field that emphasizes empiricism: terms for cultural processes, such as *sacralization*, are tested against the empirical evidence assembled from a variety of primary sources.

5. Bitton (1975) made this point outlining the many forms of expressive culture used to create a "standardized, moralized sense of the past" that was highly functional in establishing a Mormon identity (84). It is unclear, though, whether this sense of the past is emically efficacious in the way that Santino (2009, 10, 24) specifies for true ritual.

6. *Svenska Korrespondenten* (Denver), June 15, 1893, page 4. "En treflig pic nic. Sommarutflykterna bli ofta tråkiga och pinsamma, isynnerhet då man har opassande skodon på fotterna. För att verkligen få nöjsamt och må väl bör ni genast besöka A. Anderson i 811 15de gatan och köpa ett par af hans extra fina och starka skodon, och ni skall finna er främst på kapplöpningsbanan."

7. *Svenska Korrespondenten* (Denver), June 21, 1894, page 8. "nu kommer ice creamen och picnicarnes tid."

8. *Svenska Korrespondenten* (Denver), June 23, 1898, page 8. Cabinet cards were photographs printed on heavy stock the size of playing cards. "kabinettkort."

9. *Troy Weekly News*, May 11, 1906, page 7; June 22, 1906, page 4.

10. *Troy Weekly News*, June 16, 1905, page 1; June 23, 1905, page 1.

11. "Official Program," July 4 and 5, 1910, Moscow, Idaho. File 10, Oslund Family Papers. In the same file is an undated advertisement for The Fashion Shop's semi-annual sale, incorporating in a lower right-corner inset "Moscow / celebrates / July 3, 4 and 5 / a real / celebration / come."

12. Charles A. Bundsen, Speech to Vasa Order of America, at the Midsommarfest, Jefferson Park, Denver, June 24, 1912, Swedish Medical Center Collection, Folder 1, Item 26.

"att samla rundt den blå-gula fanan de för Fosterlandet förlorade söner och döttrar; ej för att motarbeta och kritisera Amerikanska förhållanden, lagar och institutioner; men för att väcka och uppehålla kärleken till Fosterlandet."

13. Ibid. "Jag glömmer aldrig den dag, just två år sedan, då jag i sällskap med Svensk-Amerikanska sångarne anlände till Fosterjorden. . . . När vi nalkades hamnen och sågo framför oss en stad prydd i blått och gult, blandad med 'The Stars and Stripes,' och öfver tio tusen landsmän som voro der för att mottaga oss; och, när 150 svenska sångare från stranden uppstämde till hällsning 'Vårt Land, Vårt Land, vårt Fosterland' då kunde tårarne ej återhållas. Med gråten i halsen svarade vi 'Jag vet ett land långt upp i höga Nord', den sången kom från hjertat; försäkrar jag eder och i nästa ögonblick voro vi omringade och omfamnade af både kända och okända."

14. *Svenska Amerikanska Western* (Denver), June 15, 1905, page 8.

15. *Troy Weekly News*, June 26, 1908, page 10.

16. *Svenska Korrespondenten* (Denver), June 16, 1898, page 8.

17. Autobiography, folder 12, Swedish Medical Center manuscript collection WH958. The play was *Ole Olson* by Gus Heege 1889; see Harvey 2001, "Performing Ethnicity," 156.

18. Here, Bundsen may have added a poetic stanza written separately on page two of the manuscript: "The land of the Midnight Sun where the nightingale sings & the brooklets run where we first saw the light & our lives begun & we live as it were, Just for fun." This was, perhaps, a reference to a Swedish or Swedish American song, although the stanza does not appear in the American Union of Swedish Singers Song Album (1909) nor in Örtengren's (n.d.) *Kvartett-Album* and the songbook *Skandia*, nor does it appear in Google searches using English and Swedish phrasing. For further analysis of this passage, see chapter 6.

19. "Swedish Am. Swedish Patriotism," folder 1, Swedish Medical Center manuscript collection WH 958.

20. It is difficult to ascertain what might have attracted Bundsen's attention to the emigration of Chinese from their homeland; the 1900s was a decade of renewed intensity in passage and implementation of Chinese exclusion legislations (McKee 1986, 171–74).

21. One such argument was raised against the celebration of Norwegian Constitution Day, May 17; see *Indlandsposten* (Great Falls, MT), March 14, 1917, page 2.

22. *Utah Korrespondenten* (Salt Lake City), June 17, 1891, page 8. "riktig nationalfest" emphasis mine.

23. *Utah Korrespondenten* (Salt Lake City), July 1, 1891, page 1. Renström's song lyrics were intended to be performed to the tune "Hvi längtar du åter til fäderneland" (Why Do You Long for the Fatherland), which was composed by Hanna Brooman for nineteenth-century Swedish poet Elias Sehlstedt's "Norrlänningens Hemlängtan" (Norseman's Longing for Home). The song was reproduced in America in the compilation *Songs of Sweden* (Gustaf Hägg 1904, 68–70).

24. *Utah Korrespondenten* (Salt Lake City), July 1, 1891, page 1. "Välkomna derför alla här, som stamma ifrån hjeltar der—från konung Ring med mannamod, från hjelten Frithjof from och god.—Se hur vi än i verlden streta; Vi må med tiden följa med! För lyckan många ständigt leta med fåfäng möda och besvär. Vi sträfva här i 'vesterns öken' som myror kräla om hvarann, omhöljda utaf moln och töcken; till målet dock vi sträfva fram, till landet bortom dödens slöja. Dit längtar trånande vår and'. O, må vi med de gode följa till sällhet uti fridens land!" I've rendered the English translation in lines reflecting the poetic style of Renström's speech.

25. *Utah Korrespondenten* (Salt Lake City), July1, 1891, page 1. Dannebrog is the Danish flag; Svear, the prehistoric people occupying the area around Lake Mälaren in Sweden. "Till midsommarsfest i det gröna!" "från Dannebrogs land . . . der 'Bøgen' står grön"

"Från Norges natursköna stränder" "från Svearnes älskade land / Med blomstrande ängar så groan"

26. "Transcript of Manuscript by Hilda," n.d. Carlson, John A., Papers, MS26, box 2, folder 8.

27. Carlson, John A., Papers, MS 26, box 1, folder 1; and John W. Carlson Collection, MS 27, box 1, folder 1, Anna Carlson letter to John W. Carlson, June 16, 1918.

28. Ibid. "Gud hafver till oss uppenbaratt / Så väl hvad honnom mishageligt / Är. Låt oss derför söka med / Allvar ock flit att göra hvad Ordet oss lär."

29. *Svenska Härolden* (Salt Lake City), July 9, 1885, page 2. ""Konstitusionen, från frihetens söner" "Skapare" "Religionsfrihet, här dyrka Gud som vi vill."

30. *Svenska Härolden* (Salt Lake City), July 23, 1885, page 3. "Snart Herrans kraft skall visa er . . . jorden fri från tyrani . . . och en hemvist bli för dem som lyda Herrans bud."

31. Rydman's poem on the occasion of this visit will be discussed further in chapter 6.

6

On Swedish Soil in Grove and Arbor
Private Celebrations in a Middle Landscape

INDIVIDUAL PARTICIPATION IN THE SPRING-TO-SUMMER holidays can be located on a private to public continuum, with some participants limiting themselves to smaller inward-turning celebrations and some more fully invested in public festivity. As we've seen in previous chapters, in the nodes of Swedish settlement such as Denver and Salt Lake City, one overarching pattern is the way in which spheres of everyday activity—domestic chores, factory hours, and farm work—impinged on and forced choices among the spring-to-summer celebrations. Yet even when participants chose planting over attending a Midsummer celebration, or celebrating Independence Day rather than Midsummer, the season as a whole represented an embodiment of human-nature connections that we can read for both ecocultural meanings and for the more specific sense of connection to Swedish soil.

Events on the private side of the private-public continuum have been described by folklorist Linda Humphrey (1979) as "small group festive gatherings." Perhaps because these are so embedded in the fabric of American life, they have received less attention than public festivities, where qualitative categories like the carnivalesque and burlesque are apparent and interesting, commanding ready attention. Humphrey lays out the common components of small group festive gatherings in America as follows:

> First, we have the idea of eating together as a form of intimate and mean-
> ingful communication which creates cohesion. Second, we have a folk
> group, not isolated, illiterate, or permanent, bound by the sharing of food
> and by eating together. And third, we have behavior, less explosive than
> that normally associated with festival, yet still a break from the ordinary,
> a release having a special time and place, and in most cases considered by
> the participants to be festive. Such gatherings provide a vehicle for various
> kinds of folkloric behavior and performance. (Humphrey 1979, 192)

DOI: 10.7330/9780874219999.c006

In this chapter, we will look at the versions of Midsummer and other spring-summer celebration that lie closer to the private pole of the private-public continuum, and we will explore the meanings generated within this type of celebration especially as practiced in the outlying areas of Rocky Mountain Scandinavian settlement. As we will see, small group versions of Midsummer, Decoration Day, Independence Day, and Pioneer Day represent a strong pattern of folkloric tradition oriented more toward implicit values of ecology and region than explicit nationalistic, ethnic, and religious identities. In comparison to the public celebrations, though, these patterns of private practice are more difficult to document. We find their traces in private writing such as letters and diaries.

Humphrey notes as a central activity the sharing of food, and that does appear to be a common focus for the Swedes and Scandinavians gathering privately for Midsummer. There is evidence of two forms of small, food-focused gatherings: coffee parties and picnics. The former, the coffee party, afforded the pleasures of companionable conversation and being outside later than one ordinarily would, at a time of year when the light lingers and it is warm enough to sit outdoors. In Scandinavian culture, coffee is served with pastries or *smörgås* (decorative open-faced sandwiches), so this was probably not a full meal but would have included more than just coffee. A brief description of regular birthday celebrations close to Midsummer for Agnes Smith Johnson of Troy, Idaho, fits this pattern, "Every June 22 . . . a group of ladies gathered at [Agnes'] . . . home, quite a crowd really, and spent the day visiting and eating delicious refreshments that they brought in her honor" (Stella Johnson 2002, 219).

The folklorist Larry Danielson observed coffee parties in Lindsborg, Kansas, where in the mid-twentieth-century celebration of Midsummer consisted of "a special coffee party and a very late evening of socializing." He characterizes this activity as taking place among "[a] very few individuals . . . up to the 1950s," Midsummer otherwise not receiving a great deal of attention. The latitudes of North America where most Scandinavians settled, with their hotter summers and earlier harvests than in the Scandinavian countries, could often interfere with Midsummer. Danielson notes that "[i]n Kansas . . . June is very warm and usually the month of wheat harvest, a task that completely engages rural families for its duration" (Danielson 1972, 294–95). Conditions are similar in most of the rural northern Rockies, with some moderation of temperatures at higher elevations.

This pattern of informal rural gatherings to converse while sharing food and beverages appears throughout the diaries of Carl and Viktorina Holm of Ammon, Idaho. Ammon was established in 1887–88 by Mormon settlers, some Scandinavian American, as a small town and farming area about five miles east of Idaho Falls (Stringham 1984, 2–3). Carl Holm, an LDS convert who emigrated from Sweden in the late 1890s, was living in the Idaho Falls area by 1896. Viktorina, another convert, emigrated in 1900 to join him, and they established their farm at Ammon in 1901. Carl's brother and father were also present in the Ammon area.[1]

The Holm family maintained a relationship with both private and public spheres in their spring and summer celebrations. Sometimes family members availed themselves of the public celebrations put on by Ammon and Idaho Falls for the spring-to-summer holidays. In 1904, for example, the family went to town for July 4, using the occasion also to have their children's photographs taken.[2] For the Holms, Decoration Day, however, was not a time for civic celebration but rather was usually an occasion for decorating graves.[3] It was at Midsummer that they most often practiced small group festive gatherings with Scandinavian American friends and relatives, either receiving visitors themselves or traveling to nearby farms in the Idaho Falls region: in 1907, 1908, 1909, 1910, 1911, and 1914. In 1909, for example, Carl wrote "I and family to Anderson's salabrating."[4] In 1910, Midsummer evoked an unusual entry in Swedish: *"vi var alla till Goshen att se Norea"* (we were all at Goshen to see Norea), the combination of Biblical proper names associated with providence giving the journey and the gathering a connotation of pilgrimage.[5]

Viktorina's diary entries, written entirely in Swedish, tell us more fully about Midsummer and provide a more domestic perspective. Her extant diary entries begin in August 1934, much later than Carl's, which may have been a function of life and family cycle changes as the couple moved out of their fertile years and their children became independent adults. By 1934, Viktorina was sixty-two, with the youngest of their children in their twenties. In poor health, she lived only ten more years. One reason that Midsummer stood out for Viktorina was that she had given birth to her daughter Olive on June 23. In 1944, for example, she visited Olive at Arimo, Idaho, on June 23.[6]

Yet, the family didn't always set aside Midsummer Eve or Day for celebration. In 1936, Viktorina listed her activities for June 23: because the men were haying, she and daughters Lillie and Vivi (Vivian) cooked for thirty-eight people that day. The next day her thoughts turned to Midsummer, and she wrote the longer, reminiscent entry quoted in chapter 4, recalling a coffee party at Midsummer in Sweden before her departure—"we . . . drank coffee at midnight"—held outdoors—"in Per Kal's arbor"—where she had enjoyed a vocal performance—"Per Kal's son . . sang "På Böljorna de Blå"

[On the Waves of Blue]." The wistfulness of her entry suggests the weight of the summer labor that had made a Midsummer gathering difficult that year. Instead, she was cooking the large midday meals required for haying crews. The press of haying season still occupied her mind as she ended her Midsummer entry with "it is nice and cool today. But the men can't do the haying because it is too wet."[7]

Small group gatherings at Midsummer time were noted by Viktorina again in 1939 and 1943. In 1939, the Holms broke with LDS custom by celebrating Midsummer on a Sunday even though that was a day later than Midsummer proper. In 1943, June 23 was again a small gathering day for the Holms, although not labeled as Midsummer: "Otto and I went over to Matilda's for a party for an old Swedish lady from Sandy, [Utah]."[8] The occasion reflects the Utah tradition of Old Folks Day, which for the Swedes was sometimes conflated with Midsummer, a day on which the oldest members of the community were recognized with attention and prizes.

This gathering prompted by the visit of an elderly Swedish American also suggests the geographical extent of the Swedish American network in southeast Idaho and Utah, a network also documented in the distribution of Swedish- and other Scandinavian-language newspapers out of Salt Lake City (Attebery 2007, 60). That network reached northward beyond the Idaho Falls area as well as south of Salt Lake City well beyond Sandy (now a suburb). Locally, the network crossed religious lines through contact with the non-LDS settlers of New Sweden, Idaho. Carl Otto noted attending many LDS conferences in Idaho Falls and other towns, but he also noted a visit to New Sweden on April 30, 1911: "Sunday / I and family to the Mission shurch [church]."[9] The New Sweden Mission Church had been established by settlers from the Midwest, principally Nebraska and Iowa, in 1895, and the congregation held services in its building at New Sweden until 1929. In 1911, the Mission Church was still holding its services in Swedish, which may have been a reason for the Holms' attendance.[10] The Holms may have also had friends in the congregation. It is difficult, of course, to establish the identities of friends and acquaintances mentioned throughout a diary, especially in the case of very common Swedish names such as Anderson. Carl's diary entries did record visits to "the Safstroms," which may have been the same extended family of Safstroms that comprised a large contingent of early members of the New Sweden Mission Church.[11]

The idea of small group festive gatherings was also used by the Holm family as an occasional alternative to attendance at public events for the other spring-to-summer holidays. Most Independence Days found Carl Otto spending a partial day at his farm work and then going to a nearby town for the public festivities: in 1912, for example, "I with family to town park salabrating / got ice cream 25¢."[12] And in 1918, the entire family traveled into Idaho Falls for an Independence Day memorable for its horse races: "All Salabrating in Idaho Falls Dolf [a son] runing his poney in race winning first place about 2.50 / Paul run Henry's horse in Cowboys race winning first prize about $6.00."[13]

But small group alternatives to these public celebrations included the practice of going into the mountains for camping and picnicking. In 1913, Carl Otto noted that his family went to Lincoln (a population center only three miles north of Ammon) for Independence Day, but "the boys Henry and Paul," probably farm hands and/or extended family members, had "gone to the hills."[14] Here, he used a vernacular expression common in Idaho dialect, meaning a trip from one's home in the valley into the nearby mountains. In 1916, he followed this pattern himself by eschewing any public celebration for a trip on July 1–4 to "the hils to salabrate" and to "the 'dam' Fishing got about 250 shubs [chubs] and suckers about 80 lbs,"[15] and again in 1942 the family picnicked in the mountains with friends. This pattern appears only once for Decoration Day, when in 1915 the Holm and Norell families joined in a Sunday trip "about 3 miles to Cranes Creek muscitoes verry bad" on May 30.[16]

For Pioneer Day, also, while the Holms frequently attended public celebrations in Ammon, Lincoln, or Idaho Falls, they instead on occasion chose small gatherings with friends or relatives: in 1906 with the Safstroms, in 1910 with Hjalmar Holm, in 1940 with friends in Ririe, and in 1944 with the Johnsons. Pioneer Day also could accommodate a trip "to the hills," as in 1918 when Carl Otto noted "Paul and Henry going to Yellowstone Park with the Ford," referring to the means of all this neighborhood gadding, the presence of automobiles in many farm families by the 1910s.[17] Model T Fords were available by 1908 and had a tremendous impact on informal visiting and leisure patterns in rural America (Berger 1979, 47–51).

Small group gatherings meant food preparation, which unfortunately is little documented in the extant sources, even those written by women. Viktorina mentioned buying and preparing food, but she did not elaborate on her shopping list or menus. In 1939, June 23, a Friday, was a marketing day for her: "We went to the city [probably Idaho Falls], bought food for the Midsummer party on Sunday."[18]

Rare documentation of another family's food patterns appears in the Oslund family papers preserved at the Latah County Historical Society. Henry and Maria Oslund established their farm at Nora, Idaho, in 1889. Accounts reflecting labor at and barter with the Johnson Lumber Mill and the Vollmer (Troy) Milling & Mercantile Company during the 1890s and purchases at the Carl Anderson and the Olson and Johnson general mercantile stores during the first two decades of the twentieth century list recurrent purchases of processed and exotic goods that one could not grow: crackers, flour, syrup, molasses, sugar, and coffee. Important parts of the purchased diet were fruits such as apples, grapes, raisins, and prunes; some of these may have been local goods bartered through the mercantile stores. In December 1917, preparatory to Christmas, purchases reflected a series of valued items including currants, walnuts, bananas, oranges, pineapple, and popcorn. Herring was a recurrent purchase from the local grocer, occasionally joined by salmon. The family may have also acquired canned and smoked fish through the Norway Pacific Fish Company's mail-order services out of Seattle, advertised to inlanders via flyer.[19]

From these purchases, we can imagine Maria Oslund, Viktorina Holm, and their daughters preparing Midsummer dishes outlined in cookbooks like *Hemmets Drottning Verldsutställningens Souvenir Kokbok* (1894, Domestic "Queen's" World Exhibition Souvenir Cookbook), *Svenska Kokboken* (Björjlund 1910, The Swedish Cookbook) or *Hemmets Kokbok* (1913, Domestic Cookbook), the latter two available via Chicago distributors of Swedish literature.[20] *Svenska Kokboken*, published by the Swedish newspaper *Tribunen-Nyheter* (Tribune-News), provided directions for preparing salmon and herring, preparing *saft* (fruit juice concentrate) from wild berries, preparing fruit soup by soaking apples that could later be used for pastries, and baking coffeecakes with the walnuts, prunes, raisins, or apples purchased or bartered at the local mercantile.[21]

Fresh fruit was highly valued at the turn of the century, an era during which the expansion of railway lines and the beginnings of refrigerated shipping were opening local markets to exotic fruits like bananas and oranges. Local harvests remained important, however, represented in the very popular practice of planting apple orchards and gathering indigenous fruits, such as the blueberry, that were abundant enough to be picked in the wild rather than cultivated.[22]

The spring-to-summer holidays were cultural sites for responding to this local, seasonal abundance, and the Swedish Americans participated enthusiastically in this pattern, which paralleled folk foodways in Sweden (Frykman and Löfgren 1987 [1979], 46). In her *History of Troy*, Stella Johnson (1992) compiles autobiographic accounts of several Troy-area Swedish American families. A recurrent theme is huckleberrying—going out to forest meadows to pick small, intensely flavored, reddish-purple berries growing, often sparsely, on low bushes.[23] The Clarence and Agnes Smith Johnson family, for example, "loved being out in the woods. Picnics, fishing and huckleberrying were favorite activities" (Stella Johnson 1992, 219). Huckleberry parties were held by the Troy women, who raced "to find the best bushes" (219).

Fresh fruit was one of Otto Rydman's excuses for skipping the public Midsummer celebration at Garfield Beach on June 24, 1892 (described in chapter 2). Rydman and his family traveled the following day, a Saturday, to visit friends in a nearby town where residents were enjoying a large strawberry harvest. In his newspaper column, Rydman noted that some enjoy Midsummer as a departure from everyday routine. But that could be achieved without a large Midsummer event: Rydman placed himself among those happy folk as he commented, in prose and verse, on the meaning of his family's private post-Midsummer excursion:

> It is not just the abundance of fruit, etc., that attracts the urbanite out to the countryside, . . . but the more pleasant tranquility and sincere friendship he experiences there. He fully enjoys the spiritual refreshment that comes to him there and returns home with new strength to persevere in the disrupting tasks of everyday life.
>
> When, free from the alarms and noise of the city
> One gets to enjoy calm and friends—
> Then the mind cools itself; and things of the heart
> Are greatly strengthened with dear remembrance.[24]

Rydman equated social, physical, and spiritual refreshment in describing his family's excursion to a natural environment for a small group gathering out of the city, where fruit was abundantly available.

Rydman's words also provide a window into understanding the many references in Midsummer texts to arbors, bowers, groves, and greenery. Swedish and English terms for these landscape features are used by turn of the century writers as though their readers would be able to visualize the setting. Hence, there is a paucity of detailed and complete descriptions of such features as arbors and groves, but clearly these were landscaping patterns that dovetailed with social and celebratory patterns.

Löfsalar (modern spelling *lövsalar*), literally "leaf-rooms," were landscaping structures present in Swedish gardens of the nineteenth century, mentioned for example in *Svensk Botanik* by Swedish naturalist Conrad Quensel (1804, 211). An alternative term used by Viktorina Holm was *berså*, translated to English as bower or arbor, a loan word into Swedish from French *berceau* (cradle) implying a sheltered outdoor space.[25] A description of a country estate in western Sweden from the latter half of the nineteenth century provides us with a sense of how arbors or bowers fit into larger landscaping patterns:

Wilhelmsberg [the name of the house and its grounds] is no large estate with fields and forests. It is a little country house out in the country, a little haven in the bosom of nature, far from the restless world of business in the nearby city [of Gothenburg]. The adjoining land consists of no more than a few acres situated between the mountain slopes. The garden, cultivated in the favorable soil between the mountains, provides crops of delicious fruit every year, and shady bowers for repose on close summer evenings. (Frykman and Löfgren 1987 [1979], 65)

This country house with its associated fields and bowers was situated in a middle landscape outside the city and between the mountains. Its land was cultivated to provide fruit, and its bowers provided "rooms" for sitting outside, especially in the summertime. It was a model for the space mentioned by Albin Widén in describing an outdoor Swedish Baptist July 4 celebration, called *lövhyddohögtiden*, in Wisconsin—"The bower [*lövsalen*] was used as the location for sermons [after the initial celebration]"—and for the outdoor spaces mentioned by Swedish Americans like Holm, or the Lovendahls of the Salt Lake City area, at whose farm they erected "big arbors" to provide shade for their visitors at the Independence Day celebration held there in 1885.[26]

August W. Carlson used *löfsalar* in describing his home landscaping at Midsummer-time in 1905 Salt Lake City: "We have enough flowers, and gardens and shrubs grow around nearly every house, so that no one thinks about other arbors."[27] Carlson's meaning is ambiguous. Possibly he meant that one need not necessarily travel farther than one's own yard to have the kind of greenery desirable for a Midsummer picnic or coffee party, even though there were celebratory excursions to groves and beaches available to Salt Lake City's residents. Or perhaps his comparison was to Sweden; Salt Lake City's gardens did not have to be considered lesser than the greenery of Sweden at Midsummer time. In either case, his version of Midsummer was a small festive gathering in the arbor he had created at home.

The term *middle landscape* was offered by American Studies scholar Leo Marx (1964) to designate the nineteenth-century modification of the idea of the pastoral in the midst of industrialization. For Marx, the pastoral shifted to incorporate the presence of industrialized machinery, the "machine in the garden." As reconsidered by Howard P. Segal, the middle landscape in industrial America

[aimed] not to escape from the cities but to balance them against the country. Manifestations . . . included . . . city parks. Their purpose was exactly to

alleviate city problems without leaving the city. For the country was either brought inside the city or, more commonly, established just at the city limits. (Segal 1977, 140)

The middle landscapes of urban America were carefully planned by designers such as Frederick Law Olmsted and Calvert Vaux, and industrialization itself was a means of planning and execution.

Middle landscapes mediate between civilization and nature, existing on the edges of human-planned spaces like cities, farms, and home-places. In America, a middle class movement toward single-family residences with landscaped yards as a form of middle landscape between perceived wilder nature and indoor spaces dates at least as far back as the popular mid-nineteenth-century Picturesque work of Andrew Jackson Downing, published in *The Horticulturalist* and elsewhere (D. Wall 2007). But the term *arbor* also became associated with the American Arbor Day, established in Nebraska in 1872 and extended to nationwide observance by the end of the century, encouraging the planting of thousands of trees on the plains and in the deserts of the far West (Olson 1972, 9–12). These arbors and bowers stemmed from European patterns of outdoor habitation.[28]

In Sweden, a celebration of the outdoors and creation of similar middle landscapes was occurring right at the time of the emigration. As Frykman and Löfgren point out, the idea that the Swedes, by virtue of their national character, are nature lovers had become a truism at least by 1910 (Frykman and Löfgren 1987 [1979], 42). The words of the immigrants themselves could lead us to this simple conclusion. Many Denverites expressed a strong connection to nature in their spring and early summer letters—emphasizing the warmth, beauty, and recreational opportunities offered by the change of seasons. Writing on May 9, 1891, Jacob Lundquist said to his sister Ellen that "the last 2 weeks we have had the finest kind of weather, almost too warm for May; but everything looks lovely here now."[29] Emma Swanson wrote on June 19, 1891, to comment on her mother's report of a beautiful flower garden at home. By contrast, she described the flowers in Denver as not so pretty as those she imagined at home.[30] August Johansson and Elin Pehrson rejoiced in the warm weather that allowed them to plant gardens.[31] Victor and Anna Hallquist enjoyed the warm Denver summer in 1898 by riding bicycles.[32] Meanwhile, Emma's brother John M. Swanson enjoyed summer excursions to fish with Swedish American friends.[33]

But, Frykman and Löfgren (1987 [1979]) resist the truism. Rather than essentializing Swedes as nature lovers, they explain the historical development of this idea. It is a complex story in which industrialization worked alongside the revival and intensification of Swedish traditions, including holiday traditions, to produce a situation in which people prized outdoor activity. Frykman and Löfgren see the latter half of the nineteenth century as a period in which the peasant understanding of land as "a sphere of production" shifted to a middle class understanding of land as "a landscape of [recreational] consumption," a romanticized view that fueled the popularity of traveling to the countryside during the summer months. Reflecting back to the trends identified in chapters 2 and 3, we can see these emergent patterns in Swedish culture as directly affecting a Swedish American excursion tradition as well as the sense of the spaces in which celebration should occur.

A phrase that appears frequently in Swedish documents surrounding the spring-summer celebrations is *i de gröna*, an idiom for "in the open" or "out of doors."[34] The literal meaning of the phrase, "in the greenery," seems to have passed away—it is a dead metonym. When one asks a native Swedish speaker today to explain the phrase, it is clear that the first meaning is simply "outdoors" and the literal reference to the qualitative experience of being outdoors among green trees and shrubbery isn't necessarily retained. But to someone for whom Swedish is not a native language, "in the greenery" is a compelling idea, especially for one whose "outdoors" is an arid environment mainly devoid of the color green. The idiom makes it clear how a Swede could simply take for granted that the outdoors is green, and its use resonates ironically when used in arid Utah, as C.J. Renström did in his song lyrics of 1891, sung in Lorin Farr's Grove, Ogden, which would have been an oasis in the Wasatch Valley. Renström referred, in his lyrics, to the gathered Scandinavians' "*midsommarsfest* [Midsummer celebration] *i det gröna! . . . Här uti naturen så sköna* [out here in nature so beautiful]."[35]

Instances of *i de gröna* in reference to spring-summer excursions seem to point not just to the state of being outdoors but also to the importance of the location as a space separate from the city and its daily activities. When Anders Gustaf Johnson of Grantsville, Utah, wrote in his LDS missionary journal on June 24, 1881, "went with the saints to Fiskeby, was out in the Green all day, had a very good time," (Johnson 2002, 77)[36] he refers to the state of being outdoors and to the respite from the missionaries' usual location and usual activities, which could be emotionally and physically arduous. The Denver *Svenska Korrespondenten* similarly located an 1891 excursion "*i de gröna.*"[37] In these uses, *i de gröna* refers not just to a generalized outdoors but to specific outdoor spaces—middle landscapes.

Like the arbor, the places used for picnicking were middle landscapes. At home one could be outdoors in an arbor or bower, holding a coffee party for family and close friends. The arbor or bower was cultivated as a liminal space between the civilized space of the home and the outdoor space of a yard. A picnic was by definition an excursion away from home. The term most frequently employed for the space used for picnics *i de gröna* was the English *grove*, even in the midst of Swedish descriptions. Perhaps in concert with the Arbor Day movement, groves became an important publicly available space during this era in the West. As with the terms *arbor* and *bower*, *grove* is used without elaboration as writer and reader seemed to share a common assumption regarding what a grove was and where the grove was located in one's home town, such that a writer could simply indicate "the grove."

Like the arbor or bower, groves were liminal, mediating civilized and wild spaces. Just as the arbor was on the edge of the house, groves tended to be on the edge of town. Troy, Idaho, had its "grove above town," used for a 1905 Independence Day celebration, which may have been the timbered area to the east described in the 1905 Sanborn map as a "hill beyond covered with timber" or may have been the area on the other side of town "west of the school house" used for the Mission church's June 24, 1905 picnic, described by the Sanborn mappers as having "no exposure around except timber."[38] These areas had two commonalities: they were just outside of the town plat, and they were wooded, providing shelter from the heat and glare of summer sun. For Americans of the early nineteenth century, they would have been considered within walking distance.

Just as Troy had its "grove above town," Helena, Montana, had its Kranich's Grove, and Butte, Montana, its Columbia Gardens. Kranich's Grove was a picnic area one mile northwest of the city limits, according to the Polk City Directory of 1893, on Ernest Kranich's land. Columbia Gardens was, according to the 1893 Polk City Directory, "2 miles east of Butte City," and a Columbia Garden Ice Company maintained ice storage houses at the same location. It was an informal picnic destination before it became a full-blown amusement park developed in 1899 by Montana entrepreneur William A. Clark ("Remembering the Columbia Gardens" 2012).

These Montana grove locations and picnic grounds on rural plots such as Kranich's Grove, Columbia Gardens, and the Lövendahl, Moses, and Calder places in the Salt Lake City area suggest how a grove might eventually become a commercially run park used for excursions. Originally located on a rural site that informally became a picnic destination, a grove could be developed into a park with amusements drawing crowds willing to pay for their use. Calder's Park, developed by George and Mary B. Calder, was "Calder's Farm" in 1886, but the Calders very early on realized the possibilities of developing a park on the edge of the city. By 1892

Figure 6.1. Participants in a Midsummer picnic held near Troy, Idaho. Photograph courtesy of Latah County Historical Society, item 15/09/05/15-11-05.

excursions were being advertised to "Calder Park" for Pioneer Day and other occasions, and the park eventually became a city park entirely surrounded by development.[39]

Photographs surviving from turn of the century festive gatherings further help us visualize these groves. A view taken in 1910 at a Troy, Idaho, celebration reads like a very large family reunion photograph: adults standing in the background with children ranged in front of them and the youngest children seated in the foreground, in all at least 150 people. The setting may well have been the "grove above town." It was a clearing or meadow in the midst of evergreen forest. The photograph evidences no picnic tables or other improvements, and for the photograph, children were seated directly on the ground.[40]

A photograph from the same era in New Sweden, Idaho, depicts about fifty people very similarly grouped. They are at the edge of farmland with a Midsummer pole and grove of trees, appearing to be either deciduous or juniper trees (called "cedar" in southeastern Idaho), in the background. Again, no tables or improvements appear in the photograph, but a separate photograph of an outdoor meal at New Sweden, not necessarily the same

Figure 6.2. An outdoor picnic at New Sweden, Idaho, dating from the 1900s. Photograph courtesy of David A. Sealander; preserved and gifted to Sealander by Anna Margaret Nygaard Cobb.

event, displays guests standing at a long table set with tablecloth and dishes. Especially striking in these photographs is the attire. People dressed in their best clothes for these outdoor events: men, in dark suits with ties and hats; women, in high-necked white or light-colored dresses with hats decorated with flowers; children, in attire very like their elders, some of the girls with flower wreaths rather than hats. This attire would have been called "Sunday best," with the variation of flower wreaths indicating a spring-summer celebration. Given the discomfort of this heavy clothing on a hot, sunny June or July day in Idaho, we have to see this attire as governed mainly by custom.

The scene depicted at New Sweden is strikingly similar to that described by Widén in Wisconsin, based on oral accounts, at the "*lövhyddohögtiden* 1869" roughly fifty years earlier on July 4. The term *lövhyddohögtiden* literally denotes a celebration in leafy bowers or huts. Its similarity to the Jewish Festival of Tabernacles, for which leafy shelters are erected, is compelling, and the Wisconsinites may have had in mind biblical parallels, although as much to the New Testament as to the Old: in the Wisconsin celebration, the Swedish Baptists of Burnett County reenacted the loaves and fish parable of the New Testament by providing an outdoor fish feast for all comers, with an after-dinner sermon and hymns accompanied on the melodeon. The feast was offered in a large *lövsal* with a long table and benches that seated one hundred, the table covered with a "white Swedish tablecloth," light red flower bouquets, and table settings, part of which had been brought from Sweden (Widén 1972, 192). This striking parallel to the scene at New Sweden helps us flesh out the kind of picnic that brought together small group festivities.

In their small group spring and summer festivities, the Swedish Americans in the Rockies expressed their perspective on human relationship to nature as well as the ethnic, nationalistic, and religious ideas already discussed in previous chapters. Natural environment, seasonal changes, and vegetative abundance were celebrated and imbued with positive connotations in the same way that Swedish and American virtues were lifted up by orators. These concerns were seamlessly joined as arbors, groves, and formally set dinner tables served to recreate spaces directly connected to those remembered from Sweden, a physical representation of hyphenated identity in which Swedishness included a positive relationship with nature.[41] This conflation of nation, ethnicity, and nature is reflected in a verse composed by Charles A. Bundsen for a February 12, 1906, banquet:

> The land of the Midnight Sun
> where the nightingale sings & the brooklets run
> where we first saw the light & our lives begun
> & we live[d] as it were, Just for fun.[42]

Although inscribed in English, these lines tantalize the reader with the possibility of a Swedish original. Swedish popular culture scholar Ulf Jonas Björk suggests that the lines can be glossed as related to Swedish song, poetry, and toasting traditions. He notes that the lines are reminiscent "of a drinking song/ *snapsvisa* in their brevity and . . . nonsensical content."

> Whether this is a translation [of a Swedish original] is hard to say,[43] but it has a definite Swedish resonance. Nightingales and brooklets (an odd word choice which must be *bäckar* [small streams] in Swedish) are frequent companions in Swedish poetry and can be found in the works of Tegnér and Stagnelius. "Saw the light" . . . looks like a mangled translation of *såg dagens ljus* (saw the light of day), a phrase meaning being born. [Possibly] . . . setting up the final line's rhyme in Swedish as *leva i sus och dus* (living it up).[44]

This brief verse in which the land where one first saw the sun is linked with the beauties of nature seen in its gentlest, most innocent phase, with singing birds and babbling brooks, appears in Bundsen's papers in the context of a longer statement—also a toast—that went beyond immigrant nostalgia to espouse Swedish Americans' retaining a sense of Swedish patriotism. Yet it seems this patriotism could not be expressed without these references to nature.

Bits of evidence in letters, grocery receipts, photographs, maps, and other documents of Scandinavian American activities allow us to add to Humphrey's list of components for small group festive gatherings.

In addition to the sharing of seasonal and ethnic foods and gathering of fellow Scandinavians in reunion-like events, these smaller spring-summer gatherings bore traces of some of the ethnic messages in the larger celebrations. But more importantly, they expressed the significance of nature as mediated—as it could be shaped through industrial means into leafy "rooms" and "groves" where nature could be experienced in a manageable way. In these surroundings the quieter traditional activities of a coffee party—conversational and musical genres—could be enjoyed with those whom one knew best.

NOTES

1. Holm Papers, box 5, folder 16, "Notes of Recollections at Three Score and Ten Years."

2. Holm Papers, box 1, folder 1.

3. Holm Papers. Visiting the cemetery was noted by Carl beginning in 1906 and continuing through 1909, then sporadically in 1911, 1913, and 1914 (box 1, folders 2, 3; box 2, folder 6; box 4, folder 15; box 5, folder 16). These visits to decorate graves may have begun when the Holms lost a daughter, Valja. In the late 1940s, Carl retired to Salt Lake City after Viktorina died. The end of May became a season for regular visits to Idaho. The Ammon cemetery was part of the itinerary of at least one of these annual trips (box 1, folders 3, 4; box 2, folders 6, 7; box 3, folder 11; box 4, folder 13).

4. Holm Papers, box 1, folder 2.

5. Holm Papers, box 2, folder 6. Goshen, fourteen miles south of Idaho Falls, had many Scandinavian settlers. It is unknown who Norea was.

6. Holm Papers, box 4, folder 15. Carl Otto noted that "Ma" was with Olive at Arimo.

7. Holm Papers, box 4, folder 12, Viktorina Holm diary entry, June 24, 1936. "Var vi i Per Kals berså och drock kaffe i midnatten. . . . Per Kals son, sjöng 'På böljorna de blå'. . . . Det är svalt och got i dag. Man männen kan inte köra hö, det är för våtte." Unfortunately, no corresponding entries exist from Carl Otto, whose 1936 diary is not extant. It is unclear whether Viktorina was still a practicing LDS member in 1936 when she wrote so enthusiastically about a coffee party (coffee is avoided by the LDS). Carl Otto reported in his autobiographical pamphlet "Notes of Recollections at Three Score and Ten Years" (1944; copy in Holm Papers, box 5, folder 16) that he had been excommunicated in 1935 for asserting his own interpretations of LDS scripture.

8. Holm Papers, box 4, folder 12. "Jag med Otto ut till Matilda på party för en svänsk gumma från Sandy." Carl Otto did not mention this gathering in his diary.

9. Holm Papers, box 2, folder 6.

10. "Co-Laborers with God," New Sweden Covenant Church, 8–9; and Anderson, Charles, *After Fifty Years*, 49–53. This was the congregation reportedly resistant to Midsummer celebrations (see chapter 1) but which did hold summer picnics.

11. Holm Papers, box 5, folder 16. For the Safstroms' role in the New Sweden Mission Church, see New Sweden Covenant Church records: Minute book, February 19, 1896; and "Co-Laborers with God," 5.

12. Holm Papers, box 2, folder 6.

13. Holm Papers, box 2, folder 9.

14. Holm Papers, box 4, folder 15.

15. Holm Papers, box 2, folder 7. The "shubs" were probably Utah chubs, native to southeastern Idaho and now considered a nuisance fish for its abundance. The Utah sucker was a food source for settlers. See American Fisheries Society: Idaho Chapter (2014).

16. Holm Papers, box 2, folder 7.

17. Holm Papers, box 5, folder 16; box 2, folder 6; box 1, folder 3; box 4, folder 15; quotation from box 2, folder 9.

18. Holm Papers, box 4, folder 13. "Vi till staden köpte mat för midsommar kalas om söndag."

19. Oslund Family Papers, files 7, 11, and 17. The flyers are included in these papers.

20. A copy of the first book, *Hemmets Drottning*, has been found in the collection of the Sealander Farm, New Sweden, Idaho.

21. Björklund, *Svenska Kokboken*, 19, 37, 132–36, and 164–66. *Hemmets Kokbok* was prepared by Fackskolan för Huslig Ekonomi i Uppsala (1913, 28–33) (The Technical Institute for Home Economics, Uppsala), and although the cookbook included many standard Swedish foods such as fruit juice-based soups, it also included a few decidedly French-influenced dishes such as wine-based soups; 28–33.

22. Wilson and Gillespie 1999, *Rooted in America*, 13, 24–25, 65–67, 121, 124–25, 127–29.

23. Genus *Vaccinium* or *Gaylussacia*.

24. *Utah Korrespondenten* (Salt Lake City), June 29, 1892, page 1. "Det är dock icke ensamt välfägnaden af frukter m.m. som lockar storstadsbon ut till landsbygden, . . . utan fast mer det behagliga lugnet och den oskrymtade vänskap han der erfar. Han njuter i fulla drag af den andliga vederqvickelse, som öppnar sig för honom och vänder hem med nya krafter att fortsätta den afbrutna hvardags-verksamheten.

> När, fri från stadslarm och brak, man här
> Får njuta lugnet och vänners lag—
> Då svalkas sinnet; och hjertats slag
> Se'n stärkas märkbart vid hågkomst kär."

Rydman's poem is similar to those quoted in chapter 4 in its oppositions of urban and rural, work and leisure.

25. It is unclear the extent to which the domestic arbor or bower corresponded to boweries, which (as mentioned in chapter 3) were constructed as temporary shelters for public festivities. In American English, the term *bowery* came from the New Amsterdam Dutch *bouwerij*, meaning "husbandry" or "farm" according to the Oxford English Dictionary.

26. *Svenska Härolden* (Salt Lake City), July 9, 1885, page 2. "stora löfsalar."

27. Carlson, August W., Letterbook. Letter to Olga, June 24, 1905, 23. "Blommor ha vi nog af och träd och buskar växa rundt om nästan hvarje hus, så att ingen tänker på andra löfsalar."

28. Not all American outdoors spaces were designed after European models. The southern porch, for example, stems from African tradition (see Deetz 1996, 219).

29. Lundquist Collection, Letter D2. Lunduist wrote in English to his sister, who was a returnee to Sweden.

30. Swanson, John M., Papers, Letter C1. That year the Swanson family would have had at least five such Swedish American-sponsored excursions to choose among in addition to small festive gatherings of their own.

31. Johansson, August, Letter E25; and Pehrson, Elin, Letter I3.

32. Hallquist, Victor A., Letters 25, 27.

33. Swanson, John M., Papers, Letter C4.

34. See the entry for *grön* (green) in *Norstedts Engelska Ordbok* 1997.

35. *Utah Korrespondenten* (Salt Lake City), July 1, 1891, page 1.

36. Johnson's translator renders the phrase literally in English.

37. *Svenska Korrespondenten* (Denver), June 4, 1891, page 8.

38. These locations appear in brief news references; see the *Troy Weekly News*, June 23, 1905, page 5; July 7, 1905, page 5. The Sanborn map for Troy, January 1905, is labeled with the town's former name of Vollmer; see Digital Sanborn Maps.

39. *Svenska Härolden* (Salt Lake City), May 20, 1886, page 3; *Utah Korrespondenten* (Salt Lake City), July 27, 1892, page 4, 8.

40. Photograph 15–9-5, Latah County Historical Society, Moscow, Idaho.

41. For an excellent exposition of the many ways Swedish and other Scandinavian Americans recreate a sense of "Swedish" spaces, see Gradén, Larsen, and Österlund-Pötzsch, "Nordic Spaces in the U.S.: Three Examples of the Performance of Nordic-American Identity."

42. This verse appears scribbled in English on the back of a longer toast, "Swedish Am. Swedish Patriotism," February 12, 1906, folder 1, Swedish Medical Center manuscript collection WH 958.

43. Both Björk and I attempted unsuccessful searches, in English and Swedish, for this verse.

44. Personal communication, June 28, 2012.

7

Uneasy Scandinavianism in the Spring-Summer Holidays

In an 1892 local news column, editors of the Swedish-language *Utah Korrespondenten* noted that there would be a Seventeenth of May celebration that year in Calder Park. *Sjötonde Mai,* or the Seventeenth of May, is the Norwegian Constitution Day, a day signifying to the Norwegians their governmental independence from Denmark and Sweden. With both countries, Norway had been a lesser partner in unions under a common monarchy, with Denmark from the mid-sixteenth century through 1814 and with Sweden from 1814 to 1905. Yet, all Scandinavians in the Salt Lake City area were cordially invited to attend the 1892 celebration. A program was planned to include speeches and music sung by a men's quartet and a choir, with a repertoire of the best-known and beloved songs from the *fosterland* (the nation of nativity, in this case Norway). Competitions were planned, with prizes for young women (a parasol, a pair of slippers), older women (a rocking chair, a carafe with glass), and men (a cane, a felt hat). The event was planned by a committee of three (John Matson, a Mr. Hoope, and a Mr. Arvidsen) that "saved neither effort nor expense to make the party enjoyable."[1] This was among the several kinds of spring and summer celebrations in Utah that used the label "Scandinavian," as noted in chapters 2 and 3, including the founding of the Scandinavian Mission, Danish Constitution Day, Midsummer, Decoration Day, Independence Day, and Pioneer Day, as well as the Seventeenth of May. In these events, we can recognize the patterns already discussed in previous chapters: celebration outdoors, speeches and songs, competitions with prizes. Clearly the Seventeenth of May fit into the spring-summer celebration paradigm established in other Scandinavian American festivities.

Throughout our consideration of Midsummer and the other spring-to-summer holidays, we have encountered many such instances of

DOI: 10.7330/9780874219999.c007

celebrations that were labeled "Scandinavian" rather than by a national designation such as Swedish, Norwegian, or Danish. But were the Scandinavians equal partners in these holidays? And were these celebrations satisfactory to participants from all corners of Scandinavia? For a Swede or a Dane there may have been little incentive—and even some disinclination—to attend a May 17 celebration, especially as toward the end of the nineteenth century, Norwegian national sentiments intensified and in turn celebrations expressing those sentiments became more important (Gustavsson 2007, 191). Alternately, Norwegians may have been disinclined to celebrate Midsummer, especially Midsummer with a (mainly Swedish) pole raising rather than a (mainly Norwegian or Danish) bonfire, as the holiday as practiced in America was implicitly more Swedish than Norwegian or Danish even when not labeled as such. We see those implicit traces in the advertisements for Scandinavian Midsummer that use the Swedish version of the Swedish-Norwegian Union flag and the appearance of a "Norden" band in Swedish blue and yellow.[2] We also see the Swedish connection to Midsummer in the efforts to create a Swedish Day close to or on Midsummer in places like Minneapolis-St. Paul.[3]

Yet in some Western settlements, circumstances provided an opportunity for what we can regard as experiments in Scandinavianism—that is, explicit or implicit promotion of a panethnicity that elided the national divisions among Norwegians, Swedes, and Danes, lumping these groups into a general rubric based on perceived language and/or cultural similarities and common social, religious, and political interests. How and why this lumping occurred, and whether it was successful, is well illustrated in two Rocky Mountain subregions: the Mormon culture area centered in Utah and the western Montana mining and smelting, and later agricultural, region.

In Utah, Scandinavianism was actively promoted through programmatic means, intentionally encouraged both by the structures of the Church of Jesus Christ of Latter-day Saints and by secular committees and organizations. In Montana, Scandinavianism was more pragmatic than programmatic; while institutions played a role, informal social patterns were important in creating and sustaining Scandinavianism. The differing historical and social contexts of Scandinavianism in these two regions during the period 1890 through the 1920s produced differing Scandinavianisms reflecting different cultural strategies. These strategies included the selection and intensification of essential parts of Scandinavian custom, as we observed in chapter 2. These efforts served "to preserve cultural values" even when the specifics of cultural practice were inexactly replicated or even replaced (Toelken 1991, 155). But they could lapse into what Herbert J. Gans calls symbolic but empty ethnic claims "free from affiliation with ethnic groups," and less satisfactory for some participants (Gans 1992, 44).

A degree of Scandinavianism can be found throughout North America during the nineteenth and early twentieth centuries. For example, Kenneth O. Bjork and Ernst Ekman point to Scandinavianism in 1860s San Francisco, where a group of immigrants, half Swedish and the remainder Norwegian and Danish, banded together in 1859 as the Scandinavian Society, a group that like many of the era pooled the members' dues for benefits to those among them who fell ill or were injured. The society also maintained a library of Scandinavian-languages books and newspapers and organized an annual children's Christmas party. With the number of founding members relatively small, seventy-four according to Ekman, and the distribution across groups rather even, a panethnic group would have made sense in 1860s California, especially when one of the motivations was garnering enough members to support the society's protective function (Bjork, 1954a, 1954b, 1955; Ekman 1974, 91–92). Bjork and Thomas Benson trace Scandinavianism, too, in California's mid-century Swedish/Norwegian religious groups, land developments, and the "Scandinavian Navy," as the coastal fishermen came to be called (Benson 1970, 8–9). As numbers of immigrants from the Scandinavian countries grew, though, Scandinavianism was in trouble; Bjork sees its dissolution in California beginning in 1875 when the Swedish Society of San Francisco was formed (Bjork 1954a, 67, 78).

When immigration from the Scandinavian countries was a trickle into places like California, Scandinavianism was an appropriate and functional cultural strategy. Moreover, nineteenth-century American Scandinavianism was bulwarked by its transatlantic counterpart, a political and cultural movement that had developed during the latter half of the eighteenth century and persisted into the mid-nineteenth century (Barton 2009, 138; Christianson 1984, 377). Arnold Barton points to "the failure of Sweden-Norway to come to Denmark's aid in its German war in 1864 . . . as the deathblow of political Scandinavianism" in the Scandinavian countries (Barton 2009, 183). Cultural Scandinavianism lingered, though, and Scandinavian religious congregations and secular societies were attempted throughout North America, with varying success (Beijbom 1972, 146–48). Scandinavianism was a strong trend in urban Norwegian and Swedish settlement, waning as those groups grew large enough to sustain national groups (Jenswold 1985). But, as we shall see, it was also possible for at least a tentative cultural Scandinavianism to develop among immigrants to the smaller, more rural settlements of the inland West throughout the nineteenth century and well into the twentieth, if the conditions were right.

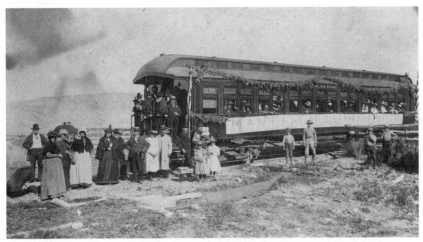

Figure 7.1. A Scandinavian choir assembled in Manti, Utah. Used by permission, Utah State Historical Society, all rights reserved; #20139.

For the Utahans, the immigration was "Scandinavian" from its inception, a matter of Mormon ideology and programmatic planning rather than mere pragmatics. This much more deeply studied migration has received considerable attention from historians, linguists, and folklorists interested in the multiethnic communities that sprang up in the latter half of the nineteenth century as European LDS converts converged on Utah.

As described in chapter 2, the LDS church attracted a mix of Norwegian, Swedish, and Danish converts, as well as much smaller numbers of Icelanders, through its mission efforts. Initially these came from among the ranks of immigrants converted in the United States, during the 1840s. But in 1849, the Mormons instigated a major effort to convert Europeans through establishing onsite missions, and the Scandinavian Mission was begun one year later by seasoned American missionary Erastus Snow, Swedish American convert John E. Forsgren, and Danish American convert Peter O. Hansen. Partly as a result of the original structure of the mission, with Snow in Denmark overseeing the work farther north, and partly as a result of Forsgren's unsuccessful initial attempts at missionary work in Sweden, Copenhagen became the center of the Scandinavian Mission until 1905, when it was split between Swedish and Danish-Norwegian missions coincident with Norwegian independence. Proximity, and the fact that Danish became the main language of translation for the mission's written materials, produced the greatest success in Denmark, followed by Sweden and then Norway. By 1905, the percentages of Scandinavian converts who had emigrated were 56 percent Danish, 32 percent Swedish, 11 percent Norwegian, and 1 percent Icelandic (Jenson 1927, 2–3, 411; Mulder 1956b; 2000 [1957], 31–39, 107).

With this mix of Scandinavians flowing into Utah throughout the second half of the century, Scandinavianism permeated several layers of culture. The vehicles for Scandinavianism included official structures, popular media, and cultural events. They also included the LDS church's divisions, newspapers and other publications, social clubs, social patterns such as intermarriage, and folklore genres such as holiday celebrations. Even though the Danish converts outnumbered Swedes, Norwegians, and other Scandinavian peoples, the LDS church established Scandinavian meetings. These met separately from the English-language services held for the same membership and used a combination of Scandinavian languages—a combination not always satisfactory, as Danish was a struggle for the Swedes (Bjork 1962, 214; Olson 1949, 6).[4] Local meetings were held weekly or monthly. Annual Scandinavian reunions or conference meetings with a combined religious and social purpose were held from 1890 through the 1920s (Henrichsen et al. 2010, 8–12). From the point of view of the LDS church, the Danes, Norwegians, Swedes, and Icelanders were *Scandinavian* immigrants.

J. R. Christianson (1984) points out that English was important in facilitating interactions among Scandinavians in America (376). Certainly the use of English by fraternal organizations such as the Scandinavian Brotherhood/ Sisterhood points to the important basis that English could provide as a leveler among Scandinavian immigrants. Because the Mormons saw English as, according to William Mulder (1956a, 11), "the Lord's favored language in which he had spoken his will in this last dispensation," the mixed Danish/ Norwegian/Swedish language services of the LDS Scandinavian Meetings were always seen as auxiliary to English-language services, and Scandinavian immigrants were members first of the English-speaking ward (a congregational unit with geographical boundaries) within which they lived and only secondarily of a Scandinavian Meeting within that ward.

Intermarriage was also affected by official structures within the LDS church. While the non-Mormon Scandinavian population in much of the Intermountain West was weighted toward single men, with the result that any single Scandinavian woman might pose a marriage interest even across nation-based ethnic lines, there was a decided preference for marrying within one's nationality if possible (Rasmussen 1989, 9, 15–16). By contrast, among the LDS Scandinavians, intermarriage patterns were complicated by polygamy, practiced by roughly one quarter of the Scandinavian Mormons

(Mulder 2000 [1957], 238). Mulder credits polygamy as "[breaking] down ethnic barriers both among the Scandinavians themselves and between them and other nationalities," citing numerous examples of Scandinavian intermarriage among Danes, Swedes, and Norwegians (Mulder 2000 [1957], 245). These polygamous unions provided opportunities for strong bonds among women within the Scandinavian LDS community.

Reinforcing these official structures was a secular Scandinavianism nurtured through social organizations and the Danish/Norwegian- and Swedish-language press. Kenneth O. Bjork sees the newspapers especially as having served as vehicles for "a persistent Scandinavianism . . . too potent to be wholly contained within the forms and routine functions of the [LDS] church" that included appeals to Scandinavians as a potential voting block and advertisements for Scandinavian events and merchants (Bjork 1962, 215). The newspapers included the Danish, Swedish, and English *Utah Skandinav* (1875); the Danish/Norwegian *Utah Posten* (1873–74), *Bibuken* (1876–1935), *Familie Vennen* (1877), a second *Utah Posten* (1885), and *Utah Pioneeren* (1895); and the Swedish *Svenska Härolden* (1885–93), *Fyrbåken* (1895), *Utah Korrespondenten* (1890–1915), *Salt Lake Bladet* (1902–11), and *Utah Posten* (1900–35) (Bjork 1962; and Mulder 2000 [1956], 258–66; Setterdahl 1981, 30). Bjork notes that *Bibuken* "came to be known as the paper of the Scandinavian Mormons" (Bjork 1962, 218). Its production was also representative of LDS Scandinavianism: written in Danish, it was edited and published by a Swedish convert, Anders W. Winberg. The paper was eventually officially underwritten by the LDS church, sponsorship also achieved by the initially controversial *Utah Korrespondenten* (Mulder 2000 [1956], 266). Through advertising in these newspapers, Utah's Scandinavians were made aware of the availability of expressly Scandinavian goods and services from Scandinavian doctors, mercantiles, apothecaries, lawyers, and so forth.

The LDS church's support for Scandinavianism among its members became a contentious issue when Otto Rydman, editor of *Utah Korrespondenten*, used his editorial position to espouse separate Swedish-language LDS meetings in Salt Lake City, especially a Swedish *julotta* (Christmas service). Rydman spearheaded the creation of a literary club, Norden, in 1896, which additionally served as a sponsor for *julotta* services until such services were finally allowed in 1913. In 1899, Rydman planned a *julotta* for Mormon Swedes but was disallowed use of LDS meeting houses in Salt Lake City. For this and his staunch anti-Scandinavianist position Rydman was excommunicated in 1902. That his position vis-a-vis the LDS church was marginal is reflected in his exclusion from the 1900 booklet celebrating the Scandinavian Mission's jubilee (*Scandinavian Jubilee Album* 1900).

Support for Rydman from some of the Swedish LDS in Salt Lake City prompted an official statement from the LDS church president that the immigrant converts should aim to "adopt the manners and customs of the American people" (quoted in Mulder 1956a, 18; see also Olson 1949, 6–10, 42). But while they assimilated, according to the church, the immigrants had the Scandinavian Meeting available to them, where a careful balance of languages was maintained in a rotation of music and speakers that always included a fair share of Swedish. For example, according to the Swedish newspaper *Svenska Härolden*, the Scandinavian meeting held in Pleasant Grove on April 17, 1886, included "7 different speakers, among whom one found our countryman the patriarch O.N. Liljenqvist." Liljenqvist, who presided over the Scandinavian meeting for decades, delivered a message without any particular ethnic content: "the union of man and woman and living a clean and holy life."[5] It was the official position to maintain this parity among ethnicities in church-organized social events labeled as Scandinavian (Mulder 1956a, 18–19). According to Ernest L. Olson, this attempt at language parity failed in part because of its denial of the degree of language and cultural differences among the Danish, Swedish, and Norwegian immigrants (Olson 1949, 6).

What Rydman's "Swedish uprising," served to do in Mormon Utah was make the programmatic intent of LDS Scandinavianism absolutely explicit, forcing the church and its members to acknowledge that their use of the panethnic label *Scandinavian* was ideological. The folklorist William A. Wilson (1979) suggests that the Scandinavian converts in Utah "did not become Yankees or English; they became Mormons—which is what the Yankees and English also became" (151). The Scandinavian Meeting was a vehicle for this transformation as much or more than it was a vehicle for panethnicity. The ethnic content, in fact, was often limited to language— Mormon hymns and doctrine translated into Danish, Swedish, Norwegian, or Icelandic.[6] Truly ethnic content would have also incorporated a religious custom such as *julotta*. For Rydman, this was a cultural strategy too empty of ethnic content to be satisfying.

Yet the LDS earnestly attempted to bridge the many cultural gaps among the church's immigrant converts, not just through Scandinavian church meetings but also through events showcasing the territory's many groups. For example, in 1887, the youth group of the Provo stake (a designation for a unit bringing together several congregations, or "wards") presented a "grand national concert" that included performances by a Welsh choir, a Danish "king and queen, with all their royal retinue," a Scottish bagpipe player, and representatives of German and Norwegian cultures, including a "duett by . . . two little girls from Lehi."[7]

Examples of similar Scandinavian events mixing Danish, Swedish, and Norwegian components abound in newspaper announcements and in surviving program booklets. Many mix secular and sacred components to the extent that it is difficult to clearly separate the two intents. Scandinavian Day, staged in Brigham City on July 12, 1908, a Sunday, is an excellent example. The event mixed religious and secular purposes, the religious function making it appropriate and acceptable to hold the event on a Sunday. And, as the newspaper reporter commented, the day's organizers included LDS leaders acting in their official capacities. Yet the pageantry and decoration that the Brigham Cityites devoted to the components of the event that were held outside of the LDS tabernacle (used for the religious components) were clearly drawn from the repertoire of spring-summer celebrations. The event was an *udflugt*, or outing. Trains arriving from north, south, and east were met by a delegation led by the city mayor and an LDS dignitary. Programs were distributed at the train station to guide attendees through the day's events. A committee provided transportation from the train station to the courthouse along a decorated route:

> On each light pole was a cross stick at each end of which flew a banner,
> beginning with one of the Scandinavian country's colors and following
> with the next and so on over again along the whole line of march. On the
> light pole at the cross roads, two American flags waived [*sic*] above the other
> colors, making a beautiful groupe [*sic*]. The color scheme was carried out
> with splendid effect at the Tabernacle and central school building.[8] At the
> entrance to each place an arch of green pine boughs, draped with bunting
> flags and the Scandinavian coats of arms, had been erected and from the
> Tabernacle gate to the building, an alley of flags and bunting had been made,
> and the front of the building was covered by two large American flags.
>   On the inside, flags, bunting, streamers and flowers had been used in
> great profusion. The west wall was draped with two large American flags,
> and the U.S. Coat of Arms. The east wall was similarly draped with the
> Swedish colors, the north wall by the Norwegian and south wall by the
> Danish colors and coats of arms.[9]

In this especially detailed description of the physical arrangements for a Scandinavian conference, we detect the patterns of sacred and secular events conflated: a worship meeting bracketed by the ideas of an excursion and a patriotic procession from one key building to another within the town—in this case, from the train station to two of the town's main institutional buildings, the tabernacle and the school. Flags, bunting, and streamers are the stuff of patriotic decorations for Decoration and Independence days, here used in the same way the American and Swedish flags were used on Midsummer poles, to express a hyphenated ethnicity. But the point was not just hyphenated ethnicity; the combination of colors and coats of arms established parity among the dominant Scandinavian groups—Norway, Denmark, and Sweden—and emphasized Mormon Scandinavianism.

This event's iconography extended to an implicit reference to Scandinavian custom with the pine bough arches framing the entryway to the public buildings. Arches made of greenery—birch boughs into which the leaves have been forced—are used today at Easter time in Sweden as church decorations, and are important signifiers of the coming of spring. Here, they seem to be extensions of the boweries built for Midsummer and patriotic events in Utah. The newspaper reporter went on to describe what appear to be *lovsalar*: "Under the trees on the school square, tables, benches and refreshment booths had been erected" where attendees ate a picnic lunch purchased at youth-run food booths, if they had not packed their own baskets.[10] Thus, we see the Scandinavian immigrants drawing upon familiar material traditions related to spring and summer as they planned the arrangements for this event.

In addition to the procession, decorations, and midday picnic (all components one would expect of a secular summer event), the day included morning and afternoon religious services and an evening concert. The mix of Scandinavian languages here was apparent in the program listed and described by the *Box Elder News*. The morning service opened with hymns by the "Scandinavian choir" directed by Julius L. Brunn, who had recently emigrated from Denmark to the United States.[11] Following this opening, second generation Swedish American Oleen N. Stohl delivered a welcoming speech in Swedish.[12] This was followed by a variety of religious speeches from Scandinavian immigrants, with Anthon H. Lund monitoring the proceedings by limiting speeches to five minutes each. Lund, a Swedish immigrant, was a president of the Scandinavian Meeting.[13] The afternoon worship service followed a similar format but was punctuated with musical performances by Blanche Larson, daughter of a Danish immigrant family living in Logan, Utah; Victor E. Madsen of Brigham City, the son of Danish immigrants; and Hagbert Anderson of Ogden, a Norwegian immigrant.[14]

One has to have respect for the engagement, or perhaps endurance, of the turn of the century audience in Utah. The day concluded with yet another set of performances at an evening concert, after which the trains left Brigham City at 11:00 p.m. In the concert, a similar mix of performers was evident. In addition to Brunn, Madsen, Larson, Anderson, and the Scandinavian Choir, the performers included a Miss H. Esterblom, Axel B. Ohlson, and Axel Nylander, all representing Sweden, and Henry and Joseph

Otte, representing Denmark.[15] Thus we see not just the mix of languages presented as a part of Scandinavianism, with Swedish and Danish dominant, but also the persistence of languages and of the idea of Scandinavianism into the second generation in Utah.

This pattern of multilingual programs attempting parity among the Danes, Swedes, and Norwegians emerges in many other reports and programs from Scandinavian events in Utah. In 1913, the booklet for the Scandinavian Christmas *Skandinavernes Julestevne* (show or competition) in Granite Stake, held on the December 27, had a multilingual program that included two Swedish-language presentations, "Veteranens Jul [The Soldier's Christmas]" and the prologue by Anna E. Holmqvist, in which she delivered a poem welcoming attendees and admonishing them not to forget their homeland. "Veteranens Jul" was billed as a historical play in one act by the Swedish-Finnish writer Zackarias Topelius. In it, a soldier returned from war makes the acquaintance of a mother and son.[16] In 1916, a "Scandinavian reunion" in Pleasant Grove included "songs in the Scandinavian tongues" including "the three national airs of Norway Sweden and Denmark . . . rendered in their several languages" creating "warm enthusiasm with the people of these nationalities," performed in a tabernacle where "American Danish, Swedish and Norwegian flags also created a good effect."[17]

The events explicitly labeled *Scandinavian* were consistent in this attempted parity among national origins even in events that might be characterized as more secular than sacred, as noted in several instances throughout previous chapters. We also see the principle of parity in the way that the LDS calendar grew through the addition of days representing the heritages of specific ethnic groups, days representing religious heritage, and days honoring the elderly. Throughout the 1890s, at the same time that Midsummer was emerging as a major holiday for Utah Scandinavians, it was common for the Scandinavians to come together for events cooperatively planned by a Scandinavian Outings Committee or Scandinavian organizations, mainly Scandia and Norden. Just in the spring-summer season, May Day, the Norwegian Constitution Day, Decoration Day, LDS leader Brigham Young's birthday on the first of June, the Danish Constitution Day on June 5, the anniversary of the founding of the Latter-day Saint Scandinavian Mission (recognized on June 14), Independence Day, and Pioneer Day could be celebrated by Scandinavians rather than just Swedes, Norwegians, or Danes.[18] Also sprinkled throughout the spring-to-summer season were other events celebrated in much the same way but not pinned to a particular holiday, outings especially for Scandinavian old timers, for example. Perhaps resonating most with Scandinavianism are the invitations in a Swedish language newspaper to all Scandinavians to celebrate the Norwegian and Danish constitution days, as exemplified in the Seventeenth of May, 1892, event in Calder Park.[19]

In contrast to the Utah LDS programmatic attempts at Scandinavianism, the Norwegians and Swedes of Montana maintained an uneasy Scandinavianism that served pragmatic purposes: where either nationality was too small to maintain effective organizations and events, their combined numbers sufficed. In Montana, Norwegians and Swedes settled alongside each other in the greatest numbers in Cascade County, with its population center in Great Falls, and in Lewis and Clark County, with its center in Helena, counties on the eastern edge of the Rockies in the Missouri River drainage. This region offered Scandinavian men employment in railroad construction, silver and coal mining, and smelting and also offered agricultural land for those with resources to start up farms and ranches (Grimsby 1926, 77–78). There were substantial contiguous Norwegian and Swedish populations, too, in Custer and Dawson counties in the Yellowstone River drainage, eastern Montana (Anderson 1974).

Scandinavianism in Montana was developed, expressed, and supported in organizational life and popular media. Churches were important as meeting places among ethnic groups, but functioned only tentatively as effective sites for Scandinavianism. Numbers of Norwegians and Swedes came into Montana only after the 1870 split between Swedish and Norwegian/Danish synods of the previously Scandinavian Augustana Synod; thus, Lutheran churches tended to be established by Norwegian, Swedish, or German national groups, whichever was dominant in the particular region, even if attended by a mix of nationalities. There were Scandinavian newspapers and secular organizations that also supported intra-group interactions.

Scandinavianism was a pragmatic strategy in the repeated and abortive attempts to establish Norwegian and Swedish newspapers in Montana. A Lutheran monthly, the Lutheran *Bergs-Väktaren*, was the only purely Swedish newspaper in Montana. Throughout the nineteenth and early twentieth century, Norwegian-language newspapers dominated the Scandinavian press in Montana. Although they were more strongly focused on Norwegian readers, these newspapers attempted to appeal to a broader readership through including news from other Scandinavian groups and including Swedish-language materials. Some newspapers labeled themselves as Scandinavian rather than Norwegian.

The Helena *Montana Posten* began in 1890 and ran through 1893 as a mostly Norwegian paper that included a Swedish page, claiming to be "the only paper in Montana published in both the Norwegian and Swedish languages."[20] The paper's advertisers followed suit, identifying themselves as Scandinavian pharmacies, butcher shops, or dentists; political advertising also encouraged Scandinavians to vote for a particular ticket. The 1893 subscribers' premiums offered a choice among Norwegian, Swedish, or English editions of John Bunyan's *Pilgrim's Progress* or Henry Davenport Northrup's *Earth, Sea, and Sky*.

Another mainly Norwegian newspaper with a good claim of serving the Scandinavian population was Butte's *Montana Skandinav*, published in 1893 but soon merged with another 1893 Butte venture, *Montana Tidende*, to become *Montana Tidende og Skandinav*, published weekly until 1895. Rather than print a separate Swedish page, this paper intermingled Norwegian and Swedish articles and features. The editors' claim, that the paper was "the only Scandinavian paper in Montana" was interestingly echoed twenty years later by the Great Falls paper *Indlandsposten* when it was begun in 1915.[21] "The Only Scandinavian Paper in Montana" appeared in English on that newspaper's masthead, generating a correction from reader Hans C. Boe of Butte in the issue of April 28, 1916, in which the paper's publishers admitted to "a general belief here in the state that Indlandsposten is the first Norwegian newspaper in Montana" and devoted a front page article to correcting their error. *Indlandsposten* was an entirely Norwegian newspaper that attempted to address the interests of Norwegian, Swedish, and Danish readers. In it we find features, advertisements, group announcements, and church announcements inviting Scandinavians, not just Norwegians, to take part in Scandinavian activities and commerce. Like its predecessors, *Indlandsposten* lasted but a few years, into 1917. A post-World War I paper with similar ambitions, but addressing a specifically Lutheran audience and using English rather than Norwegian, was *The Rocky Mountain Skandinavian*, a weekly begun in 1920 and published in Helena. It lasted less than one year.

The Swedish and Norwegian Lutherans were late in establishing churches in Montana, and once established those churches experienced a slow growth. Language-specific church groups like the Swedish Mission Covenant church and the Swedish Baptists were, in comparison to the Lutherans, even smaller and quite scattered (Olsson 1962, 466–67; Westman 1931, 333–34). The Covenant minister in Butte, where a chapel had been established in 1899, despaired of ministering to the Swedes there, in "a nest of Satan filled with sin and shame" (Olsson 1962, 467). Norwegian Lutheran missionaries began work in Montana in 1885 with the visit of Reverend P. J. Reinertsen to Big Timber, where services included an afternoon session in English to accommodate the mixture of peoples who were interested in attending: Scots, French, and Native Americans as well as a mix of Scandinavians (Grimsby 1926, 99). Traveling to Bozeman, Montana, Reinertsen encountered "a number of Scandinavian people in the city" but did not hold services. "They did not desire any religious service. They were too contaminated with Mormonism" (Grimsby 1926, 99).[22]

Swedish Lutheran missionaries visited Montana about ten years later than the Norwegians (Johnson 1984, 158), and many Montana communities with Norwegian and Swedish residents eventually developed Lutheran congregations affiliated with the Norwegian and Swedish Lutheran synods throughout the 1890s and 1900s, alongside similar institutions affiliated with the German Lutherans. The presence of numerous nationally oriented churches brought ministers to Montana whose interaction could promote bridges across doctrinal and language divisions as they cooperated locally (Grimsby 1926, 114), and some of the local church bodies, however clear their members may have been about their Swedish or Norwegian orientations, were ascribed as Scandinavian by outsiders. In Helena, which according to O. M. Grimsby became "the head station for mission work" in Montana (107), the 1891 Polk directory listed a "Scandinavian Lutheran Church," with pastor N. N. Boe, who was a Norwegian synod missionary sent to nurture the organization of Lutheran congregations. This was just prior to the congregation's formal organization as the Trinity Evangelical Lutheran Church (115). The same directory listed a "First Evangelical Scandinavian Church" ministered to by Reverend J. F. Frederickson. This was a Swedish Mission Covenant church that had been organized the previous year (Westman 1931, 334).

Churches could be sites for Scandinavianism, but for Lutherans there was a strong pull toward the synods related to each of the Swedish, Norwegian, and German American ethnicities and languages, with the attendant importance of liturgy in one's native language. Avis R. Anderson's examination of Lutheran congregations in Custer and Dawson counties provides a case study of how shaky the attempts at a Norwegian-Swedish combination could be in a religious context. Anderson documents the formation of the Glendive Lutheran congregation as an affiliate of the United Norwegian Lutheran Church of America. It was recorded in the church's Norwegian-language minute books as a "meeting of all interested Scandinavians" (Anderson 1974, 34) even though Norwegians outnumbered the Swedes in Dawson County from settlement well into the twentieth century (105), as evidenced in the importance of Glendive's annual May 17 celebration (185). Nevertheless, the church was both perceived by the surrounding English-speaking community as Scandinavian and self-ascribed as a Scandinavian Lutheran church (41, 45).

According to Anderson, the Glendive church fostered First Lutheran in Miles City, Custer County, where a "more equal balance of Swedes to Norwegians" led to more Swedish influence in the religious practices even though the official affiliation was Norwegian American (153–55, 165) and Norwegian was used in worship services (143). On the other hand, the Miles City church took its minutes in Swedish (142). The mixture produced tensions. According to one long-time resident interviewed by Anderson, "the Swedes and Norwegians had a misunderstanding in the early days so the Swedes threatened to leave and take their money along. . . . They also did not like the idea that the pastors in Miles City were always Norwegians" (143).

Also indicative of the perceived affinity between language and religious practice was *Bergs-Väktaren*, published by the Swedish Lutherans of the Evangelical Lutheran church (St. John's) in Helena. It was begun as a monthly in 1898 and ran at least until 1899. In the first issue the editors, Reverend C. E. Frisk of Helena and Reverend A. E. Gustafson of Missoula, couched their claim to be editing the first and only Swedish newspaper in Montana in terms of national loyalty, thus conflating religion and hyphenated ethnicity: "we hope therefore that it will be highly valued by all of our patriotic Montana citizens," Frisk and Gustafson wrote, offering the first issue free of charge.[23]

Some churches explicitly reached out to Scandinavians. The Great Falls Swedish Baptist church's newspaper notices during 1915 ended with the statement that "Scandinavians are cordially welcome."[24] As indicated by its name, the Scandinavian Methodist church in Butte, organized in 1892, made a more intentional effort at Scandinavianism, receiving criticism for the attempt. In an 1893 opinion column, *Montana Posten* correspondent "Frederick" was skeptical of the feasibility of organizing Swedes and Norwegians "under the banner of Scandinavia." In his view, the idea was good in theory but had yielded little results.[25] One should note that Frederick appears to have maintained a tone of skeptical cynicism in most of his columns. The small organization remained, though, reporting twenty-five members in 1905 (*R.L. Polk & Co.'s Butte City Directory* 1905, 70). In 1915, Great Falls had an active Scandinavian Methodist congregation that held a Christmas tree celebration on Christmas evening, to which all Scandinavians were welcomed with their children,[26] thus selecting a holiday tradition that could unite Scandinavians across national lines. The following month this congregation invited all Scandinavians to a series of meetings, including an English-language speech by evangelist Lars Andersen.[27]

Secular organizations in Montana freely subscribed to a pragmatic Scandinavianism. As had been the situation in California at mid-century,

in turn-of-the-century Montana a Scandinavian benevolent society made
sense. The main such organization documented in Montana was the Scandinavian Brotherhood of America and its auxiliary the Scandinavian Sisterhood of America, which had lodges in Butte (two lodges organized in 1891
and 1912), Helena, Kalispell (a lodge disbanded in 1911 and then reestab-
lished in 1924), and Great Falls.[28]

With the membership requirement that one be of Scandinavian "birth
or descent," the Scandinavian Brother- and Sisterhood of America had
an intentionally panethnic membership. Lodge programming was three-
pronged: members could progress through steps toward an Odin degree,
beneficial members had death and illness benefits available to them, and
social members planned and attended numerous social events throughout
the year. Explicit Scandinavianness seems to have been limited to the first
of these, with the reference to Norse mythology. In the period for which
we have documentation, the 1910s and early 1920s, the many social events
planned through the joint efforts of fraternity and sorority were not explicitly
marked as Norwegian, Swedish, Danish, or even Scandinavian: summer picnics and outings with music and dancing, a Leap Year ball, evening card parties, progressive whist, a masque ball for Thanksgiving, and a barn dance on
New Year's Eve; nothing labeled as a celebration for May 17, Midsummer,
or *jul*.[29] Combined with the fact that minutes were taken in English, the panethnic content of this Scandinavianness seems entirely empty unless, following Orm Øverland (2000), one considers that the purpose of the group
included assimilation strategies to espouse that the Scandinavians were
especially American, an appropriate strategy in this period of Nativist sentiment in the United States. But even earlier, during the 1895–1910 period
of ethnic renewal and consolidation for the Scandinavians, according to
historian Jorgen Dahlie, among the Scandinavian fraternal organizations,
the Scandinavian Brotherhood and Sisterhood had a "strong emphasis on
Americanization" (Dahlie 1967, 161).

In addition to the Scandinavian Brotherhood and Sisterhood, Montana's
towns had, in 1890 through the 1920s, several scattered secular organizations with Scandinavian (or more expressly Swedish or Norwegian) orientations
that selected and intensified particular, representative celebrations such as
the Seventeenth of May. In the multiethnic mining town of Butte, alongside the Scandinavian Brotherhood/Sisterhood there were a Svea Lodge of
the International Order of Odd Fellows and a Sons of Norway branch.[30]
In 1916, the latter organization held an Ibsen Fest at the Norwegian
Lutheran church.[31] Yet the Scandinavians of Butte came together for their
1893 Midsummer celebration and for a summer outing with rail service

to Columbian Garden. The summer outing was figured by both *Montana Posten* and the English-language *Butte Miner* as a successful event drawing all Scandinavians—"all Scandinavians were on their feet and taking part in the celebration"—and the *Miner* correspondent connected the event with the claim that "Norsemen" had "no small amount of historic glory" in the discovery of the Americas.[32] In contrast to this reportedly successful Scandinavian event, the Midsummer celebration was reported as a "fiasco" by a newspaper correspondent who pointed specifically to the mixture of Swedish dialects and Scandinavian languages heard there, hence questioning the viability of achieving a truly syncretic Scandinavian event.[33] As in Utah, the deal breaker was language.

Yet the Scandinavian population of Butte was active enough as a body during the mid-1890s to consider erecting a Scandinavian assembly building.[34] It is unclear whether these plans eventuated in the Scandinavian Hall that appears in the 1895 Polk directory as a meeting place for the Scandinavian literary society and temperance society. This two-story building must have had some sponsorship from the Scandinavian Methodist Episcopal Church. It was located across Alaska Street from the church, and Sanborn mappers labeled it "meeting/church rooms."[35]

In Helena, Swedish, Norwegian, and Scandinavian groups included a Svea Society and Society Scandia as early as 1891 and throughout the 1890s, and an Odin singing group.[36] In addition to their regular meetings, these groups sponsored summer picnic outings, including a May 17, 1893, Scandia celebration of the Norwegian Constitution Day.[37] Of this event the Norwegian language newspaper *Montana Posten* reported enthusiastically that the celebration was a success, attended by Norwegians, Swedes, and "other nationalities," and that it featured a performance by the brothers Berg, much appreciated with thundering applause. The hall used for this indoor affair was full to congestion, and the festivities lasted until 3:00 a.m. But the editor of *Posten* also complained about a misinformed announcement that had appeared in the English-language *Helena Independent*, that the Scandia association would be giving a ball "in celebration of the union between Norway and Sweden." Members of the panethnic group Scandia included some of the most intelligent of Helena's Norwegians, the editor protested; was it possible that none of them knew the significance of May 17? The editor concluded that the announcement must have been a misprint.[38] From the solely English-speaking community members' point of view, all Scandinavians could be lumped into a common heritage group. The important distinctions of Norway versus Sweden in the issue of the Union were simply invisible to them.

Figure 7.2. An early twentieth-century Norwegian American picnic in Bonner, Montana. Norwegians typically gathered for the Seventeenth of May, the Norwegian Constitution Day. Photoboard #128, Jack L. Demmons, photographer; Archives and Special Collections, Mansfield Library, The University of Montana-Missoula.

Helena's Svea organization also sponsored an expressly Swedish Midsummer in 1893, inviting all Scandinavians—"no Scandinavian should miss it . . . 50¢ admission . . . women free"—to attend the event scheduled to correspond to Svenskarnas Dag (Swedish Day) at the World's Fair in Chicago.[39] Scandinavians in the Helena area were also urged to come together at a series of Sunday picnics with musical entertainment planned at Kranich's Grove. These were planned by Robert Lindquist and an A. Mcleary, who reportedly engaged Helena's best musicians for the events.[40]

Great Falls, receiving a slightly later wave of Norwegian and Swedish immigration into new agricultural developments, had Sons and Daughters of Norway chapters as well as the Scandinavian Brotherhood/Sisterhood. The Seventeenth of May was celebrated there in 1916 and 1917 with Sons of Norway sponsorship, even though Scandinavian Montanans were well aware of the controversy over doing so as America entered World War I in Europe, when displays of ethnicity were often seen as disloyal.[41]

On both sides of the Atlantic, Scandinavianism had been an uneasy union. The turn-of-the-century attempts in the Rocky Mountain West reflect this larger pattern. In both Montana and LDS Utah, whether merely pragmatic or carefully programmatic, efforts at forming truly Scandinavian organizations, events, and even religious unions were not entirely without question. Some attempts existed more in name than practice, as in the claimed Scandinavianism of the Scandinavian Meetings, their materials translated from English originals, and of the Scandinavian Brotherhood/Sisterhood, their social events lacking ethnic and panethnic content. Certainly, to critics like Rydman and the Montana correspondent "Frederick," the Scandinavianism attempted in the Rockies was merely symbolic and therefore unsatisfying. Other Scandinavian blendings achieved some success through careful selection of holidays or practices recognized throughout Scandinavia, intensifying *jul* and Midsummer as panethnic, for example, even when the results, such as Midsummer picnics, were adaptations in an American environment.

Were the Scandinavians equal partners in these holidays? However programmatically or pragmatically the planners approached the idea of a Scandinavian Seventeenth of May or Danish Independence Day, these holidays were strongly marked in the immigrants' minds with traditional associations from their European homelands and with the context of ongoing events such as the dissolution of the Norwegian-Swedish Union and Nativist pressures prior to United States involvement in World War I. And in America, parity among groups also broke down not just under the disproportions of population distribution but also under the disproportionate activism of groups like the Swedes in Utah, who with their musical and organizational abilities held their own in a Danish majority. The strongly patriotic bent of the American spring-to-summer holidays brought these nationalist sentiments to the fore as Norwegians, Swedes, and Danes incorporated their special days into a vaguely Scandinavian American calendar.

NOTES

1. *Utah Korrespondenten* (Salt Lake City), May 11, 1892, page 8. "icke sparat hvarken möda eller utgifter för att göra festen angenäm."

2. See these instances at the 1891 Draper's Park, Utah, celebration discussed in chapter 2.

3. See Albin Widén's efforts described in chapter 1.

4. In my own experience, Danish is much easier to read, if one knows Swedish, than to comprehend aurally, pronunciations being counterintuitive from a Swedish point of view.

5. *Svenska Härolden*, April 29, 1886, page 3. "7 olika talare, bland hvilka befann sig vår landsman patriark O.N. Liljenqvist" "de band, som äro knutna mellan man och qvinna, och att lefva ett rent och heligt lif."

6. Rydman was critical also of the quality of the Swedish hymn translations produced by LDS Swedish missionary Frans S. Fernström's son (Olson 1949, 95).

7. "Saturday Night's Entertainment." *The* [Provo, Utah] *Daily Enquirer Newspaper*. October 4, 1887, page 3.

8. In most LDS villages, a tabernacle and public school would be located in the town's central square. The 1907 Sanborn Fire Insurance map for Brigham City identifies only a court house in the central square, leaving the precise end location for this procession a mystery.

9. "Scandinavian Day." [Brigham City, Utah] *Box Elder News*, July 16, 1908, page 1.

10. Ibid.

11. 14th Census of the United States 1920. Salt Lake City Ward 1, Salt Lake, Utah, Roll T625_1865, page 6A, enumeration district 89, image 1044.

12. Stahl was born in Utah in about 1865 to Swedish immigrant parents. 13th Census of the United States 1910. Brigham City Ward 3, Box Elder, Utah, Roll T624_1602, page 9B, enumeration district 0007, image 232.

13. See Jennifer L. Lund (2003), on Lund's career.

14. 12th Census of the United States 1900. Ogden Ward 3, Weber, Utah, Roll 1688, page 4B, enumeration district 188.

15. H. Esterblom may have been H. Charlotte Esterblom, a stenographer who lived in Salt Lake City in 1908 (US City Directories 1821–1989). The name is probably Swedish. An Axel B. Ohlson emigrated from Sweden to Utah in 1906 (14th Census of the United States 1920, Salt Lake City Ward 4, Utah, Roll T625_1865, page 4A); an Axel Nylander, from Sweden to Utah in 1900 (15th Census of the United States 1930, Salt Lake City, Utah, Roll 2420, page 1B, enumeration district 87, image 649). The Otte family was probably the Henry Ottes of Logan, Henry having emigrated from Denmark and Joseph living in the same household as a student (US City Directories 1821–1989).

16. The program was labeled Sunday, December 27, 1913. December 27 was a Saturday in 1913; hence it is uncertain whether this program was a Saturday or a Sunday program. "Skandinavernes Julestevne i Granite Stav" 1913.

17. "Scandinavian Reunion Best Ever Held," *American Fork* [Utah] *Citizen*, September 23, 1916, page 7. http://chroniclingamerica.loc.gov/lccn/sn85058027/1916-09-23/ed-1/seq-7/.

18. *Utah Korrespondenten* (Salt Lake City), July 1, 1891; July 1, 1892; May 25, 1893; July 12, 1894.

19. *Utah Korrespondenten* (Salt Lake City), May 11, 1892; June 1, 1893.

20. *Montana Posten* (Helena, MT), August 15, 1891, page 1.

21. *Indlandsposten* (Great Falls, MT), November 26, 1915, page 1.

22. The reference is interesting, as Montana was not a center for Mormonism in this period and would have been regarded by the LDS as a missionary field. But in this field Reinertsen felt uncompetitive.

23. *Bergs-Väktaren* (Helena, MT), October 1898, page 2.

24. *Indlandsposten* (Great Falls, MT), November 26, 1915, page 7.

25. *Montana Posten* (Helena), August 13, 1893, page 3.

26. *Indlandsposten* (Great Falls, MT), December 17, 1915, page 7.

27. *Indlandsposten* (Great Falls, MT), January 21, 1916, page 8.

28. Butte (Montana) Lodge No. 11, By-laws and minutes; Kalispell (Montana) Lodge No. 233, Minutes; and *Indlandsposten* (Great Falls, MT), June 9, 1916, page 8.

29. Ibid.

30. *R.L. Polk & Co.'s Butte City Directory* 1905; *Indlandsposten* (Great Falls, MT), November 26, 1915, page 7.

31. *Indlandsposten* (Great Falls, MT), March 24, 1916, page 4.

32. *Montana Posten* (Helena), July 20, 1893, page 1. The *Miner* comment was quoted in *Posten*. "Alle Skandinaver var paa Benene og deltog i Festen."

33. *Montana Posten* (Helena), June 22, 1893, page 4; June 29, 1893, page 1.

34. *Montana Tidende og Skandinav* (Butte), February 9, 1894, page 1.

35. R.L. *Polk & Co.'s Butte City Directory* 1895; and Butte, 1900, Sheet 7, Digital Sanborn Maps 1867–1970.

36. R.L. *Polk & Co.'s Helena City Directory* 1891–96; *Montana Posten* (Helena), August 15, 1891, page 3.

37. *Montana Posten* (Helena), February 23, 1893, page 2; May 18, 1893, page 2; June 22, 1893, page 4.

38. *Montana Posten* (Helena), May 11, 1893, page 4; and May 18, 1893, page 2.

39. *Montana Posten* (Helena), June 22, 1893, page 4.

40. *Montana Posten* (Helena), May 25, 1893, page 3; June 1, 1893, page 3.

41. *Indlandsposten* (Great Falls, MT), March 24, 1916, page 8; March 14, 1917, page 2; and April 11, 1917, page 4.

8

Shifts in Spring-Summer Celebration
Modes, Media, and Messages

T HE LATE NINETEENTH-CENTURY HOLIDAYS OF the spring-to-summer season were occasions for the Swedish and Scandinavian Americans to turn
inward, celebrating together in what resembled oversized family reunions.
They gathered to speak and sing Swedish, Norwegian, and Danish, and
to remind themselves of their common values, secular and sacred. Their
verbal and physical activities took many forms, from dancing and racing
to choral performance to formal speech making to informal inscriptions
in memorandum books, but their messages were similar: We Swedes (or
Scandinavians) are patriotic ethnic Americans. We value character traits
such as honesty and industry, piety and freedom of worship. In this season of warmth and beauty, we also value being in landscaped natural surroundings, an experience that is not just pleasurable but also esthetically,
in nineteenth-century terms, Picturesque. These practices, expressions, and
meanings are so important to us that we have to return to them in celebrations that crowd our calendars and to speak them and write them
abundantly and redundantly.

This pattern differs from contemporary spring-to-summer celebrations in four ways: mode, medium, message, and audience differ. We should
therefore be hesitant to read back one hundred years with any assumptions
about the nature of calendar custom events based on contemporary practices. Realizing these shifts in practice also leads us to further considerations
of how ethnic events have been reshaped in the mid- to late-twentieth century and our own early twenty-first-century era.

In studying the Swedish American community of Lindsborg, Kansas,
during the 1960s, Larry Danielson (1972; 1974) gleaned evidence about the
shaping of a festival, Hyllnings Fest, that has become iconic of Swedish
America. Hyllnings Fest is a several-day autumn festival during which

DOI: 10.7330/9780874219999.c008

townsfolk celebrate and display their Swedish heritage, *hyllning* meaning homage or tribute. Among the ways in which the festival is an Americanization is the simple fact that Swedish tradition lacks a major autumn holiday. Hyllnings Fest is still observed today and has more recently been studied by the folklorist Lizette Gradén, who began her fieldwork in Lindsborg in the mid-1990s (Gradén 2003).

Danielson (1972) interviewed people who were directly involved with the first Svensk Hyllnings Fest in Lindsborg in 1941. The October 1941 event was scheduled as Lindsborg's contribution to a statewide "Founders Day" recognizing not Swedish settlement but Coronado's legendary entry into the region (Gradén 2003, 97). Danielson (1972) points out that the 1941 event was regarded by the community as the beginning of the tradition.

However, the Lindsborg creation narrative for Hyllnings Fest assigns a beginning point that, according to Danielson, overlooks a number of previous events. These were "based on the costume-music-dance complex which evolved into the three-day Svensk Hyllnings Fest" (Danielson 1972, 147). Danielson dates the first of these events to the first decade of the century and considers that they incrementally set—or "evolved into"—a pattern for mid-century celebration. In the early 1900s, Bethany College's Male Chorus was an active generator and perpetuator of a Swedish American song repertoire. In 1912, a series of May festivals were organized with the understanding that they drew on Swedish heritage.[1] These established a pattern of pageantry combining music, dance, and costume. During the 1920s, a series of pageants held in November included a "Pioneer Day" component celebrating heritage and old-timers' role in creating the town.[2] The patterns established in these prior events can be seen as coalescing not in 1941 but rather in 1938 with the town's Swedish Day, one of the many recognitions in Swedish American communities nationwide of the summer-long jubilee celebration of the New Sweden, Delaware, colony (Barton 1994, 314, 326–27).[3]

Danielson's tracing of the development of Hyllnings Fest suggests the gradual process through which more inwardly directed community events could develop into publicly directed festivals inviting visitors into the community. Arnold Barton (1992) points to similar processes in many Swedish American communities throughout the United States during the 1920s through 1970s in his article "Cultural Interplay Between Sweden and Swedish America," emphasizing the role of transatlantic connections in nurturing these events.

The formation of Denver's Vasa lodge and of the Swedish Club of Denver in the first half of the twentieth century offers interesting cases in point, in which we see continuities, consolidations, and conscious rejuvenations of traditional practice, all moving toward increased focus on modes of display to the public. As we've seen in chapter 2, Midsummer events were a longtime Denver tradition sponsored by a variety of Swedish organizations. In the first half of the twentieth century the tradition continued, eventually coalescing into a cooperative project of the city's Vasa lodge and other groups with the express label Swedish Day, although a few rival events continued to be offered as alternatives.

Midsummer was a typical activity for Vasa Order of America (VOA) lodges throughout the country during this period, enhanced by the lodges' building pavilions and parks (Hanson 1996). Denver's Enighet lodge sponsored celebrations of Midsummer beginning in 1911 and throughout the 1910s and 1920s.[4] But by 1929, there was still more than one Midsummer celebration. Planned for Sunday, June 23, were both the Vasa Midsummer at Jefferson Park and a "Svenskarnas Dag Midsommar-Fest" planned at Hollywood Grove by the Valhalla Lodge of the Foresters of America, the Dagmar Lodge of the Independent Order Ladies of Vikings, the Frigg Lodge of the Independent Order of Vikings, and the Orpheus Svenska Sångföreningen.[5] By June 1930, the Vasa lodge had acquired a Vasa park and pavilion, and the celebration that year brought together the Enighet Lodge of the VOA with these other groups, a consolidation of sponsorship that continued through the next decades. By 1960, *Western News* editor Enoch Peterson, a second generation Denver Swedish American, could comment in his promotional announcement of the event:

> Svenskarnas Dag is an annual event that has been carried on for a number of years, in fact as far back as we can remember. . . . The committee in charge promises to do everything possible to make this year's picnic better and more enjoyable than ever before, and when they say so, they really mean it.[6]

Western News was an almost entirely English-language newspaper descended from *Svenska Korrespondenten* and *Westerns Nyheter.* The newspaper served as a main source of publicity for events planned by the city's Swedish American population.

Peterson used the label Svenskarnas Dag (Swedish Day) for the event. This appellation first appears in the advertisements for Midsummer celebrations in 1929 with the Valhalla-Orpheus-Dagmar-Frigg Midsummer and continued in the use by this cooperative when the Vasa lodge joined in and provided its park and pavilion. This shift in labeling occurred throughout the United States. In the communities that she has studied, Barbro Klein sees the change in the holiday name as indicative of changes in meaning and also as a form of Americanization:

> When one turns a midsummer celebration into *Sweden* Day one is following a general tendency [in America] to transform celebratory customs that are associated with the annual cycle of agrarian-religious practices and meanings into ethnic, political or national displays. (Klein 1989, 63)

The label *Sweden* points to a reimagining of the purpose of a calendar custom as a national day that renders Swedishness understandable and available to Americans. Another such attempt to bridge to the American context was *Western Nyheter*'s gradual shift to English. In the 1920s, English appeared in many advertisements; in the 1930s selective headlines and content appeared in English—ironically, including the 1934 program for Svenskarnas Dag and a 1936 article "Midsummer, Sweden's Greatest Holiday." By 1937, the newspaper's content was a mix of Swedish and English, and by 1942, the newspaper had become a mainly English newspaper with the masthead "The Western News."[7]

In many ways, the mid-twentieth-century Swedish Day, as planned by the combined Swedish fraternal/sororal lodges, testifies to strong continuities with late-nineteenth-century practices. Also continuous are the supporting patterns of transatlantic contact, updated in this period through new technologies. The 1949 Swedish Day Picnic was held on a Sunday, a pattern followed by numerous Swedish spring and summer picnics organized by Denver's Swedish organizations in the 1890s. Activities closely followed those practiced fifty years earlier: picnicking, a program of music and speeches, the singing of "Du Gamla Du Fria," competitive sports, including races and horseshoe pitching, and a social dance lasting well into the evening. The 1949 address by Reverend L. B. Swan of the Methodist Church focused on "the wonderful Swedish traditions and how our forefathers have helped build this nation," themes continuous with those of the 1890s' hyphenated Swedish Americanness.[8]

The availability of rival events was also continuous with the earlier turn-of-the-century era Midsummers of Denver, although pared down in total number. Throughout the post-World War II era, the Vasa and other lodges' Swedish Day Picnic was scheduled very closely to and sometimes conflicting with at least two other annual Midsummer events. At the historic Ryssby church north of Denver an annual festival included Swedish services followed by a midday picnic. This event usually occurred the same day as Denver's Swedish Day. A second event usually held on a Saturday was the Salvation Army Midsummer Fest, including music, readings, costumes, refreshments, and a string band.[9]

In 1956, an additional Saturday Midsummer Festival was promoted by a commercial venture, The Tepees, a roadside attraction in a "tipi" style with motel rooms, restaurant, dance floor, and picnicking grounds located eighteen miles west of Denver. The Tepees promoters emphasized that their event offered music, song, and folk dancing around a Midsummer pole on the same day as Midsummer in Sweden. A photograph after the event depicted the coronation of a Queen of the Festival, a Swedish tourist posed in front of the Midsummer pole.[10] A Tepees event did not receive newspaper publicity the following year, so this may have been a unique occurrence.

Up through 1954, Denver's Orpheus Singers were an important part of these celebrations, another continuity with the earlier era. This group consisted of first and second generation Swedish men who had mastered a repertoire of Swedish and American songs. Their activities included visits to Sweden, where they could interact with fellow men's choral groups. By 1955, though, the group was no longer a regular part of Swedish Day, and by 1959, we see the headline "Singers Needed for Swedish Choir" as plans were being made for a Colorado Centennial Swedish Day at the Civic Center. According to the planners, it was not necessary to know Swedish or to have a trained voice to join the choir being assembled.[11]

Transatlantic contact experienced in the earlier era by the Orpheus Singers, as related by Bundsen in his 1912 speech, had regularly renewed interest in and content of Denver's Swedish ethnicity. This was evident too in the era of air transport. In 1948, airline travel was still a relatively new fascination, and *Western News* editor Peterson was also a travel agent. Throughout this period we see advertisements for air travel and ocean liner travel alongside each other. Ocean travel was advertised for providing leisure as well as passage to Europe. But air travel offered speedy convenience. In 1948, the Scandinavian Airlines System (SAS) advertised in *The Western News*, "This Summer! Only 14 Hours to Europe."[12] An American Airline advertisement later the same year highlighted the significance of this new technology, declaring that "One Visit to Sweden Is Worth 1000 Letters," with a sketch depicting an older couple greeting a man disembarking from an airline.[13] The *Western News* spotlighted air travel with articles and columns devoted, for example, to the christening of a new SAS DC–6 and airline arrivals and departures of notables such as the Denver Danish Vice-Consul.[14]

Air travel enhanced Swedish Americans' ability to maintain an easier and more direct contact with Swedish culture. Swedish films could be sent

via air parcel post to the states. Denver's Swedish Americans enjoyed show-
ings at the Alameda theater of popular comedies such as the 1945 film *The
Happy Tailor* with Edvard Persson, showing in September 1948, and had
special viewings available of informational film lectures such as "Eyes on
Scandinavia" with travel lecturer Russell Wright.[15] Touring choirs and lec-
turers also took advantage of the new availability of air travel. These were
continuities, though, rather than new practices, with air travel and air post
merely enhancing effectiveness and with films added to live theater and
musical performance as offerings.

   Yet in the midst of these continuities, connections, and cooperative
consolidations, the Swedish Club of Denver perceived itself as renewing
traditions that were in danger of languishing. Patterned on the idea of
Swedish men's clubs elsewhere in the country—a Swedish Club of Seattle
had existed since 1892 (Carlson 1983, 307)—the Swedish Club of Denver
began in late 1958. Its first meeting was labeled a "tremendous success" by
a *Western News* headline of December 18. During its first few years, the club
was engaged in sponsoring a St. Lucia festival and a spring banquet as well
as other social gatherings sprinkled throughout the year. The *Western News*
boosted the club and its membership drive, giving it considerable column
space on the newspaper's front page.

   In creating the all-male club, its members noted "the modern day 'inte-
gration' of the Swedes" and a need to preserve heritage, culture, and tradition in their rapidly modernizing environment. A main vehicle, besides
the club itself and its activities, was to be a "Swedish Headquarters,"
where "year-round genuine smörgåsbord could be enjoyed; where meetings, large and small, could be held; where distinguished visitors could
be accommodated; where gifts and other Swedish merchandise could be
purchased and displayed."[16]

   Eventually the Swedish Club of Denver had a regular column *"Tre
Kronor"* [three crowns, signifying the three crowns of the Swedish mon-
archy] in the *Western News*, where the club's activities were advertised and
reported. In April of 1962, the Swedish Ice Hockey Team visited Denver,
lunching with club members at the Park Lane Hotel. April also brought a
membership dinner with the Swedish consul, at which Enoch Peterson was
awarded the Vasa Order. The club's 1962 activities also included eclectic
excuses to get together without any express ethnic content: attendance at a
play "Anna Christie," a tour of the Air Force Academy, a card party, and a
New Year's Eve ball. At least one 1962 event crossed ethnic lines: on March
17, the Swedish Club and the Viking and Vasa fraternal groups sponsored a
joint St. Patrick's Day dance.

In its institution of St. Lucia as a regular practice and its desire for a "genuine smorgasbord," we see the same kind of invention of tradition to heighten ethnic identity that Arnold Barton finds throughout Swedish America, yet the club's involvement with Midsummer was a story of renewal and alteration rather than revival or invention (Barton 1992). The Swedish Club of Denver began to take a proprietary interest in Swedish Day in 1962 when the club joined with the Vasa lodges to assist in sponsoring the event. In the process, the Club expressed a sense that it was reviving the event and emphasized the costume-music-dance complex of events like Hyllnings Fest. Change was already in the air with a 1958 move of Svenskarnas Dag away from the Vasa Park location that had been used since 1930 to the Jefferson County Fairgrounds, which was "on the way to the mountains," a nod to the recreation movement.[17] In 1962, according to "Tre Kronor," the club's sponsorship created "a revival of Svenskarnas Dag. . . . This will long live as the number ONE for 1962! We served 745 people at this one," suggesting that making ethnic fare available to a public audience was an important purpose. Taking over sole responsibility for Svenskarnas Dag in 1963, the Swedish Club arranged for dance lessons prior to the event. In March 1963, the Bookstrom Folk Dancers offered instruction in Swedish folk dance to prepare those who intended to attend Svenskarnas Dag on June 23, 1963. The club's other 1963 activities included an excursion to the Lindsborg Hyllnings Fest, suggesting how contacts and mutual influences could occur within Swedish America.[18]

At the beginning of the twenty-first century, the midwinter St. Lucia event is still one of the Swedish Club of Denver's main focuses, while Midsummer has become a large regional festival held even farther into the mountains at Estes Park, and has become the work of several Scandinavian American groups along the Front Range of the Rockies. This two-day event begins with a Saturday morning Midsummer pole rais-ing scheduled for a brief half hour, followed by opening ceremonies and a line up of folk dance and song performances, repeated throughout the day so that attendees can sample these offerings. Sunday's events begin with a church service followed by a similar line up of offerings, and con-cluding with a raffle. Throughout, the audience is invited to participate in the folk dances.[19]

These newly privileged modes and media of the middle of the twen-tieth century—dance, music, costume, folk foods, and pageant—shifted attention away from the earlier range of expressive forms, as they offered Midsummer attendees the opportunity to sample representative bits of Swedish culture. Audience members can sample a food and move on to view a dance or hear a song but without fully engaging or understanding the samples beyond their indexically pointing to Swedishness.

The digital age has made us ever more aware of the significance of these kinds of modal and medial changes. Social semiotician Gunther Kress (2009) notes that "changing uses and functions of different modes should be revealing of social changes" in laying out methods for the study of multi-modal texts (46). To illustrate the impact of modal changes Kress examines an example of change that predates the digital revolution. The use of visual images in print publications such as magazines changed in the middle of the twentieth century. Previously used mainly to illustrate the information provided in an article or essay, visual images changed to become conveyers of content not otherwise present in the accompanying print text. By the beginning of the twenty-first century, according to Kress, this shift has continued so that now image and print have "equal semiotic status" (Kress 2009, 46).

In the case of Midsummer and other spring-summer Scandinavian American holidays, the semiotic change was from the wordiness of nineteenth-century Rhetorical Culture, in which one introspectively spoke (oral-aural modes) and wrote (graphic-visual modes) about one's cultural activities while practicing them in an inward-turning group, to the bodily activity of publicly displaying markers—indexes and icons—of ethnic culture through kinesthetic, visual, musical, and gustatory modes that had been present in earlier celebrations but had not been as dominant. The choice of modes for immigrant/ethnic expression shifted, as did the audiences. Underpinning the change was loss of the privileged insider Scandinavian languages and adoption of English—a language in common across immigrant groups and in common with the host American culture. Barbro Klein notes, writing of ethnic American tradition in general, that "among the immigrants' descendants, material culture—based on sound, sight, smell, or taste—often takes on a new and unique position" as this language loss occurs (Klein 1989, 63). Kress would call this a change in "modal reach" (Kress 2009, 11).

But the shift in modalities to the semiotic ensemble that Danielson (1972, 147) calls a complex did not necessarily signify the same meanings as did the speeches and writings of the immigrants. Messages shifted along with modes and media. Those immigrants fluent in a Scandinavian language and in English, conversant with verbal texts being produced on both sides of the Atlantic, were able to use their multilinguality to consider abstractions such as fosterland, heritage, patriotism, and Swedishness. These subjects usually were dealt with in a serious rhetorical tone, as they were related to the immigrants' intimate and painful experiences of uprooting and transplantation.

In contrast, through song, dance, and pageantry, one is able to consider images and representations of ethnicity using mainly English and some recreational Scandinavian-language words and phrases, and these modes and media lend themselves to a celebratory or even humorous tone and welcome outsiders who are "wannabe" Scandinavians. Those using these modes of expression—outsider and inside alike—can quickly index the idea of Swedish ethnicity through a simple reference to coffee drinking, for example.

The late twentieth century has brought yet another set of tools to the domain of identity expression. Just as in previous eras, Swedish and Scandinavian Americans have readily taken up these new technologies to both continue ethnic expression and reshape it for new purposes and new audiences. Among the most recent means of public display of messages are social media. Facebook provides a site where anyone who is a site participant (a reported one billion in autumn of 2012; "Facebook Hits One Billion" 2012) can search for and "like" the Swedish Club of Denver; the Scandinavian Midsummer Festival, Estes Park; the Swedish-American Chamber of Commerce Colorado; or the Seattle Swedish Cultural Center. For these organizations, social media are augmenting or replacing their use of print and oral communications—flyers, mailings, newspaper announcements, public service announcements, newsletters, direct mailings, phone trees, and face-to-face conversation.

The Swedish Club of Denver joined Facebook in April 2012, when members posted photographs of the 2011 Santa Lucia Festival. It has since used its Facebook page to advertise a September smorgasbord raffle and to post the story of an old Swedish bible. The Facebook page of the Scandinavian Midsummer Festival, Estes Park, was one of the main vehicles for publicizing the 2014 Midsummer event. In January 2014, it had 165 "likes." The Swedish-American Chamber of Commerce in Colorado maintains an active Facebook page, begun in September 2011, posting information and comments about business and industry events, as well as social and cultural events. The organization's mission is encouraging commercial exchange between Sweden and Colorado, and its Facebook page is a tool for links to other websites. The Seattle Swedish Cultural Center also maintains a heavily used site. Joining Facebook in May 2009, the center boasted nearly 950 "likes" in October 2012, and its users saw regular updates for events.

For some of these groups, an even stronger Internet presence is maintained through their own websites. The Swedish Club of Denver's website was, in October 2012, an active site with up-to-date information regarding activities planned for 2012–2013. Its news link displayed photograph galleries of events from the past year. Its calendar link listed events planned through September 21, 2013, several with printable images of programs and reservation forms. Clicking on "Links," one found a list of live links to key Swedish American organizations throughout the United States, from the Swedish American Chamber of Commerce to the Swenson Swedish Immigration Research Center to Denver's chapter of the Swedish women's group SWEA (Swedish Women's Educational Association).

Pragmatically, of course, these Facebook and website nodes in Internet networks allow organizations to get the word out regarding the festivities they plan and offer to the public. But they also communicate an idea of Swedish Americanness. These sites enact the idea of ethnic networking itself, through links and likes, and the posting of photographs allows abbreviation of Swedishness in presentation of images: the Midsummer pole, a blond dance couple dressed in folk costume, a blond young woman with a wreathe of flowers. These images abbreviate ethnicity into a shorthand.

Twenty-first-century Swedish Americans also make use of Tumblr, a blog hosting Internet site that provides free templates to those wanting to create a Tumblr blog. Those using Tumblr tend toward self-conscious display of their creative efforts or social commentary. Visitors to a Tumblr site can comment on postings, and those maintaining a site can reblog from others' blogs. One Swedish American organization using Tumblr to good effect is the American Swedish Institute of Minneapolis. The institute is a museum, arts and cultural center, and library/archives established in 1929. Housed in a Chateauesque mansion, the institute added a modern cultural arts space to its campus in 2012 and has been recognized for its innovative outreach and programming, to which the use of social media contributes.

In addition to maintaining a very active website, the American Swedish Institute blogs and reblogs responses to its events, exhibits, and restaurant through Tumblr. In an October 2012 example, the Institute reblogged a posting that, like the Institute's name, invoked both the American and the Swedish halves of hyphenated identity. The blogger described a visit to the Institute in "The Adventures of Baby Cap in the 21st Century." "The Adventures" traces a Captain America stuffed toy's visits to numerous venues, represented with photographs of the toy at those locations. According to the site description, "Steve 'Baby Cap' Rogers is trying to make his way through the 21st century. Here you can see what he's up to, and request things for him to do" ("One of the Fun Things Thor and I Did" 2012). Baby Cap and his anonymous handler enjoyed their trip to the Institute with, appropriately, fellow stuffed toy Thor: "we saw a great goat mascot that is actually named after Thor's mama, Freya! Thor liked seeing all the Scandinavian things and his likeness throughout the museum" ("One of the Fun Things Thor and I Did" 2012). Via recent movie adaptations, comic books, and their spin-off merchandise, the Scandinavian pantheon has been pulled into the twenty-first century, as this blogger emphasizes, and into the American superhero metanarrative of the Avenger comics and film, placing Thor and Freya alongside Ironman and Black Widow, a significant disassociation from the antiquarian Scandinavianness one could reference through this mythology at the end of the nineteenth century. The author of the Baby Cap Tumblr not only playfully places Thor back in—or at least closer to—his Scandinavian environs, but also uses these new associations to reflect on the casual gaze of museum tourists.

Tumblr is an interactive medium that goes beyond the more static "pages" of a website. Clearly, most of the material posted by the American Swedish Institute is intended as publicity designed to attract a younger set of visitors to the museum, archives, and their programs as a reliable cohort of mostly midwestern Swedish American visitors and supporters ages. The degree to which the younger cohort "talks back" via postings can be taken as a measure of Tumblr success. One of the modes added to ethnic expression in the twenty-first century is shared across turn of the twenty-first-century texts—statistics. Twenty-first-century Western societies, enamored with digital technologies, have elevated counting things and the manipulation of the resulting statistics, "metrics" or "big data," to decision-making power, as if this mode were more reliable than any other. Our actions as consumers of ethnicity are enumerated at chain grocery stores, for example, so that if one is a regular consumer of Gevalia coffee, the computerized system at the check-out counter obligingly spits out Gevalia coupons for future purchases. So, too, the American Swedish Institute is able to count visitors to its online sites as well as its museum building. Its Facebook site had 4,879 "likes" on November 19, 2012; its Twitter account, 1,323 followers; its YouTube channel, 26 subscribers and 14,403 views. With the right programming and training, a site manager is able to refine these statistics to check "hits" on particular content.

Beyond the ability to count visitors, though, what are the modal qualities of Facebook, websites, and Tumblr? Interestingly, although they attract our interest and engagement first as viewers, through visual images, and offer us the sometimes dubious insights of statistics, they also are capable of taking us back to the turn-of-the-century focus on words. On the Internet and in social media the communicative strengths of both visual and logocentric communications are present. In *Multimodality*, Kress (2009) points to the way in which visuality as a mode is static, suspended in time, expressing meaning through spacial relationships. This mode requires the theory and established method of art criticism. Logocentric forms instead are arranged linearly, in Western culture at least, representing a perception of the flow of time in narrative or logical patterns in which one idea precedes another, the provenance of literary scholarship (Kress 2009, 81–82). This bifurcation was already complicated before invention of the Internet by modal ensembles such as film—"moving pictures"—and the graphic novel, in which images are sequenced. Film, the graphic novel, and social media combine modes to allow viewers/readers to dwell on successive images and text and to respond with their own images and narratives.

Through their new orchestration of modes, social media and websites demonstrate yet another shift in modalities through which ethnic expression is being reshaped in our own era. And, just as the modes are multiple and interactive, the messages can be complex. It is possible to sustain a digitally enabled discussion about Swedish and Scandinavian American ethnicity in the twenty-first century. A June 2012 Tumblr posting by American Swedish Institute President and CEO Bruce Karstadt is an excellent case in point (Jaworski 2012). Karstadt's posting reframed and extended a parody begun by satirist Stephen Colbert on his television show *The Colbert Report*, available also on the Colbert website (Colbert 2012). Karstadt's posting requires considerable back story to be fully appreciated because Colbert's parody was itself a reframing of an event in Sweden that had hit the international news that month. During 2012, Sweden's public @sweden Twitter account managers invited ordinary Swedes to take over the account for one week each, posting in English to a presumably international audience. This risky but earnest and egalitarian experiment, called "Curators of Sweden," was intended to counter common Swedish stereotypes and promote international tourism to Sweden. In June, the experiment misstepped with posting of messages that appeared to be anti-Semitic (Goodman 2012).

The incident was quickly picked up across the Atlantic by American comedian Stephen Colbert, who perceived how it raised the issue of whether there is anything we can call ethnic authenticity in the context of global networks. Colbert (2012a) broadcast his spot "Operation Artificial Swedener" on June 12, 2012, just after the questionable posts regarding "what's the fuzz about Jews." In "Operation Artificial Swedener," Colbert posed an argument for his being trusted—even though (mostly Irish) American— as one of the one-week @sweden account Tweeters (or "Tweeders"). His initial argument rested on metrics and expertise. The statistical argument played upon the image of Sweden as a small country (in spite of its large land mass) in regards to its impact: Colbert pointed to his 3.5 million followers, as opposed to @Sweden's 33,816. The argument based on expertise played on stereotypes of dumb ethnic Swedes, not entirely competent and speaking broken, musical English, through allusion to the Muppets character the Swedish Chef. Colbert's "herny shmerny," as he articulated it, was demonstrated not while cooking but while texting. What would have been the Swedish Chef's spoon in a Muppet skit, tossed over the shoulder after it was used, became a cell phone. The changed content hailed those in the audience who were in tune with all things Swedish, including the origins of the cell phone.

In his two follow-up spots broadcast on June 18, 2012, and June 21, 2012, "Operation Artificial Swedener—Sweden's Response" and "C'mon Sweden, Take a Chance on Stephen," the allusions to Swedish and Swedish American stereotypes became richer. Colbert (2012b, 2012c) and his writers deftly assembled indexes and icons of Swedishness to reflect on the idea of authenticity referenced in the title "Artificial Swedener." What is it to be authentically Swedish in the twenty-first century? Is it St. Lucia crowns, the American cartoon strip *Hagar the Horrible*, or Swedish meatballs sold at the Swedish-based chain store IKEA? The smartest of these references reflected that Colbert and his writers had delved into immigration history: Colbert claimed to have "Swedish fever," a parody of the "America fever" of the nineteenth-century immigrants. Stirring his coffee with his cell phone (possibly an allusion to the logger of American balladry who stirs his coffee with his thumb), Colbert threw the phone over his shoulder, then noted that in America our streets are "paved with cell phones," a reference to the "streets paved with gold" idea conveyed in immigrant rhetoric.[20]

Throughout the series of skits, Colbert raised the issue of Swedish authenticity in the twenty-first century, an era of rapidly shifting technologies that allow us to play with images and labels. These concerns are at the heart of the American Swedish Institute's mission, and Director Bruce Karstadt was well positioned to join in the conversation with an answer to the question of authenticity. Reblogging the June 21 broadcast on the Institute's Tumblr, Karstadt invited Colbert to Tweet for the institute, preferably in conjunction with its late June opening of the long-anticipated institute building addition:

> It has come to our attention that you've been angling to take over the official Twitter account for the country of Sweden . . . . [T]he American Swedish Institute, one of the largest Swedish American organizations in the U.S., would like to offer you control of our American Swedish Twitter

feed for one day this week or next. . . . [A]s a major hub of American-Swedish relations, we hope you will find it an acceptable short-term substitute. . . . You can tweet in English, Swedish, or in some hilarious, fakey mix of the two. We leave the comedy up to you, sir. . . .

Yours in Swedishness,
(the American kind) (Jaworski 2012)

According to Karstadt, American Swedishness was viable in early twenty-first century Minnesota as the next best thing to "genuine" Swedishness, but he was happy to have it represented in a "hilarious, fakey mix," bringing to mind, for the American Swedish Institute audience, Swenglish, the mixed Swedish and English spoken among immigrant Swedish Americans of the upper Midwest, and again reflecting on the ways in which the boundaries of Swedishness have been stretched and reshaped in America.

In the one-sided Colbert-Karstadt virtual exchange (we have no evidence of their meeting in person nor of Colbert replying), representations of Swedish American ethnicity are transmitted in a rapid-fire series of references to an anonymous, broadly public, and potentially global audience. Even though the texts of the exchange are brief, as we interpret them we realize that they combine some of the expressive power of nineteenth-century rhetoric with the public performativity of the mainly nonverbal modes of mid-century. Logocentric wordplay is an important component of early twenty-first-century multimodal expression, but always creating meaning through its interaction with other modes such as gesture and visual image—the "herny-schmerny," the cell phone, and the toss over the shoulder.

It is not my task here to develop a complete history of modes, media, and messages in ethnic American life, but our visit to three time periods is nonetheless suggestive. In spite of the shared logocentricity of digital technology and turn of the twentieth-century expression, nothing today seems parallel to the degree of emphasis on vocal performance explicated in chapters 4 and 5. In the years between, at mid-century, words seem to have fallen away along with the Scandinavian languages themselves. The mimetic modes of dance, instrumental music, pageantry, and costume emerged as dominant. These modes were perhaps the best solution to the dilemma of how to preserve ethnic tradition in the midst of language loss, and they are evidence of the degree to which the generations after immigration wanted to hold on to a sense of tradition.

The New Sweden, Idaho, Midsummer celebration described in chapter 1 exemplifies some of the mid-twentieth-century patterns. By Dave Sealander's generation, Swedish was not regularly spoken in New Sweden, nor in the nearby Swedish-Baptist community of Riverview, or the several southeastern communities with substantial LDS Scandinavian American populations. Language had receded to recreational use, invoked among old friends, and sung by a few old-timers who still knew Swedish hymns and secular lyrics.

In the early twentieth century, Midsummer observances in these agricultural southeast Idaho communities had followed the rural, informal pattern of visitations and large picnics. One would have had to travel over two hundred miles south to Salt Lake City for any large, public celebration of Midsummer. While these communities certainly had strong orientations toward sacred practices, their sacralization of spring-summer holidays was more limited than examples in the heartland of Mormonism, Salt Lake City. On the public-to-private continuum of ethnic expression, they kept Midsummer closer to the private end of the scale and Independence Day closer to the public. Correspondingly, Swedishness or Scandinavianness was claimed less explicitly.

In this environment, and somewhat parallel to the Lindsborg, Kansas, story told by Danielson, a New Sweden Pioneer Association was established in 1919, and its members, all those who had come to the area by 1904, met in summer picnics throughout the 1910s, '20s, and '30s. No annual pageantry of the scope of Hyllnings Fest grew out of this picnic tradition, but the picnics did include musical performances. In 1939, rather than consolidate their celebratory patterns into a regional festival of a Swedish Day, the New Sweden Pioneer Association decided to write its history, and in 1941, the resulting *After Fifty Years* was printed for the association by Caxton Printers, Caldwell, Idaho. But, as with the community's celebrations, the book elided New Sweden's ethnicity into Western Americanness (Anderson 1994, 84–92).[21]

With the static finality of print, *After Fifty Years* clearly established the community preference for English and by bracketing off the community's first fifty years suggested that a chapter had come to an end, perhaps what we could label as the first generational or the immigrant chapter. What was left to second and third generation mid-century New Sweden descendants who cared about ethnic tradition? In melody, dance, costume, and other material culture and activities, one could recapture meanings no longer accessible through words. Dave Sealander's establishing a Midsummer celebration in 1985, which became an annual event, built on the ongoing picnic tradition at the same time that it satisfied a need for ethnic expression.

The quasi-public/quasi-private participant-audience at the New Sweden, Idaho, Midsummer that assembled during the 1990s had some of the freedoms and responsibilities of creating the ethnic message, and parts of that

Figure 8.1. Musicians Sheila Hadden, David Sealander, David Combs, and Kristi Austin admire the Midsummer pole at New Sweden, Idaho, as they prepare to perform for dancing around the pole, June 2007. Susan Duncan, photographer, Idaho State University Photographic Services.

message remained implicit, rather than being acknowledged as ethnic. Like their Rocky Mountain predecessors, the participants at New Sweden added to tradition and blended its elements. Represented and preserved in the New Sweden Midsummer were the core patterns that we have identified in the celebration in America: the tendency to mix traditions in Scandinavianness and to stage their celebration during a window of summertime regardless of the precise day, the focus on gathering outdoors at the beginning of summer time, the preference for a day-long event for which one leaves home (an excursion or visitation, an *utflykt*), the sharing of food, the flying of flags, interaction with and influences from associations and folklorists, mixing of traditions across summertime holidays, and layering of modalities that together communicate both to and among participants.

Many twenty-first-century Midsummer celebrations follow these core patterns, yet these celebrations also follow the overall trajectory of twentieth century change in ethnic expression, which has moved from insider audience to a broad and potentially global audience, and from insider language to a language used worldwide. Organizers and participants do so when they anticipate the event with social media and website postings and conversations and when they re-experience it through videos and vlogs.

The experience of participants has shifted to include both the immediacy of oral speech and embodied expression of dance and song and the disembodied exchanges of digital text and image. The audience has shifted to include some who have only the latter, disembodied, experience of Midsummer. The incremental nature of these changes as they can be plotted across the twentieth century makes "emergent culture" a better model for understanding twentieth century ethnicity than the model of "ethnic revival," a term that emphasizes loss and suggests nostalgic replication of old patterns. Our evidence for Midsummer in the twentieth century suggests instead that groups and individuals creatively embrace and manipulate new media that combine modes of expression in new ways, allowing for interesting new messages about identity: We Swedes (or Scandinavians) are patriotic ethnic Americans who are aware of our global connections. We value our culture and America's diverse cultures. We enjoy our ongoing connections with Sweden, which is the country of Nordic skiing and IKEA as well as Midsummer poles. We value this season of warmth and beauty and value being in natural surroundings close to the wilderness. We value our ethnicity but are playful with it, too. We invite all Scandinavians and Wannabes to join us in celebration.

NOTES

1. Both Danielson and Barbro Klein note that this event was instead an adoption of the British May Day tradition (Danielson 1974, 26; Klein 1989, 63).

2. Similar in function to the Latter-day Saint Pioneer Day, this was not an LDS celebration. It is unclear why the autumn was chosen for these Pioneer Days.

3. Barton notes that 1938 celebrations of the three hundredth anniversary of the New Sweden colony occurred in Sweden as well as Swedish America.

4. *Westerns Nyheter* (Denver), June 20, 1929, page 1; and June 18, 1936, page 1. Bundsen's 1912 speech (discussed in chapters 4 and 5) would have been at the second annual Vasa sponsored Midsummer in Denver.

5. *Westerns Nyheter* (Denver), June 20, 1929.

6. *Westerns Nyheter* (Denver), June 9, 1960, page 1.

7. *Westerns Nyheter* (Denver), June issues 1925–42.

8. "Svenskarnas Dag Midsummer Picnic," *Western News* (Denver), June 23, 1949, page 1.

9. *Western News* (Denver), June 16, 1949, page 1; June 22, 1950, page 1.

10. *Western News* (Denver), June 14, 1956, page 1; June 21, 1956, page 1; July 5, 1956, page 1; and July 12, 1956, page 1.

11. "Singers Needed for Swedish Choir," *Western News* (Denver), May 7, 1959, page 2.

12. *Western News* (Denver), July 8 1948.

13. *Western News* (Denver), September 16, 1948.

14. Scandinavian Airline System's Plane Christened." *Western News* (Denver), July 1, 1948, page 1; "Mr. and Mrs. Wolf C. Hansen Visit Denmark." *Western News* (Denver), June 17, 1954, page 1.

15. *Western News* (Denver), September 2, 1948, page 1; April 21, 1949, page 1.

16. "First Meeting of Swedish Club Proves to Be Tremendous Success," *Western News* (Denver), December 18, 1958. I have no evidence of such a meeting place being built.

17. *Western News* (Denver), June 5, 1958, page 1.

18. Newspaper clippings from January 3, 1963 and March 28, 1963, 1963–64 clipping book, Swedish Club of Denver collection, WH1976, Denver Public Library.

19. In 2013, the Scandinavian Midsummer Festival was canceled by the Fjellborg Vikings, Boulder, due to an accident that had occurred at the 2012 festival. The City of Estes combined with the Swedish Folkdance Club of Denver to hold an alternative Midsummer Dance Festival. In 2014, Estes City and the folkdance club worked together again to plan a "Scandinavian Midsummer Festival" (2012). See also *Vesterheim News* (Boulder, CO), May–June 2013, http://www.vesterheimlodge.com/template1_images/Nwsltr_MAY_JUNE-13.pdf, accessed January 11, 2014. According to the *Vesterheim News,* the Fjellborg Vikings had been involved in sponsorship of the Midsummer Festival for the previous five and a half years.

20. Utopian immigrant formulas for America are analyzed in Attebery 2007. See pages 98–99.

21. See Attebery 2001 for my critique.

References

American Fisheries Society: Idaho Chapter. 2014. http://www.idahoafs.org/index.php

American Union of Swedish Singers Song Album; Male Choruses. 1909. Chicago: American Union of Swedish Singers.

Anderson, Avis R. 1974. "Scandinavians and Lutherans in Custer County and Dawson County, Montana." Master's thesis, Utah State University, Logan, UT.

Anderson, Chase E. (Original work published 1941) 1994. *Century of Progress in New Sweden: After Fifty Years.* Caldwell, ID: Caxton Printers.

Anderson, Orlando. 1983. "Interview by Marsha C. Martin, 16 June 1983, Logan, Utah." *LDS Family Life Oral History Project.* Provo, UT: Charles Redd Center for Western Studies, Brigham Young University Library Special Collections.

Aronson, Albert H., and Bertha D. Aronson. Collection MSS 1079. Denver, CO: Colorado State Historical Society.

Asad, Talal. 2003. *Formations of the Secular: Christianity, Islam, Modernity.* Stanford, CA: Stanford University Press.

Aspen Daily Chronicle. 1888. July 6, 1. http://www.coloradohistoricnewspapers.org/Default/Skins/Colorado/Client.asp?Skin=Colorado&AW=1266783801220&AppName=2.

Attebery, Jennifer Eastman. 1995. "Transplantations of Swedish America in Idaho: The Role of the Churches." *Swedish-American Historical Quarterly* 46 (2): 122–40.

Attebery, Jennifer Eastman. 2001. "Claiming Ethnicity: Implicit and Explicit Expressions of Ethnicity among Swedish Americans." In *Not English Only: Redefining "American" in American Studies,* ed. Orm Øverland, 12–28. European Contributions to American Studies, no. 48. Amsterdam: VU University Press.

Attebery, Jennifer Eastman. 2007. *Up in the Rocky Mountains: Writing the Swedish Immigrant Experience.* Minneapolis: University of Minnesota Press.

Barrows, T. Eugene. 1986. "Celebrating the Fourth of July in Fort Benton, 1910." *Montana: The Magazine of Western History* 36 (3): 76–79.

Barton, H. Arnold. 1984. "Albin Widén (1897–1983)." *Swedish Pioneer Historical Quarterly* 35 (2): 179–80.

Barton, H. Arnold. 1992. "Cultural Interplay between Sweden and Swedish-America." *Swedish-American Historical Quarterly* 43 (1): 5–18.

Barton, H. Arnold. 1994. *A Folk Divided: Homeland Swedes and Swedish Americans, 1840–1940.* Carbondale: Southern Illinois University Press.

Barton, H. Arnold. 1997. "Skansen and the Swedish Americans." *Swedish-American Historical Quarterly* 48 (4): 164–80.

Barton, H. Arnold. 2009. *Essays on Scandinavian History.* Carbondale, IL: Southern Illinois University Press.

Beijbom, Ulf. 1972. "The Societies—A Worldly Alternative in the Swedish Chicago Colony." *Swedish Pioneer Historical Quarterly* 23:135–50.

Beijbom, Ulf. 1985. *Albin Widéns Samling: Description of the Albin Widén Collection, Including a Brief Biography.* Växjö, Sweden: Emigrant Institute.

Beijbom, Ulf. 2004. "Tegnér and America." In *Scandinavians in Old and New Lands: Essays in Honor of H. Arnold Barton,* ed. Philip J. Anderson, Dag Blanck, and Byron J. Nordstrom, 159–83. Chicago: Swedish-American Historical Society.

DOI: 10.7330/9780874219999.c009

Bellah, Robert N. 1967. "Civil Religion in America." *Daedalus* 96 (1): 1–21.

Benson, Thomas I. 1970. "Gold, Salt Air, and Callouses." *Norwegian-American Studies* 24:193–220.

Berger, Michael L. 1979. *The Devil Wagon in God's Country: The Automobile and Social Change in Rural America, 1893–1929.* Hamden, CT: Archon Books.

Berry, Mildred Freburg. 1978. "Memories of a Swedish Christmas." *Palimpsest* 59:20–3.

Billington, Sandra. 2007. "Early Pagan Midsummer Traditions in North-western Europe: Fact or Fiction?" *The Ritual Year and Ritual Diversity.* Proceedings of the Second International Conference of the SIEF Working Group on The Ritual Year, 65–73. Göteborg, Sweden: Institute for Language and Folklore, in association with the Department of Ethnology and the Department of Religious Studies, Göteborg University.

Billington, Sandra. 2008. "The Midsummer Solstice as It Was, or Was Not, Observed in Pagan Germany, Scandinavia, and Anglo-Saxon England." *Folklore* 119 (1): 41–57. http://dx.doi.org/10.1080/00155870701806167.

Bitton, Davis. 1975. "The Ritualization of Mormon History." *Utah Historical Quarterly* 43 (1): 67–85.

Björjlund, Gustafva. 1910. *Svenska Kokboken.* Chicago: Svenska Tribunen-Nyheter.

Bjork, Kenneth O. 1954a. "Scandinavian Experiment in California, Part I." *Swedish Pioneer Historical Quarterly* 5:67–78.

Bjork, Kenneth O. 1954b. "Scandinavian Experiment in California, Part II." *Swedish Pioneer Historical Quarterly* 5:100–16.

Bjork, Kenneth O. 1955. "Scandinavian Experiment in California, Part III." *Swedish Pioneer Historical Quarterly* 6:26–34.

Bjork, Kenneth O. 1962. "A Covenant Folk, with Scandinavian Colorings." *Norwegian-American Studies* 21:212–51.

Blanck, Dag. 1988. "History at Work: The 1888 New Sweden Jubilee." *Swedish-American Historical Quarterly* 39:5–20.

Blanck, Dag. 1995. "History and Ethnicity: the Case of the Swedish Americans." *Swedish-American Historical Quarterly* 46 (1): 58–74.

Blanck, Dag. 2006. *The Creation of an Ethnic Identity: Being Swedish American in the Augustana Synod, 1860–1917.* Carbondale: Southern Illinois University Press.

Brennen, Bonnie. 2008. "From Religiosity to Consumerism: Press Coverage of Thanksgiving, 1905–2005." *Journalism Studies* 9 (1): 21–37. http://dx.doi.org/10.1080/14616700701768006.

Bringéus, Nils-Arvid. 1976. *Årets Festseder.* [*Calendar Customs*] Stockholm: LTs Förlag.

Bringéus, Nils-Arvid. 1994. "Vår Hållning till Döden." [Our Deportment toward Death] *Dödens Riter,* [*Rites of Death*] ed. Kristina Söderpalm, 9–31. Stockholm: Carlsson Bokförlag and Gothenburg: Göteborgs Stadsmuseum.

Brunvand, Amy. 2000a. "Contra Dance." *Catalyst* (March): 33.

Brunvand, Amy. 2000b. "Pagans and Propriety at the English Country Dance." *Catalyst* (May): 24.

Bungert, Heike. 2001. "Demonstrating the Values of 'Gemüthlichkeit' and 'Cultur': The Festivals of German Americans in Milwaukee, 1870–1910." In *Celebrating Ethnicity and Nation: American Festive Culture from the Revolution to the Early Twentieth Century,* ed. Geneviève Fabre, Jürgen Heideking, and Kai Dreisbach, 175–93. New York: Berghahn Books.

"Butte Lodge No. 11, Scandinavian Fraternity of America, By-laws and minutes." Microfilm SC226 and 227. Swenson Swedish Immigration Research Center, Augustana College, Rock Island, Illinois.

Campbell, Åke, and Åsa Nyman. 1976. *Atlas over Svensk Folkkultur. II Sägen, Tro och Högtidssed, 1. Kartor, 2. Kommentar. [Atlas of Swedish Folk Culture. II. Legends, beliefs, and holiday customs. 1. Maps, 2. Notes]* Uppsala: Kungl. Gustav Adolfs Akademien.

Cannon, Hal. 1985. "New Sweden Pioneer Day." In *Idaho Folklife: Homesteads to Headstones,* ed. Louie W. Attebery, 68–80. Salt Lake City: University of Utah Press.

Carlson, August Wilhelm. 1819. *Letterbook, MSS A.* Salt Lake City: Utah State Historical Society.

Carlson, Dale A. 1983. "The Swedish Club in Seattle." *Swedish-American Historical Quarterly* 34 (4): 306–11.

Carlson, John A. Papers, MS 26. Logan: Utah State University Special Collections.

Census of the United States. 1900. "12th Census." Records of the Bureau of the Census, Record Group 29. Washington, DC: National Archives. Accessed September 5, 2012. Ancestry.com.

Census of the United States. 1910. "13th Census." Records of the Bureau of the Census, Record Group 29. Washington, DC: National Archives. Accessed September 5, 2012. Ancestry.com.

Census of the United States. 1920. "14th Census." Records of the Bureau of the Census, Record Group 29. Washington, DC: National Archives. Accessed September 5, 2012. Ancestry.com.

Census of the United States. 1930. "15th Census." Records of the Bureau of the Census, Record Group 29. Washington, DC: National Archives. Ancestry.com

Christianson, J. R. 1984. "Cooperation in Scandinavian-American Studies." *Swedish-American Historical Quarterly* 35:374–86.

Clawson, Mary Ann. 1989. *Constructing Brotherhood: Class, Gender, and Fraternalism.* Princeton, NJ: Princeton University Press. http://dx.doi.org/10.1515/9781400860500.

Cohn, William H. 1976. "A National Celebration: The Fourth of July in American History." *Cultures* 3 (1): 141–56.

Cohn, William H. 1977. "Popular Culture and Social History." *Journal of Popular Culture* 11 (1): 167–79. http://dx.doi.org/10.1111/j.0022-3840.1977.1101_167.x.

Colbert, Stephen. 2012a. "Operation Artificial Swedener." *The Colbert Report.* Episode 08110, aired June 12. http://www.colbertnation.com/the-colbert-report-videos/415197/june-12-2012/operation-artificial-swedener.

Colbert, Stephen. 2012b. "Operation Artificial Swedener—C'mon Sweden, Take a Chance on Stephen." *The Colbert Report.* Episode 08116, aired June 21. http://www.colbert-nation.com/the-colbert-report-videos/415706/june-21-2012/operation-artificial-swedener-c-mon-sweden-take-a-chance-on-stephen.

Colbert, Stephen. 2012c. "Operation Artificial Swedener—Sweden's Response." *The Colbert Report.* Episode 08113, aired June 18.

Connolly, William E. 2002. *Neuropolitics: Thinking, Culture, Speed.* Minneapolis: University of Minnesota Press.

Dahlie, Jorgen. 1967. "A Social History of Scandinavian Immigration, Washington State, 1895–1910." PhD dissertation, Washington State University, Pullman, WA.

Dahllöf, Tell G. 1980. "A List of Swedish-American Literary Pseudonyms." *Swedish-American Historical Quarterly* 31 (1): 51–9.

Dahlquist, Lars Andersson. Collection SC 58. Helena: Montana Historical Society Archives.

Danielson, Larry. 1972. "The Ethnic Festival and Cultural Revivalism in a Small Midwestern Town." PhD dissertation, Indiana University, Bloomington, IN.

Danielson, Larry. 1974. "Public Swedish-American Ethnicity in Central Kansas: A Festival and Its Functions." *Swedish Pioneer Historical Quarterly* 25 (1): 13–36.

Davison, Stanley R. 1964. ""Christmas in Montana." *Montana.*" *Magazine of Western History* 14 (1): 2–9.

Deetz, James. 1996. *In Small Things Forgotten: An Archaeology of Early American Life*, revised and expanded edition. New York: Anchor.

Deloria, Philip J. 1998. *Playing Indian*. New Haven, CT: Yale University Press.

Dennis, Matthew. 2002. *Red, White, and Blue Letter Days: An American Calendar*. NY: Cornell University Press.

"Digital Memories" 2001. University of Idaho Library, Special Collections and Archives. April. http://www.lib.uidaho.edu/special-collections/dm/dm2001/npwarphotos.htm.

Ekman, Ernst. 1974. "Wetterman and the Scandinavian Society of San Francisco." *Swedish Pioneer Historical Quarterly* 25:87–102.

Eliason, Eric A. 2002. "The Cultural Dynamics of Historical Self-Fashioning: Mormon Pioneer Nostalgia, American Culture, and the International Church." *Journal of Mormon History* 28 (2): 139–73.

"Elim Lutheran Church records, Ogden, Utah, 1889–1944." S–340. Rock Island, IL: Swenson Swedish Immigration Research Center, Augustana College.

Evans, Brad. 2005. *Before Cultures: The Ethnographic Imagination in American Literature, 1865–1920*. Chicago: University of Chicago Press.

Fabre, Geneviève, and Jürgen Heideking. 2001. "Introduction." In *Celebrating Ethnicity and Nation: American Festive Culture from the Revolution to the Early Twentieth Century*, ed. Geneviève Fabre, Jürgen Heideking, and Kai Dreisbach, 1–24. New York: Berghahn Books.

"Facebook Hits One Billion" 2012. *Wall Street Journal, Eastern Edition*. October 6, C4.

"Fackskolan för Huslig Ekonomi i Uppsala." 1913. *Hemmets Kokbok*. Chicago: Dalkullan Publishing and Importing.

Farrell, Thomas B. 1995. *Norms of Rhetorical Culture*. New Haven, CT: Yale University Press.

Fessenden, Tracy. 2007. *Culture and Redemption: Religion, the Secular, and American Literature*. Princeton, NJ: Princeton University Press.

"The Festival of Saint Lucia." 2014. Saint Peter, MN: Gustavus Adolphus College. Accessed June 16. http://gustavus.edu/events/stlucia/.

Flygare, Nils C. Collection MSS 1496. Provo, UT: Brigham Young University Special Collections.

Foley, John Miles. 1991. *Immanent Art: From Structure to Meaning in Traditional Oral Epic*. Bloomington: Indiana University Press.

Frigga Lodge No. 42, Independent Order Ladies of Vikings, Salt Lake City. Minutes, 1927–28. SC151. Rock Island, IL: Swenson Swedish Immigration Research Center, Augustana College.

Frykman, Birgitta Skarin. 1994. "Det Skulle Visas Utåt att Man Hade Lik i Huset." [As with a House, It Should Represent What One Had] In *Dödens Riter*, [*Rites of Death*] ed. Kristina Söderpalm, 93–101. Stockholm: Carlsson Bokförlag.

Frykman, Birgitta Skarin. 2007. "Sista Ordet: En Revolution i Stillhet; Om Arbetarbegravningarnas Sociala Språk." In *Arbetarrörelse och Arbetarkultur: Bild och Självbild*, ed. Lena Johannesson, Ulrika Kjellman, and Birgitta Skarin Frykman, 32–173. Stockholm: Carlssons.

Frykman, Jonas, and Orvar Löfgren. (Original work published 1979) 1987. *Culture Builders: A Historical Anthropology of Middle-Class Life*. Trans. Alan Crozier. New Brunswick, NJ: Rutgers University Press.

Gabbert, Lisa. 2011. *Winter Carnival in a Western Town: Identity, Change, and the Good of Community*. Logan: Utah State University Press.

Gadd, John D. C. 1968. "Saltair: Great Salt Lake's Most Famous Resort." *Utah Historical Quarterly* 36 (3): 198–221.

Gans, Herbert J. 1992. "Comment: Ethnic Invention and Acculturation, a Bumpy-Line Approach." *Journal of American Ethnic History* 12 (1): 42–52.

Gaudet, Marcia. 1990. "Christmas Bonfires in South Louisiana: Tradition and Innovation." *Southern Folklore* 47 (3): 195–206.

Goodman, J. David. 2012. "On Sweden's Democratic Twitter Account, Some Odd Questions About Jews." *New York Times,* June 12. http://thelede.blogs.nytimes. com/2012/06/12/on-swedens-democratic-twitter-account-some-odd-questions-about-jews/.

Gordon, Sarah Barringer. 2000. "Blasphemy and the Law of Religious Liberty in Nineteenth-Century America." *American Quarterly* 52 (4): 682–719. http:// dx.doi.org/10.1353/aq.2000.0045.

Gowers, Richard. 2001. "Race and National Holidays: The African American Fourth of July, 1865–1905." *Melbourne Historical Journal* 29: 79–84.

Gowers, Richard. 2005. "Contested Celebrations: The Fourth of July and Changing National Identity in the United States, 1865–1918." Dissertation, University of New South Wales, Australia.

Gradén, Lizette. 2003. *On Parade: Making Heritage in Lindsborg, Kansas.* Studia Multiethnica Upsaliensia 15. Uppsala, Sweden: Acta Universitatis Upsaliensis.

Gradén, Lizette. 2004. "Christmas in Lindsborg." In *Creating Diversities: Folklore, Religion and the Politics of Heritage,* ed. Anna-Leena Siikala, Barbro Klein, and Stein R. Mathisen, 276–91. Helsinki: Finnish Literature Society.

Gradén, Lizette, Hanne Pico Larsen, and Susanne Österlund-Pötzch. 2012. "Nordic Spaces in the U.S.: Three Examples of the Performance of Nordic-American Identity." *American Studies in Scandinavia* 44 (1): 67–98.

Grimsby, Oscar Melvin P. 1926. "The Contribution of the Scandinavian and Germanic People to the Development of Montana." MA Thesis, University of Montana, Missoula.

Guglielmo, Thomas A. 2003. *White on Arrival: Italians, Race, Color, and Power in Chicago, 1890–1945.* New York: Oxford University Press.

Gustavsson, Anders. 2007. "Celebrations of National Holidays in a Norwegian-Swedish Border Perspective." In *The Ritual Year and Ritual Diversity,* 191–200. Proceedings of the Second International Conference of the SIEF Working Group on The Ritual Year. Göteborg, Sweden: Institute for Language and Folklore, in association with the Department of Ethnology and the Department of Religious Studies, Göteborg University.

Hägg, Gustaf, ed. 1904. *Songs of Sweden: Eighty-seven Swedish Folk- and Popular Songs.* New York: Schirmer Internet Archive; http://www.archive.org/details/ songsofswedeneig00hg.

Hallquist, Victor A. Collection 22: 4: 14: J. Växjö, Sweden: Emigrant Institute.

Hanson, Henry. 1996. "The Vasa Order of America: Its Role in the Swedish-American Community, 1896–1996." *Swedish-American Historical Quarterly* 47 (4): 236–44.

Hartley, William G. 1983. "Childhood in Gunnison, Utah." *Utah Historical Quarterly* 51 (2): 108–32.

Harvey, Anne-Charlotte. 2001. "Performing Ethnicity: The Role of Swedish Theatre in the Twin Cities." In *Swedes in the Twin Cities: Immigrant Life and Minnesota's Urban Frontier,* ed. Philip J. Anderson and Dag Blanck, 149–72. St. Paul: Minnesota Historical Society Press.

Hedblom, Folke. 1965. "Swedish Speech and Popular Tradition in America." *Swedish Pioneer Historical Quarterly* 16 (3): 137–57.

Hedblom, Folke. 1967. "Research of Swedish Speech and Popular Traditions in America." *Swedish Pioneer Historical Quarterly* 18 (2): 76–92.

Hemmets Drottning Verldsutställningens Souvenir Kokbok. [*Domestic "Queen's" World Exhibition Souvenir Cookbook*] 1894. Chicago: Fort Dearborn Publishing.

Henrichsen, Lynn, George Bailey, Timothy Wright, John Brumbaugh, Jacob Huckaby, and Ray LeBaron. 2010. "Building Community by Respecting Linguistic Diversity: Scandinavian Immigrants in Nineteenth Century Utah." *Utah Historical Quarterly* 78 (1): 4–22.

"Hepatica nobilis Schreb. var. obtusa (Pursh) Steyerm. roundlobe hepatica." 2011. Plants Database, Natural Resources Conservation Service, United States Department of Agriculture. Accessed June 9. http://plants.usda.gov/java/profile?symbol=HENOO.

Historical Census Browser. 2004. Geospatial and Statistical Data Center, University of Virginia. mapserver.lib.virginia.edu.

"History of Latah County" 2012. *Latah County Historical Society.* Accessed May 23. http://users.moscow.com/lchs/history.html#troy.

Holm, Carl Otto. Papers MSS 1894. Provo, UT: Special Collections, Brigham Young University Library.

Hull, Betty Lynne. 2003. *Denver's Elitch Gardens: Spinning a Century of Dreams.* Boulder, CO: Johnson Books.

Humphrey, Linda T. 1979. "Small Group Festive Gatherings." *Journal of the Folklore Institute* 16 (3): 190–201. http://dx.doi.org/10.2307/3813824.

Hutchison, William R. 1998. "The Emperor's Old Clothes: A Comment on Hartmut Lehmann's 'Christianization of America and Dechristianization of Europe in the 19th and 20th Centuries.'" *Kirchliche Zeitgeschichte* 11 (1): 137–42.

Hutton, Ronald. 1994. *The Rise and Fall of Merry England: The Ritual Year, 1400–1700.* New York: Oxford University Press. http://dx.doi.org/10.1093/acprof:oso/9780198203636.001.0001.

Isaacson, Carl. 2003. "The American Moberg: Lillian Budd's Swedish-American Trilogy." *Swedish-American Historical Quarterly* 54 (2): 111–32.

Jacobson, Matthew Frye. 1998. *Whiteness of a Different Color: European Immigrants and the Alchemy of Race.* Cambridge: Harvard University Press.

Jacobson, Matthew Frye. 2006. *Roots Too: White Ethnic Revival in Post-Civil Rights America.* Cambridge: Harvard University Press.

Jarvi, Raymond. 1996. "Report: Emigrants and Immigrants in Swedish History 1846–1996: Celebrating the Sesquicentennial: Part I." *Swedish-American Historical Quarterly* 47 (1): 40–48.

Jaworski, Michelle. 2012. "American Swedish Institute Offers Twitter Account to Stephen Colbert." *The Daily Dot,* June 21. http://www.thedailydot.com/news/stephen-colbert-american-swedish-institute-twitter/.

Jenson, Andrew. 1927. *History of the Scandinavian Mission.* Salt Lake City: Deseret News Press.

Jenswold, John R. 1985. "The Rise and Fall of Pan-Scandinavianism in Urban America." In *Scandinavians and Other Immigrants in Urban America,* ed. Odd S. Lovall, 159–70. Northfield, MN: Saint Olaf College Press.

Johannesson, Kurt, Olle Josephson, and Erik Åsard, eds. 1998. "Esaias Tegnér Prisar Reformationen och den Lagbundna Friheten 1817." In *Ordet Är en Makt: Svenska Tal från Torgny Lagman till Carl Bildt och Mona Sahlin,* 249–56, Stockholm: Norstedts.

Johansson, August. Collection 9: 6: 10: E. Växjö, Sweden: Emigrant Institute.

Johnson, Cleo J. 1982. "The Scandinavian Organization." *Snake River Echoes: A Quarterly of Idaho History* 11 (2): 82–85.

Johnson, Emeroy. 1984. "The Beginnings of Swedish Lutheran Church Work in Montana." *Swedish-American Historical Quarterly* 35: 151–61.

Johnson, Niel M. 1992. "Swedes in Kansas City: Selected Highlights of their History." *Swedish-American Historical Quarterly* 43 (1): 19–40.

Johnson, Stella E. 1992. *History of Troy.* Troy, ID: Stella E. Johnson.

Johnson, William Eugene, ed. 2002. *"History and Journals of Anders Gustaf Johannesson."* MS 1995. Salt Lake City: University of Utah Special Collections.

Kalispell (Montana) Lodge No. 233, Scandinavian Fraternity of America. Minutes. Microfilm 228. Rock Island, IL: Swenson Swedish Immigration Research Center, Augustana College.

Kaufmann, Michael W. 2007. "The Religious, the Secular, and Literary Studies: Rethinking the Secularization Narrative in Histories of the Profession." *Literary History* 38 (4): 607–28. http://dx.doi.org/10.1353/nlh.2008.0004.

Kimball, Richard Ian. 2001. "'All Hail to Christmas': Mormon Pioneer Holiday Celebrations." *BYU Studies* 40 (3): 6–26.

Kinney, Martha E. 1998. "'If Vanquished I Am Still Victorious': Religious and Cultural Symbolism in Virginia's Confederate Memorial Day Celebrations, 1866–1930." *Virginia Magazine of History and Biography* 106 (3): 237–66.

Klein, Barbro. 1989. "Den Gamla Hembygden eller Vad Har Hänt med de Svenska Folktraditionerna USA?" In *Bland-Sverige: Kulturskillnader och Kulturmöten,* ed. Åke Daun and Billy Ehn, 43–67. Stockholm: Stiftelsen Sveriges Invandrarinstitut och Museum.

Klein, Barbro. 1996. "Symbol Building at the Summer Equinox: the Midsummer Pole in Sweden and Finland." *Michigan Folklife Annual,* 12–21.

Kolchin, Peter. 2002. "Whiteness Studies: The New History of Race in America." *Journal of American History* 89 (1): 154–73. http://dx.doi.org/10.2307/2700788.

Korsbaneret: Kristlig Kalender. 1880–1950. Rock Island, IL: Augustana Book Concern.

Kress, Gunther. 2009. *Multimodality: A Social Semiotic Approach to Contemporary Communication.* New York: Routledge.

Kvist, Roger. 1999. "A Social History of the Swedish Ethnic Units from Illinois in the Civil War." *Swedish-American Historical Quarterly* 50 (1): 20–42.

"Lagoon Welcomes the Swedish Societies." 1939. Pamphlet PAM 5219. Salt Lake City: Utah State Historical Society.

Lamm, Richard D. 1983. "The Fourth of July in Colorado: A Perspective and a Hope." *Colorado Heritage* 3: 28–33.

Lavin, Maud. 2004. *The Business of Holidays.* New York: Monacelli.

Lehmann, Hartmut. 1998. "The Christianization of America and the Dechristianization of Europe in the 19th and 20th Centuries." *Kirchliche Zeitgeschichte* 11 (1): 8–20.

Lenhammar, Larry. 1998. "The Christianization of America and the De-Christianization of Europe, Particularly of Sweden, in the 19th and 20th Centuries." *Kirchliche Zeitgeschichte* 11 (1): 41–50.

Liljenquist, Emma. n.d. "Pioneers' Observance of the Sabbath Day, Hyrum." MSS A 478–3. Salt Lake City: Utah State Historical Society.

Liman, Ingemar. 1983. "The Skansen Dancers' Tour of America, 1906–1907." *Swedish-American Historical Quarterly* 34 (3): 224–34.

Linder, O. A. 1880–1930. Clipping Collection, SSIRC MSS P: 7. Rock Island, IL: Swenson Swedish Immigration Research Center, Augustana College.

Litwicki, Ellen M. 2000. "'Our Hearts Burn with Ardent Love for Two Countries': Ethnicity and Assimilation at Chicago Holiday Celebrations, 1876–1918." *Journal of American Ethnic History* 19 (3): 3–34.

Litwicki, Ellen M. 2003. *America's Public Holidays, 1865–1920.* Washington, DC: Smithsonian Books.

Lofgreen, Peter Anderson. 1896–1919. Autobiography and journal MSS A 40. Salt Lake City: Utah Historical Society.

Lord, Albert B. 2000. *The Singer of Tales.* 2nd ed. Ed. Stephen Mitchell and Gregory Nagy. Cambridge: Harvard University Press.

Lund, Jennifer L. 2003. "Out of the Swan's Nest: The Ministry of Anthon H. Lund, Scandinavian Apostle." *Journal of Mormon History* 29 (2): 77–105.

Lundquist, Jacob. Collection 29: 4: 8: D, 2–4, and E 21. Växjö, Sweden: Emigrant Institute.

Marx, Leo. 1964. *The Machine in the Garden: Technology and the Pastoral Ideal in America.* New York: Oxford University Press.

Matson, Paul R. 1979. *"The Life of Peter Matson, 1851–1919."* Copy deposited at Brigham Young University Library. Provo, UT: Special Collections.

Mauritzson, Jules. 1994. *Looking West: Three Essays on Swedish-American Life*, trans. Conrad Bergendoff, and ed. Ann Boaden and Dag Blanck. Rock Island, IL: Augustana Historical Society.

Måwe, Carl-Erik. 1971. *Värmlänningar I Nordamerika: Sociologiska Studier i en Anpassningsprocess.* Säffle, Sweden: Säffle-Tidningens Tryckeri.

McDonald, Myrtle. n.d. *No Regrets: The Life of Carl A. Carlquist.* Copy at Brigham Young University Library, Special Collections, Provo, UT.

McKee, Delber L. 1986. "The Chinese Boycott of 1905–1906 Reconsidered: The Role of Chinese Americans." *Pacific Historical Review* 55 (2): 165–91. http://dx.doi.org/10.2307/3639528.

McMahon, David. 1997. "Rediscovering a Swedish Ethnic Past: the National Park Service and Baillytown, Indiana." *Swedish-American Historical Quarterly* 48 (1): 26–52.

"Midsommar 2011" 2011. Swedish Heritage Society of Utah. http://www.swedishheritagesociety.com/2011/06/.

"midsummer, n." 2011. *OED.com.* Oxford University Press. http://www.oed.com/view/Entry/118247?redirectedFrom=midsummer#eid.

Milich, Klaus J. 2004. " 'Oh, God': Secularization Theory in the Transatlantic Sphere." *Amerikastudien* 49 (3): 409–29.

Monnett, John H. 1987. *A Rocky Mountain Christmas: Yuletide Stories of the West.* Boulder, CO: Pruett.

Mulder, William. 1956a. "Mother Tongue, 'Skandinavisme,' and 'The Swedish Insurrection' in Utah." *Swedish Pioneer Historical Quarterly* 7: 11–20.

Mulder, William. 1956b. "Norwegian Forerunners among the Early Mormons." *Norwegian-American Studies and Records* 19: 46–61.

Mulder, William. (Original work published 1957) 2000. *Homeward to Zion: the Mormon Migration from Scandinavia.* Minneapolis: University of Minnesota Press.

Nelson, Axel T. Papers MS355. Boise: Idaho Historical Society.

Nelson, Peter S. Papers MSS P: 227. Rock Island, IL: Swenson Swedish Immigration Research Center, Augustana College.

New Sweden Covenant Church records, New Sweden, Idaho. 1896–1931. S–459. Rock Island, IL: Swenson Swedish Immigration Research Center, Augustana College.

"New Sweden, Maine 2012 Midsummer Festival June 22, 23 & 24." 2012. Accessed June 8 2012. http://www.maineswedishcolony.info/midsom/2012/MidsommarBrochure2012.pdf.

"News." 1995. *Swedish-American Historical Quarterly* 46 (2): 153–60.

Nilsson, Hjalmar, and Eric Knutson. 1898. *Svenskarne i Worcester, 1868–1898.* [The Swedes in Worcester] Worcester, MA: Skandinavias Bok-och Tidningstryckeri.

Nissenbaum, Stephen. 1997. *The Battle for Christmas: A Social and Cultural History of Christmas That Shows How It Was Transformed From An Unruly Carnival Season Into The Quintessential American Family Holiday.* New York: Alfred A. Knopf.

Norelius, Eric. 1851–1916. Papers SSIRC MSS P: 1. Rock Island, IL: Swenson Swedish Immigration Research Center, Augustana College.

Norman, Hans, and Harald Runblom. 1988. *Transatlantic Connections: Nordic Migration to the New World after 1800.* Oslo: Norwegian University Press.

Norstedts Engelska Ordbok. 1997. 3rd ed. Sweden: Norstedts.

Olsen, Steven L. 1996–97. "Celebrating Cultural Identity: Pioneer Day in Nineteenth-Century Mormonism." *BYU Studies* 36 (1): 159–77.

Olson, Ernest L. 1949. "Otto Rydman, Satirist: An Immigrant Editor's Views of the Scandinavian Scene in Utah." MA thesis, University of Utah, Salt Lake City.

Olson, James C. 1972. "Arbor Day: A Pioneer Concern for Environment." *Nebraska History* 53 (1): 1–13.

Olsson, Karl A. 1962. *By One Spirit.* Chicago: Covenant Press.

"One of the Fun Things Thor and I Did" 2012. *Adventures of Baby Cap.* http://adventuresofbabycap.tumblr.com/post/33268676542/.

Ong, Walter J. 1982. *Orality and Literacy: The Technologizing of the Word.* London: Routledge. http://dx.doi.org/10.4324/9780203328064.

Örtengren, J. R., ed. n.d. *Kvartett-Album: Äldre och Nyare Kvartetter för Mansröster.* Chicago: Engberg-Holmberg.

"Oslund Family Papers." n.d. Moscow, ID: Latah County Historical Society.

Øverland, Orm. 2000. *Immigrant Minds, American Identities: Making the United States Home, 1870–1930.* Urbana: University of Illinois Press.

Pehrson, Elin. Collection 10: 2: 16, folder I, letters 1–5. Växjö, Sweden: Emigrant Institute.

Quensel, C. 1804. *Svensk Botanik.* Stockholm: J.W. Palmstruch.

Ralph, Charles. 2011. "Opera in Old Colorado." Fort Collins, CO. http://www.operaoldcolo.info/index.html.

Rasmussen, Janet E. 1989. "'I Met Him at Normanna Hall': Ethnic Cohesion and Marital Patterns among Scandinavian Immigrant Women." *Norwegian-American Studies* 32 (4): 71–89.

"Remembering the Columbia Gardens." 2012. Montana PBS. Accessed August 9. http://watch.montanapbs.org/video/1524524498/.

Restad, Penne L. 1995. *Christmas in America: A History.* New York: Oxford University Press.

Rhodes, Wanda. 1988. *The History of River Heights.* Logan: River Heights Civic Club.

Risley, Kristin A. 2003. "Christmas in Our Western Home: The Cultural Work of a Norwegian-American Christmas Annual." *American Periodicals: A Journal of History, Criticism, and Bibliography* 13 (1): 50–83. http://dx.doi.org/10.1353/amp.2004.0009.

Ritchie, Susan J. 2002. "Contesting Secularism: Reflexive Methodology, Belief Studies, and Disciplined Knowledge." *Journal of American Folklore* 115: 443–56.

R.L. Polk & Co.'s Butte City Directory. 1895. Butte, MT: R.L. Polk.

R.L. Polk & Co.'s Butte City Directory. 1905. Butte, MT: R.L. Polk.

R.L. Polk & Co.'s Helena City Directory. 1891–1899. Helena, MT: R.L. Polk.

Robbins, Vernon K. 1994. "Oral, Rhetorical, and Literary Cultures: A Response." *Semeia* 65: 75–91.

Robbins, Vernon K. 2006. "Interfaces of Orality and Literature in the Gospel of Mark." In *Performing the Gospel: Orality, Memory, and Mark,* ed. Richard A. Horsley, Jonathan A. Draper, and John Miles Foley, 125–46. Minneapolis: Fortress Press.

Rodgers, Lawrence, and Jerrold Hirsch, eds. 2010. *America's Folklorist: B.A. Botkin and American Culture.* Norman: University of Oklahoma Press.

Rosenzweig, Roy. 1983. *Eight Hours for What We Will: Workers and Leisure in an Industrial City, 1870–1920.* Cambridge, UK: Cambridge University Press.

Runeberg, Johan Ludvig. 1870. "Sköna Maj, Välkommen." *Samlade Skrifter.* Project Runeberg. http://runeberg.org/runeberg/0_01.html.

Salomonsson, Eric J., William O. Hultgren, and Philip C. Becker. 2005. *Swedes of Greater Worcester Revisited.* Charleston, SC: Arcadia.

Sanborn Digital Maps. 1867–1970. http://sanborn.umi.com/.

"Sancta Lucia Festival" 2014. *Bethlehem Lutheran Church*. http://www.blcelgin.org/blce/
    sancta_lucia_festival_20141.
Santino, Jack. 1994. *All Around the Year: Holidays and Celebrations in American Life*. Urbana: Uni-
    versity of Illinois Press.
Santino, Jack. 1996. *New Old-Fashioned Ways*. Knoxville: University of Tennessee Press.
Santino, Jack. 2004. "Performative Commemoratives, the Personal, and the Public: Spon-
    taneous Shrines, Emergent Ritual, and the Field of Folklore (AFS Presidential
    Plenary Address, 2003)." *Journal of American Folklore* 117 (466): 363–72. http://
    dx.doi.org/10.1353/jaf.2004.0098.
Santino, Jack. 2009. "The Ritualesque: Festival, Politics, and Popular Culture." *Western Folklore*
    68 (1): 9–26.
Scandinavian Jubilee Album. 1900. Issued in Commemoration of the Fiftieth Anniversary of
    the Introduction of the Gospel to the Three Scandinavian Countries by Elder Erastus
    Snow and Fellow Laborers. Salt Lake City: Church of Jesus Christ of Latter-day Saints.
    California Digital Library. http://www.archive.org/details/scandinavianjubi00churrich.
"Scandinavian Midsummer Festival." 2012. Swedish Club of Denver. Accessed June 8.
    http://www.estesmidsummer.com/ and http://www.estesmidsummer.com/schedule
    _2012.htm.
"Scandinavian Reunion Best Ever Held." 1916. *American Fork Citizen* (American Fork, UT),
    September 23. http://chroniclingamerica.loc.gov/lccn/sn85058027/1916-09-23/
    ed-1/seq-7/.
Schmidt, Leigh Eric. 1995. *Consumer Rites: The Buying and Selling of American Holidays*. Princ-
    eton, NJ: Princeton University Press.
Scott, Franklin D. 1965. "Literature in Periodicals of Protest of Swedish-America." *Swedish-
    American Historical Quarterly* 16 (4): 193–215.
Scott, George W. 2005. "Scandinavians in Washington Politics." *Swedish-American Historical
    Quarterly* 56 (4): 231–69.
Sealander, Dave. 2001. Personal conversations. New Sweden, Idaho. July 6 and 19.
Segal, Howard P. 1977. "Leo Marx's 'Middle Landscape': A Critique, a Revision,
    and an Appreciation." *Reviews in American History* 5 (1): 137–50. http://
    dx.doi.org/10.2307/2701782.
Setterdahl, Lilly. 1981. *Swedish-American Newspapers*. Rock Island, IL: Augustana College
    Library.
Sinor, Jennifer. 2002. *The Extraordinary Work of Ordinary Writing: Annie Ray's Diary*. Iowa City:
    University of Iowa Press.
"Skandinavernes Julestevne i Granite Stav." 1913. Bringham Young University Library Spe-
    cial Collections.
Skårdal, Dorothy Burton. 1977. "Scandinavian-American Literature: A Frontier for
    Research." *Swedish-American Historical Quarterly* 28 (4): 237–51.
Skarstedt, Ernst. 1879. *Våra Penn-Fäktare*. San Francisco: Vestkustens Tryckeri.
Sollors, Werner. 1986. *Beyond Ethnicity: Consent and Descent in American Culture*. New York:
    Oxford University Press.
Stokker, Kathleen. 2000. *Keeping Christmas: Yuletide Traditions in Norway and the New Land*. St.
    Paul: Minnesota Historical Society Press.
Strecker, Ivo, and Stephen Tyler, eds. 2009. *Culture and Rhetoric*. Oxford, UK: Berghahn
    Books.
Stringham, Miranda. 1984. *Old Ammon, Idaho, U.S.A.* Rexburg, ID: Ricks College Press.
Sundberg, Charles J. 1914. *Kyrklig Förvirring Gentemot Gudomligheten I Naturen: En Afhandling
    Om Äldre Och Nyare Religions-fantasier Samt Framtidens Religion Eller Människans Rätt Till
    Individuell Själf-ständighet På Det Andliga Området. Tillikamed En Kortfattad Granskning Af
    Den Föregifna Urkunden "Mormons Bok."* Pleasant Grove, UT: Författarens förlag.

Sundberg, Charles J. 1917. *The Mysterious Book of Mormon: Does It Appear Truthful?* UT: Sandy.
Svensk Almanack För År. 1883, 1884, 1888–93, 1895. New York: Amerikanska Emigrant Kompaniet.
Svensk-Amerikansk Almanacka och Kalendar. 1901, 1904, 1906–1925, 1989. New York: S. Nielsen.
Svensk-Amerikanska Kalendern. 1911–1912. Worchester, MA: Karl G. Fredin.
Svenska Amerikanarens Almanack. 1915–1916, 1918–1923, 1925–1928, 1930–1932. Chicago: Svenska Amerikanaren Hemlandet.
Svenska Monitorens Almanacka. 1911–1915. Sioux City, Iowa: Svenska Monitorens Trycheri.
Svenska Postens Almanack och Kalender. 1912. Rockford, Illinois: Svenska Posten.
Svenskt Porträttgalleri. 1895–1913. Vol. 21, Tonkonstnärer och Sceniska Artister. Stockholm: Hasse W. Tullbergs Förlag. Project Runeberg. Accessed January 18 2011. http://rune berg.org/spg/21/.
Svensson, Birgitta. 1992. "Prärieblomman (1900–1913): A Swedish-American Cultural Manifestation." *Swedish-American Historical Quarterly* 43 (3): 156–69.
Swahn, Jan-Öjvind. 1997. *Maypoles, Crayfish and Lucia: Swedish Holidays and Traditions.* Stockholm: Swedish Institute.
Swanson, John M. Papers 10: 2: 19: B and C. Växjö, Sweden: Emigrant Institute.
Swanson, Lynne. 1996. "Celebrating Midsummer in Brevort." *Michigan Folklife Annual*, 22–28.
Swedish Club of Denver Papers. WH1976. Denver: Denver Public Library.
Swedish Evangelical Free Church Collection. MSS 1540. Denver: Colorado Historical Society Library.
Swedish Medical Center Collection. WH 958, box 12. Denver: Denver Public Library.
Tallgren, Henrik. 1999. *Skandi-Fest: En Antropologisk Studie av Skandinav-Amerikanskt Festivalfirande i Kalifornien.* [*Skandi-Fest: An Anthropological Study of a Scandinavian-American Celebration in California*] SANS (Socialantropologiska Skrifter) 7. Göteborg, Sweden: Sociolantropologiska Institutionen, Göteborgs Universitet.
Tellefsen, Ole Christian. Diaries MSS B 87 box 1, folder 5. Salt Lake City: Utah State Historical Society.
Thompson, Kenneth. 1991. "Transgressing the Boundary between the Sacred and the Secular/Profane: A Durkheimian Perspective on a Public Controversy." *SA. Sociological Analysis* 52 (3): 277–91. http://dx.doi.org/10.2307/3711362.
Thorp, Rollin L. Diary M 780. Denver: Denver Public Library.
Tidholm, Po, and Agneta Lilja. 2004. *Det Ska Vi Fira: Svenska Traditioner och Högtider.* Stockholm: Svenska Institutet.
Toelken, Barre. 1991. "Ethnic Selection and Intensification in the Native American Powwow." In *Creative Ethnicity: Symbols and Strategies of Contemporary Ethnic Life,* ed. Stephen Stern and John Allan Cicala, 137–56. Logan: Utah State University Press.
Toelken, Barre. 1996. *The Dynamics of Folklore,* revised edition. Logan: Utah State University Press.
Tonsing, Ernest F. 2000. "Transforming Swedish Immigrants into Swedish Americans: The Function of a Speech by Governor John A. Martin, Lindsborg, Kansas, 5 July 1886." *Swedish-American Historical Quarterly* 51 (3): 222–35.
Torgny Lodge No. 61, Independent Order of Vikings, Salt Lake City. 1927–1928. Minutes SC155. Rock Island, IL: Swenson Swedish Immigration Research Center, Augustana College.
Trotzig, E. G. 1977. "Early Swedish Settlements in the Dakota Territory." *Swedish Pioneer Historical Quarterly* 28 (1): 106–17.
Tschannen, Olivier. 1991. "The Secularization Paradigm: A Systematization." *Journal for the Scientific Study of Religion* 30 (4): 395–415. http://dx.doi.org/10.2307/1387276.
Turner, George E. Collection WH415, microfilm 119. Denver: Denver Public Library.

Ulrich, Laurel Thatcher. 2001. *The Age of Homespun: Objects and Stories in the Creation of an American Myth*. New York: Vintage.

US City Directories. 1821–1989. Online database, accessed September 6, 2012. Ancestry.com.

Välkommen to Lindsborg, Kansas. Calendar, December 8, 2012. http://lindsborgcity.org/Calendar.aspx?EID=2651.

Waits, William B. 1993. *The Modern Christmas in America: A Cultural History of Gift Giving*. New York: New York University Press.

Wall, David. 2007. "Andrew Jackson Downing and the Tyranny of Taste." *American Nineteenth Century History* 8 (2): 187–203. http://dx.doi.org/10.1080/14664650701387920.

Wall, Tora. 2007. "Magic at Midsummer: Past and Present Beliefs Concerning Love and Divination." *The Ritual Year and Ritual Diversity*, 58–64. Proceedings of the Second International Conference of the SIEF Working Group on The Ritual Year. Göteborg, Sweden: Institute for Language and Folklore, in association with the Department of Ethnology and the Department of Religious Studies, Göteborg University.

Warner, W. Lloyd. 1962 [1953]. *American Life: Dream and Reality*. Chicago: University of Chicago Press.

Wendelius, Lars. 1990. *Kulturliv i ett Svenskamerikanskt Lokalsamhälle. [Cultural Life in a Swedish American Community]* Uppsala, Sweden: Centre for Multiethnic Research, Uppsala University.

Westman, Erik G., ed. 1931. *The Swedish Element in America*. Chicago: Swedish-American Biographical Society.

Widén, Albin. 1937. *Svenskar Som Erövrat Amerika. [Swedes Who "Conquered" America]* Stockholm: Nordisk Rotogravyr.

Widén, Albin. 1948. "Those Who Left." Trans. John E. Norton; originally published as "De som drog ut" in *Svenska Turistföreningens Årsskrift*. *Swedish-American Historical Quarterly* 47 (1): 5–18.

Widén, Albin. 1966. *Amerikaemigrationen i Dokument. [The American Emigration through Documents]* Stockholm: Bokförlaget Prisma.

Widén, Albin. 1972. *Nybyggarliv i Svensk-Amerika: Minnesbilder och Kulturtraditioner. [Settlers' Life in Swedish America: Reminiscences and Cultural Traditions]* Stockholm: LTs Förlag.

Widén, Albin. Collection 15: 7. Boxes 6, 8, and 10–13. Växjö, Sweden: Emigrant Institute.

Williams, Anna. 1991. *Skibent i Svensk-Amerika: Jakob Bonggren, Journalist och Poet*. Uppsala, Sweden: Avdelningen för Litteratursociologi vid Litteraturvetenskapliga Institutionen.

Wilson, David Scofield, and Angus Kress Gillespie, eds. 1999. *Rooted in America: Foodlore of Popular Fruits and Vegetables*. Knoxville: University of Tennessee Press.

Wilson, William A. 1979. "Folklore of Utah's Little Scandinavia." *Utah Historical Quarterly* 47: 148–66.

Wood, Fred E. 2005. *Fire on Ice: The Story of Icelandic Latter-day Saints at Home and Abroad*. Provo, UT: Religious Studies Center, Brigham Young University.

Youngquist, Eric V. 2002. "Growing up Swedish." *Swedish-American Historical Quarterly* 53 (4): 236–57.

Zelinsky, Wilbur. 1984. "Oh Say, Can You See? Nationalistic Emblems in the Landscape." *Winterthur Portfolio* 19 (4): 277–86. http://dx.doi.org/10.1086/496189.

Zion Evangelical Lutheran Church records, Salt Lake City, Utah. 1882–1942. S–339. Rock Island, IL: Swenson Swedish Immigration Research Center, Augustana College.

About the Author

JENNIFER EASTMAN ATTEBERY is professor of English at Idaho State University, where she teaches folklore and also chairs the Department of English and Philosophy. She has twice enjoyed sojourns in Sweden, in 1988 as a Fulbright Senior Scholar at University of Gothenburg and in 2011 as the Fulbright Distinguished Chair in American Studies at Uppsala University. Attebery is the author of *Up in the Rocky Mountains: Writing the Swedish Immigrant Experience* (University of Minnesota Press, 2007), a study of letters as vernacular writing. Her studies of Swedish culture in the Rocky Mountain West have also been published in *Scandinavian Studies* and *Swedish-American Historical Quarterly*.

Index